Private Choices and Public Health

Private Choices and Public Health

The AIDS Epidemic in an Economic Perspective

Tomas J. Philipson and Richard A. Posner

Harvard University Press
Cambridge, Massachusetts
London, England   1993

Library of Congress Cataloging-in-Publication Data

Philipson, Tomas J.
    Private choices and public health : the AIDS epidemic in an
    economic perspective / Tomas J. Philipson and Richard A. Posner.
        p.   cm.
    Includes bibliographical references and index.
    ISBN 0-674-70738-9
    1. AIDS (Disease)—Economic aspects—United States.   I. Posner,
    Richard A.   II. Title.
RA644.A25P484   1993
338.4'33621'96979200973—dc20
93-17417
        CIP

Contents

Preface

This book presents the first full-scale economic study of communicable disease and its social control, focused on the most feared and discussed such disease of the twentieth century. Although there is a thriving field of health economics, economic analysis of public health in general, and of the control of communicable diseases in particular, has lagged. This is unfortunate from the standpoint of both social science and social policy.

Like most communicable diseases that are fatal or potentially so, infection with the Human Immunodeficiency Virus (HIV) that causes AIDS (Acquired Immune Deficiency Syndrome) has evoked extensive public intervention, consisting of a variety of regulatory measures plus subsidies for research, education, treatment, testing, and counseling. Unlike most communicable diseases, however, fatal or otherwise, AIDS is spread primarily by voluntary intimate contacts between human beings. Sexual intercourse and the sharing of hypodermic needles by intravenous drug users are the principal means of transmission. The disease is therefore avoidable by what may appear to be simple, straightforward changes in personal behavior—in short, by voluntary choice. On both counts—public intervention and voluntary exposure—AIDS is a natural topic for economic analysis. It is also a neglected one. In this book we attempt to remedy the neglect, and, in doing so, to advance the understanding and control not only of AIDS but also of other communicable diseases, most of which have elicited forms of public intervention similar to those used or proposed to be used against HIV and AIDS and many of which are also avoidable by behavioral change. The book has the further aim of illustrating the power of economic analysis to illuminate nonmarket behavior that is remote from the conventional subject matter of economics.

By analyzing the AIDS epidemic—and therefore the public and private responses to the disease—from an economic perspective, we hope to make a contribution to answering a number of questions, both positive (descriptive) and normative (prescriptive): What are the social as distinct from the private costs of the epidemic? What are its fiscal implications? To what extent is the epidemic self-limiting through voluntary behavioral changes by persons at risk? Do epidemiological models take adequate account of private incentives to make such changes? Why are there such large differences in prevalence and response across groups defined by race or gender? Is testing for the AIDS virus, whether on a voluntary or a mandatory basis, likely to retard or to accelerate the epidemic? What restrictions, if any, should government impose on behavior that increases the risk of transmitting the virus? What is the proper role of government subsidies in combating the epidemic? What accounts for the actual pattern of regulations and subsidies? And how does the risk of AIDS interact with other risks of sex, such as that of an unwanted pregnancy?

Most people who write about AIDS believe that it is *the* public health crisis of the twentieth century and requires massive public intervention on both the regulatory and fiscal fronts. Its magnitude and lethality cannot be denied, even if the recent prediction by the Global AIDS Policy Coalition (1992, pp. 3, 107 and tab. 2.10) that by the year 2000 as many as 110 million people will have been infected with the AIDS virus since the epidemic began—and as many as 8.2 million in North America—turns out to be exaggerated, as have many previous predictions about the magnitude of the epidemic. We believe that standard epidemiological models do exaggerate the likely growth of a disease like AIDS that is spread largely through voluntary behavior, and that economics can be used to increase the predictive and explanatory power of such models. We find, for example, that the AIDS population (that is, the cumulative number of AIDS victims minus the cumulative number of AIDS deaths) in the United States has stabilized (see Chapter 2). Whether or not the growth of the disease has been exaggerated, economics suggests that the case for public intervention, whether regulatory or subsidizing, designed to curb that growth has been exaggerated. Some public intervention is warranted on economic grounds, but much may not be—including the most common, which is to encourage people at risk of HIV to be tested for the virus. Many proposals for further intervention are actually perverse from an epidemiological standpoint because they are more likely to accelerate than to curtail the spread of the disease. This point has been missed because the standard epidemiological approaches fail to consider the role of incentives in shaping private responses both to the communicable disease itself and to programs aimed at controlling it.

Our criticisms of public intervention and of the public health community may appear to give this book a "conservative" cast. If so, the appearance is misleading. Unlike many conservatives, who are libertarian when it comes to economic markets (narrowly defined) but turn interventionist when issues of morality appear to be at stake, we do not take a stand on the political and ethical issues that ultimately determine the choice of public policies. A number of proposals that we criticize—including mandatory testing for the AIDS virus and quarantining persons who test positive—come from conservatives. And our analysis provides support for such quintessentially "liberal" policies as recognizing rights to abortion and to homosexual marriage. But liberals will be disappointed by our failure to discover a compelling economic case for publicly subsidizing AIDS research and education as heavily as is being done today, by our suggestion that not only has the cost of the epidemic to Medicaid and other public programs been exaggerated but the epidemic may actually save public resources, and by our contention that the spread of the disease is self-limiting because of the effect of disease risk on incentives.

Economics was first called "the dismal science" because of Malthus's gloomy (and erroneous) thesis that the growth of population would outrun the growth of agricultural output. Today it is noneconomists who are more likely to be the prophets of doom and economists who like to point out that gloomy prophecies—such as that the world is about to run out of this or that natural resource—neglect the effect of scarcity in driving up prices, which in turn increases incentives to economize. Our analysis is in the spirit of such observations. We believe that predictions of the spread of AIDS have been exaggerated because of a failure to recognize that the increase in the prevalence of a disease is (with certain qualifications) the equivalent of an increase in the price of behavior that creates a risk of contracting the disease, inducing behavioral responses that limit further spread.

When the epithet "dismal" is applied to economics today, it is because of the economist's propensity to insist that everything has a cost and to analyze even the most private, emotional, and morally charged human behavior and experiences, including life and death themselves, with clinical detachment. These propensities may seem heartless and even inhuman when applied to a subject such as AIDS, which has caused so much suffering, fear, and anger. However, the current polarized discourse, in which the left regards anyone who does not accept the most radical proposals of AIDS activists as a homophobe and the right regards anyone who does not consider the problem of AIDS a consequence of immoral behavior as a radical, will not generate intelligent approaches to dealing with the disease. The reasoned, disinterested approach of the economist is a needed antidote to the emotionalism of much of the current debate over AIDS. It should be unnecessary to add that in analyzing the disease as a problem for social science, we do not mean to disparage either the sufferings of its victims or the sincere concern of much of the public with behaviors and attitudes that contribute to the spread of the disease.

Because we believe that economics has a significant role to play, along with immunology, epidemiology, law, and other disciplines, in understanding AIDS and controlling its spread, we seek an audience among all who have a professional interest in AIDS and other communicable diseases, not merely economists. To that end we have subordinated economic terminology to plain English and provided detailed verbal explanations of our occasional algebraic and geometrical formulations.

We do not claim to have said the last word on AIDS. Not only is economics only one voice in the multidisciplinary chorus, but knowledge of the disease is growing and changing daily. Even as a contribution merely to the economic analysis of AIDS, the book makes no pretense to being definitive. This is a new area of economics, and our analysis is tentative and exploratory. But we think it is an exciting area for economics, rich with promise.

We thank Benjamin Aller, Jonathan Cohen, Lynne Engel, Theodore Frank, Wesley Kelman, Jin Kim, Harry Lind, Monica McFadden, Richard Madris, Rishi Sood, Brian Weimer, and John Wright for helpful research assistance, Michael Aronson for advice and encouragement, and Michael Altmann, Gary Becker, Richard Epstein, William Eskridge, David Friedman, Sherry Glied, Victor Goldberg, Samuel Hellman, Penelope Hitchcock, Louis Kaplow, Daniel Klerman, Lawrence Lessig, Derek Neal, Martha Nussbaum, Robert Ohsfeldt, Charmaine Picard, Laura Pincus, Charlene Posner, Kenneth Posner, Stephen Stigler, Cass Sunstein, James Wiley, Richard Zeckhauser, and participants in workshops at the University of Chicago, Harvard University, UCLA, the University of Montreal, and the Western Economic Association for many helpful comments. None of the persons whom we have thanked should be blamed for any of our mistakes or conclusions.

Private Choices and Public Health

Introduction

The AIDS epidemic is the most discussed public health crisis of this century.[1] The obvious reasons—its lethality, insidiousness, rapid growth, and worldwide extent—are not the only ones. AIDS erupted at a time when, in wealthy nations like the United States, incurable communicable diseases much graver than the common cold were widely believed to be a thing of the past. In 1969 Surgeon General William H. Stewart "told the U.S. Congress that it was time to 'close the book on infectious diseases,' declare the war against pestilence won, and shift national resources to such chronic problems as cancer and heart disease" (Garrett 1992). AIDS is, moreover, primarily although not exclusively a sexually transmitted disease, and in the wealthy nations of the world such as the United States one especially prevalent among homosexuals.[2] Because of its connection to sex in general (especially when promiscuous), and in

1. The scholarly literature is immense. We estimate from Medline, a computerized database of medical publications, that by the end of 1992 almost 50,000 articles on HIV and AIDS had been published—excluding articles in legal and social scientific journals, which Medline does not survey. Cf. Elford, Bor, and Summers (1991). For a useful although incomplete literature review, see the monthly *AIDS Literature and News Review* published by University Publishing Group in Frederick, Maryland. For a good introduction to the scholarly literature, see Turner et al. (1989), and for a good general introduction, emphasizing AIDS policymaking, see Panem (1988).

2. Throughout this book, we use "homosexual" and "homosexuality" to refer exclusively to male homosexuals, since the transmission of the AIDS virus by lesbian practices is negligible. Although the homosexual community prefers the term "gay" for male homosexuals, "homosexual" remains the more neutral term. We use it with no pejorative intent. Incidentally, for the world as a whole, the rate of heterosexual transmission of the AIDS virus exceeds the rate of homosexual transmission.

particular to sexual practices such as unshielded anal intercourse with multiple partners that are more prevalent among homosexuals than among heterosexuals, proposals for dealing with AIDS have stirred intense controversy in many countries, especially the United States— which, half-libertine, half-puritan nation that it is, has long had difficulty formulating and implementing consistent policies for the social control of sexually transmitted diseases (Brandt 1985). The transmission of the AIDS virus (HIV) through the sharing of hypodermic needles by drug addicts has reinforced the moral charge that the epidemic carries. But despite its seemingly unique attributes, AIDS is not the first, and it will probably not be the last, fatal communicable disease to afflict the world; Surgeon General Stewart's overly optimistic assessment may have reflected a historically unique lull in disease epidemics. Even today, AIDS is not the only serious, and imperfectly controlled, sexually transmitted disease. A better understanding of the AIDS epidemic and of the methods employed or proposed for dealing with it may thus confer benefits on future generations as well as on our own.

Previous Approaches

Two approaches dominate scholarly as well as popular discussion of AIDS. One, the biomedical, draws on such disciplines as microbiology, medicine, and public health, including epidemiology, the study of the occurrence of disease in a population (Bailey 1975; Anderson and May 1991). The biomedical approach seeks to determine the behavior of the AIDS virus; to use this knowledge to predict the spread of the epidemic and to propose behavioral changes, such as greater use of condoms or more extensive HIV testing, designed to control the disease; and to find a vaccine or a cure and, pending either, treatments aimed at prolonging the lives of HIV or AIDS victims, such as the drug AZT. The biomedical approach implicitly assigns a very large role to the public sector in the control of communicable diseases, because the approach generally assumes away private incentives to avoid disease, even though the feasibility of avoidance is generally greater with communicable than with noncommunicable diseases. Behavioral change is a more feasible preventive of HIV infection than of most cancers.

The other common approach to the issue of AIDS is ethical, a term we use in a broad sense to describe the variety of moral, legal, and political perspectives that have been brought to bear on the epidemic (Mohr 1988, pt. 4; Dalton and Burris 1987; Levine and Bayer 1989; Jarvis et al. 1991; Daniels 1992; Hunter and Rubenstein 1992). The focus of this approach is twofold. First is the question of what normative evaluation society should place on the disease. Should society regard it, as some conservatives propose, as God's or nature's punishment for unnatural or irresponsible behavior, a punishment that can be averted only by reversing the sexual revolution of the twentieth century and returning to sexual abstinence outside of marriage? As a consequence of genocidal impulses of whites, as some blacks believe? Or as a product of benighted social attitudes toward sex and drug addiction, as some liberals believe? The second and closely related aim of the ethical approach is to determine what if anything should be done as a matter of social justice to arrest the epidemic, consistent with civil liberties, fiscal limitations, and other constraints.

The biomedical and ethical approaches are so frequently conjoined that a virtual orthodoxy has emerged, which holds that the AIDS epidemic is a problem for solution primarily by public-sector activities guided by medical and public health professionals but subject to constraints imposed by considerations of justice, morality, civil liberties, and similar legal-ethical concerns. The idea that AIDS might be approached from the standpoint of *economics* has received, in contrast, little attention.[3] It is not surprising that the biomedical community would slight incentives and behavioral change as factors in spreading or controlling an epidemic, since these are not biological or medical phenomena. It is a little more surprising that the social science, and especially the economics, research community would do so. Of course it is understood that AIDS has financial effects, and not only on the victims of the disease and their families. Providers of medical services, health insurers, employers that have health plans for their employees, government welfare programs, industries such as the fashion industry in New York City that have been hard hit by the death and disability of key workers as a result

---

3. A recent paper argues that the control of sexually transmitted diseases in general and AIDS in particular "is possible only if *all* workers in the field of STD [sexually transmitted disease] research (clinicians, microbiologists, molecular biologists, epidemiologists, psychologists, sociologists, and public health administrators) are aware of the multiple overlaps among their disciplines and collaborate effectively" (Sparling and Aral 1991; emphasis added). Notice the omission of any reference to economists. Richard Mohr's philosophical analysis of AIDS (Mohr 1988, pt. 4), however, addresses the issue of the external costs of AIDS from an implicitly economic standpoint. Economics and philosophy overlap in another way: Normative economics is an ethical system. Throughout this book, however, we use "ethical" to refer to ethical systems other than normative economics.

of AIDS—all have suffered financial consequences from the epidemic, and those consequences have elicited a body of useful economic analysis illustrated by Bloom and Glied (1991), Greeley (1989), and Schwefel et al. (1990). But it is a more limited use of economics than we attempt in this book.[4]

Our approach is to examine the *full range* of private and public responses to the AIDS epidemic from the perspective of economic theory, with its emphasis on the responsiveness of human behavior to changes in incentives. This means, first, treating the individual's choice between safe and risky sex (and other choices that affect the transmission of the disease, such as a decision to be tested for the virus) as a rational decision in the sense of one responsive to incentives. Second, it means using economics to predict and evaluate the effects of public policies concerning AIDS, such as subsidies for medical research, for AIDS education, and for voluntary HIV testing; mandatory HIV testing; insurance regulations; subsidized distribution of condoms or (for drug addicts) hypodermic needles; registration of prostitutes; and control of immigration (for example, forbidding the entry of HIV carriers into the United States). In its evaluative aspect this analysis is normative, but intelligent normative economic analysis is not conducted in an empirical vacuum. Because the behavioral responses to policy are as critical in evaluating policy as the behaviors that the policy seeks to regulate, normative economic analysis relies heavily on positive analysis to determine the actual effects of existing policies and the probable effects of proposed ones. It also provides the impetus for the branch of positive economic analysis, often called public choice, that tries to explain the divergence between actual and optimal public policies by emphasizing the self-interested behavior of political actors.

---

4. Bloom and Glied (1991, p. 1802), however, discuss the social costs of AIDS, and the possible social benefits of HIV testing, although very briefly, while Hay (1989) analyzes the value of life of AIDS victims, and Weinstein and colleagues (1989) discuss several AIDS-preventive measures from a cost-benefit perspective, as does Lloyd (1991), whose approach is closest to ours. The relative lack of interest that health economists have evinced in AIDS—Phelps's textbook, for example, despite its recency, confines discussion of AIDS to a single page, dealing with contaminated blood (Phelps 1992, p. 437)—may reflect the heavy emphasis in the literature of health economics on the demand for medical care and on the structure and behavior of the health-care industry. Nevertheless, we do draw heavily on the findings of health economics in Chapters 4 and 7 and elsewhere. For a lucid review of the health-economics literature in its bearing on issues of public health, see Drummond (1991).

Some scientific and social scientific literature that is not explicitly economic is implicitly so or uses models that are isomorphic with economic models. Examples abound in population biology, law, political science, and even philosophy (see note 3). However, with only a few exceptions the biomedical and ethical literatures on communicable diseases in general and AIDS in particular are not of this character. As a result, these literatures leave a large gap for an explicit economic approach to fill—an approach, moreover, that challenges many of the assumptions and conclusions of the more familiar approaches. Epidemiologists generally assume away issues involving the *choice* of individuals to expose themselves, or to avoid exposing themselves, to the risk of infection. They thus slight the interrelated issues of information, incentives, and behavioral change. Most epidemiological models of the AIDS epidemic, for example, assume random sorting of HIV-positive persons to HIV-negative persons in sexual transactions and ignore the demand for safe sex. Yet much of the governmental and organized private response to AIDS consists of efforts (such as HIV testing, partner notification, and public education) to generate and disseminate information on risk, prevention, and infection status—information that people can and do use to *avoid* random sorting and risky sex. The epidemiological models cannot explain the private or public demand for such information; and the fact that such information is actually used to guide behavior falsifies the assumptions of the epidemiological models. In contrast, behavioral responses to a changing environment of risk, information, and opportunity are central to economic analysis.

The Economic Approach to Human Behavior

We shall, in short, be proceeding on the assumption that the market for risky sexual "trades" (or, what is analytically similar, for the sharing of hypodermic needles that have not been decontaminated) is, in its relevant features, much like other markets that economists study. The quotation marks are only to make clear that our analysis is not limited to prostitution; we refer to "trade" in the standard economic sense of an activity perceived as mutually beneficial to the persons engaged in it. Compare credit markets, where lenders, facing a risk of default that is analytically similar to the risk of infection faced by people who trade in a sexual market, take measures to adjust to this risk. We present empirical as well as theoretical reasons for believing that persons contemplating sexual intercourse, or the sharing of a hypodermic needle, take optimal measures (which will sometimes mean no measures) to adjust to the risk of infection.

We should explain the tradition in economics out of which such a study of rational choice in "nonmarket markets" arises. To most people who are not economists—indeed to many economists as well—the proper domain of economics is the study of explicit markets and hence of transactions in which money is the standard of value and the medium of exchange. Yet ever since Jeremy Bentham and Thomas Malthus began writing in the latter part of the eighteenth century, economic theory has also been used to analyze nonmarket behavior—in Bentham's case, primarily the behavior of criminals, and in Malthus's case, population growth. The economics of nonmarket behavior has burgeoned in recent decades. Not only the subjects that interested Bentham and Malthus, but many other nonmarket phenomena, notably education, litigation, politics and legislation, the common law, the institutions of primitive and ancient societies, racial and sexual discrimination, and—of particular relevance to this book—health, safety, accidents, addiction, the family, and sex, have been brought under the lens of the economist.[5]

Such work is premised on the view that people do not leave off acting rationally—do not suddenly cease responding to incentives—when they leave the marketplace and go home, or for that matter (we would add) to a singles bar, a homosexual bathhouse, or a "shooting gallery" where addicts inject themselves with needles shared among strangers. Once rationality is assumed, almost the entire apparatus of economic theory can be brought to bear, though it is important to note that most prices of nonmarket goods and services are shadow prices. That is, they are not explicit money prices; they are costs, which need not be pecuniary costs, incurred in consequence of making a particular choice. Just as the shadow price of fast driving is the expected cost of an automobile accident, and the shadow price of working in a dangerous occupation is the expected cost of the accidents associated with that occupation, and the shadow price of cigarette smoking is the expected cost of the diseases associated with smoking, so the shadow price of engaging in an act of unsafe sex is the expected cost, both pecuniary and nonpecuniary (with the latter predominant in this example), of becoming infected with the

5. See, for example, G. Becker (1975, 1976, 1991); Becker, Grossman, and Murphy (1991); Fuchs (1982a); Grossman (1972); Phelps (1992); Posner (1981, 1992); Shavell (1987); Stigler (1975); Tolley, Kendel, and Fabian (1992); Viscusi (1985); Weisbrod (1983); and for an excellent survey, Hirshleifer (1985).

AIDS virus. It is another form of accident, or, like a disease caused by smoking, another form of avoidable illness.

The assumption of rationality may seem misplaced when applied to so emotional an activity as sex, or such a self-destructive one as drug addiction. The question of how far the assumption can reasonably be pressed is the largest question about the economics of nonmarket behavior in general, and it is, we acknowledge, especially acute when one is considering the particular behaviors that result in most cases of AIDS. But there is little purpose in debating the question in the abstract.[6] If behavior in the face of the risk of AIDS is irrational, the economic approach to it is unlikely to be illuminating. The existing literature, a sample of which we cited in note 5, suggests that the economic approach to nonmarket behavior is fruitful and therefore that the assumption that such behavior is rational, however implausible the assumption may seem, is a useful one. Of particular relevance is the literature on rational behavior with respect to contraception,[7] since sex is the principal mode of transmitting AIDS and since pregnancy and disease are closely related risks of sex. (We explore that relation in Chapter 9.)

We do not claim that *every* decision that results in the transmission of the AIDS virus is a rational one, any more than every purchasing decision by a consumer or even every business decision is rational or optimal. Common sense—not always, but here, a reliable guide—teaches that impulsive, compulsive, forgetful, illogical, self-deceptive, weak-willed, short-sighted, even crazed behavior is found in most domains of human activity, notably including the sexual and the addictive (and sex may have addictive characteristics). So we do not expect every act of risky sex or risky needle sharing to be explicable in terms of rational choice. In general, and certainly in the area of interest to us in this book, economics does better at predicting average behavior and central tendencies than at explaining the totality of individual behavior. In this respect it is like physics. Many of the laws of physics are strictly true only if there is no friction; in the real world they hold only as approximations. It is the same (if we substitute hyperrationality for frictionlessness)—only more so—with the laws of economics.

Our project will seem more plausible if the reader understands that

---

6. Though it is worth noting that a growing literature challenges the conventional view that emotions are irrational (for example, de Sousa 1987).

7. See discussion and references in Posner (1992, p. 268); also Tanfer, Cubbins, and Brewster (1992), and other references in Chapter 9 of this book.

"rational choice" in economic analysis need not be conscious, delibera-tive, cool, or informed. In most versions of economics, including the one employed in this book, a choice is rational if it maximizes expected util-ity, where "utility" refers to the subjective welfare of the actor and "ex-pected" to the presence of uncertainty, which may make the choice—for example, unsafe sex—that was best ex ante (that is, when made) a poor choice ex post (after it is made). When the obtaining or absorbing of information is costly, an uninformed choice, for example one that either overestimates or underestimates the risk to health or safety of some con-templated course of action, may still be expected-utility-maximizing; "rational ignorance" is not an oxymoron. And while many choices are habitual rather than deliberated, they may have become habitual *because* they are such obviously good choices (an example is brushing one's teeth after meals) that there is nothing to be gained from mulling them over every time.

As these examples suggest, rationality implies nothing more, really, than suiting means to ends, whatever those ends may be. This should help to make clear that economic or rational-choice theory is not a the-ory of mental states, conscious or not, or a guide to introspection. It does not aspire to reveal the phenomenology of sexual intercourse or of the injecting of illegal drugs. It is a source of explanations and predictions concerning behavior, including behavior toward the dangers posed by AIDS, whether behavior by persons engaged in risky sexual trades or by voters, medical professionals, politicians, or others concerned with the health and fiscal consequences of AIDS.

Because economics has both positive and normative—that is, descrip-tive and evaluative—components, it enables the analyst both to predict the effect of a particular policy on rational actors, for example a policy of mandatory testing for the AIDS virus, and to evaluate the policy in terms of normative economic criteria, such as efficiency. Although we discuss a number of specific policies, and therefore our analysis has ines-capable normative overtones, our primary interest is in positive analysis. We want to improve the understanding of AIDS policies, actual and pro-posed, by improving the understanding of the behavioral responses of rational persons to them. But our analysis can also clarify the normative issues presented by AIDS. Most experts on the disease take the goal of policy to be to minimize the spread of the epidemic, subject to a variety of constraints, such as the welfare of existing victims of AIDS, who might be helped by drugs that postpone conversion to the active disease state while at the same time prolonging the period during which an infected person is infective. Call this goal *constrained disease minimization*. By focusing on the ex post consequences of risky behavior, it leaves out of account preference satisfaction, or ex ante utility. The ex ante utility of two persons who are contemplating sexual relations might be increased by risky sex even though safe sex would be better from the standpoint of limiting the spread of the disease. Of course, these persons' utility is not the only thing to be considered, since their decision to engage in risky sex may impose disutility on other persons, for example their future sexual partners. These points lead some normative economists and many utilitarian philosophers to specify *utility maximization* as the goal of social policy, with utility understood in ex ante terms and aggregated across all members of society.

The emphasis that economists place on the ex ante perspective is related to their emphasis on rationality. Rationality implies choice on the basis of one's best estimate of the nature, magnitude, and probability of the consequences of the alternatives among which one can choose in an effort to maximize one's utility. The ex ante perspective is missing from most noneconomic analyses of the AIDS epidemic. The epidemiologist, for example, in predicting the future growth or decline of the disease, is apt to abstract from the volitional element—the decision whether or not to engage in potentially transmittive behavior (or how frequently to engage in it)—that the economist expects will play a central role in that growth or decline until a vaccine or cure is developed, and maybe afterward as well.

Despite our emphasis on ex ante utility, we often in this book evaluate policies in terms of their contribution to the goal of reducing the spread of disease regardless of ex ante utility. Policies can be analyzed for the efficiency with which they achieve or pursue their goals, even if the goals are not those that an economist would be likely to choose. This point is important because not all economists agree that the ex ante perspective is the correct one from the standpoint of evaluating social welfare, or that utility can be aggregated across persons or should be measured without regard to its distribution across persons, or what the relevant society is—one's own nation, the world's human population, or some even broader aggregate. We do not have to get into these questions. It is enough for our purposes that ex ante utility is *a* social value (as would be obvious if the question were whether to fix a speed limit of 3 miles per hour on interstate highways in order to reduce the number of highway accidents) and that costs, broadly defined to include all sources and forms of disutility, are relevant to the evaluation of public policies, so that a draconian anti-AIDS policy that reduced the spread of the disease might be undesirable if the cost of the policy to homosexuals was even greater than the cost of the illness that the policy prevented. We do not claim that the economist has a monopoly on ethical insight and therefore should have the whip hand in the formulation of policy toward AIDS. We do claim that the economic perspective deserves a significant place in the scholarly and public response to the epidemic and to communicable diseases in general. It deserves this because of its unremitting focus on and systematic analysis of behavioral responses, a focus essential to normative as well as positive analysis of AIDS but missing from the other approaches.

The analysis that we lay out in the remaining chapters has led us to conclude tentatively that the optimal governmental role in controlling the epidemic is, while not zero—we do not advocate laissez-faire— smaller than, and also different from, that urged by either liberals or conservatives. The fundamental reasons for our conclusion (which is limited to the United States, the only country whose HIV/AIDS problems and policies we consider in detail) are that people are responding to the epidemic by altering their behavior in ways that make public intervention at once less necessary and less effective, and that the social and private costs of the epidemic diverge less than has been assumed. We find, for example, that the size of the AIDS-infected population (cumulative cases of AIDS minus deaths from AIDS) has stabilized (see Chapter 2) and that the social and fiscal costs of the epidemic have been exaggerated (Chapter 4).

Our conclusion that the public sector probably is overinvolved in AIDS has led us to search for supplements or alternatives to economic efficiency, disease minimization, or other versions of the public interest, including majoritarian preferences, as explanations of public policy in this area. We emphasize the role of interest groups—self-interested political pressure groups—in the formation of public policy. We see AIDS policy as redistributive, as well as allocative, in character: specifically, as redistributing wealth from low-risk to high-risk segments of the population and to the public health community.

Plan of the Book

In Chapter 1 we present our basic model, on which all the subsequent chapters build, of rational choice between safe and risky sexual activity. The risk we are interested in is, of course, that of becoming infected by the AIDS virus. Although sex is not the only method by which the virus is transmitted, it is the main one, and to simplify exposition we focus on sexual transmission. We discuss other methods, primarily needle-sharing by intravenous drug users, where appropriate.

Blood transfusion was an important source of contagion in the early days of the disease; but because of careful screening of would-be donors and the testing of all blood for the AIDS virus, it is no longer, so we largely ignore it. Granted, testing all donated blood for the AIDS virus is not foolproof; as we shall see, there can be a lag of several months between a person's becoming infected and his body's manufacturing the AIDS antibodies for which the tests test. Screening all potential donors in an effort to exclude those who are at risk of being HIV-positive is not foolproof either, since those who are selling rather than giving away their blood have a financial incentive to conceal any characteristics that would cause the blood bank to refuse to buy from them. However, the *combination* of testing all donated blood with screening all potential donors is estimated to have reduced the probability of becoming infected with HIV as a result of a blood transfusion to less than 1 in 200,000 (American Health Consultants 1992b). Similarly, the screening of blood has largely eliminated the transmission of the virus to hemophiliacs in blood concentrations that contain the clotting factors needed to treat that disease. Because AIDS is still a relatively new and incompletely understood disease, however, attempts to quantify the risks associated with it, such as the 1/200,000 risk of getting the disease from a blood transfusion, should be taken with a grain of salt. This caveat should be borne in mind throughout the book.

In addition to expounding the basic model in Chapter 1, we explain there the model's assumptions and derive its implications, emphasize the fundamental distinction between ex ante and ex post evaluations of policy, refine the model by (for example) distinguishing between altruistic and egoistic sexual actors, and contrast its predictions concerning the growth of AIDS with those of the epidemiological models. In Chapter 2 we confront the economic model with data concerning levels and rates of growth of AIDS both generally and within selected subpopulations, such as blacks, women, intravenous drug users, and homosexuals, and also concerning behavioral changes within those subpopulations. Many of the data that we use in Chapter 2 and in other chapters as well are data that we have extracted from the AIDS Public Information File Data Set. Created and maintained by the Centers for Disease Control[8] of the

---

8. Recently (and redundantly) renamed the Centers for Disease Control and Prevention. We shall stick with the old, better-known name.

U.S. Public Health Service, this data set contains in machine-readable form detailed information on each of the more than 200,000 U.S. AIDS cases reported to date. On the basis of these and other data we find substantial evidence, both direct and indirect, of behavioral change and conclude that the economic approach, with its emphasis on information, incentives, and behavior, provides a better explanation for the patterns revealed by the data than any purely epidemiological approach has been able to do.

In Chapter 3 we use the economic model to analyze the effects of the main public response to the epidemic: the encouragement and facilitation of voluntary HIV testing. (Mandatory testing is discussed in Chapter 5.) We distinguish between "partner-observed" and "partner-unobserved" voluntary testing[9] and show, contrary to the implicit (and frequently explicit) view of virtually the entire public health community, that HIV testing may increase the growth of the epidemic rather than retard it. The reason is that persons who test negative can use their test result to obtain risky sexual trades that they could not obtain otherwise, while nonaltruistic persons who test positive have a diminished incentive to choose safe sex. Since testing can thus increase the demand for unsafe sex and consequently the volume of risky sexual trades, it can lead to an increase in the spread of the virus[10]—can, not must. When the model is refined to take dynamic and other complicating factors into account, the clarity of its prediction concerning the effect of voluntary testing on the spread of the disease is diminished. A safe conclusion, however, is that there is no compelling theoretical or empirical reason for believing that voluntary testing will actually reduce the spread of the disease.

Even without governmental encouragement and subsidization, there would be, as we explain in Chapter 3, a demand for HIV testing; hence that chapter straddles the private and public responses to the epidemic. In Chapter 4 we set the stage for further evaluation of the public responses by considering the *social* costs of the epidemic and hence the extent to which its spread reflects a market failure that would, in princi-

---

9. A "partner-observed" test is one in which the sexual partner of the person who is tested learns the test result. One might think that the partner would never have warranted confidence in what the person told him was the result of the test, but we argue that in some circumstances such confidence is warranted.

10. The point has been overlooked because epidemiologists generally do not ask *why* people ever want to be tested for HIV.

ple anyway, justify public intervention on purely economic grounds.[11] The qualification "in principle" is important. Public intervention is never warranted merely because a market appears to be performing badly; it is warranted only if the intervention is likely to improve performance, as it may not be if it is costly or ineffectual, even if not perverse in the sense of producing the opposite of the intended result—although it may be that too.

Before even considering the costs and efficacy of public intervention, we have to decide whether the market for sexual relations or needle-sharing is in fact incapable of producing the economically optimum level of HIV infection. Economists have tended to regard communicable disease as a textbook example of an activity that generates a negative externality—that is, imposes a cost that the persons engaged in the activity that produces it do not take into account (because it is not a cost to them) in deciding whether or how much of the activity to engage in. This conventional view is not wrong, but it is incomplete, especially when applied to a disease that is a by-product of voluntary behavior and can be, but often is not, avoided by changes in that behavior.[12] Horrible as AIDS is, most though not all of its costs are internal to the "markets" in sexual intercourse and intravenous drug use. And this implies that a level of the disease considerably greater than zero may be economically optimal simply because many people demonstrate by their behavior ("revealed preference") that they consider the cost of reducing the risk of the disease to zero through a change in behavior to be greater than the expected cost, in disease, disability, and death, of the risk itself. Of course they would prefer that there be no disease, but the costs of eliminating it may be prohibitive.

---

11. "Private costs" are prices, whether or not pecuniary; they are what influence private behavior. "Social costs" are costs (that is, reductions in value through the consumption of scarce resources), by whomever borne, whether or not the costs are prices to particular persons and therefore affect individual behavior. If the social costs of an activity are not reflected in private costs, the free market may generate too much output from the standpoint of overall social welfare.

12. Public health professionals distinguish between a "contagious" disease, in the sense of one transmitted by air, water, insect or animal bites, or other involuntary routes, and an "infectious" disease, transmitted only by voluntary contact between persons. The distinction can be criticized because it dichotomizes a continuum. Contagious diseases (in the narrow sense) can often be avoided, and not necessarily at any higher cost than that of avoiding an infectious disease, by keeping away from an infected person or population. We prefer the term "communicable disease" to describe both contagious and infectious diseases.

The notion that the "optimal" level of a fatal disease such as AIDS, once it gets a foothold in the population, might be greater than zero may strike the noneconomist as strange, even repulsive. Does it mean that we think AIDS is a good thing for society to have? It does not, any more than we think highway accidents are a good thing. The point is only that it may not pay for society to try to reduce a bad thing to zero, either because the costs of totally extirpating it may exceed the benefits (as would be dramatically the case if, for example, carbon dioxide pollution were eliminated by forbidding people to breathe) or, what comes to the same thing, because it is an unavoidable by-product of a highly valued activity. Thus, a positive level for AIDS would be "optimal" only in the sense that it would not pay to reduce the level further.

Although fiscal cost and economic cost are different—the latter being the loss of value from consuming a scarce resource, the former a budget entry on the government's books—there is a natural concern with the potential fiscal cost, in government health and welfare expenditures, of the AIDS epidemic. In Chapter 4 we argue that this cost, too, has been exaggerated. AIDS may even produce a net saving to the taxpayer—despite the almost $5 billion in annual federal expenditures on AIDS research, education, and (mainly via Medicaid) treatment, and hundreds of millions more in state expenditures[13]—by killing people who, had they lived, would have been a net deficit item on the government's tax-spending books. This does not, to repeat, mean that AIDS is on balance a good thing. Indeed, the economic perspective is helpful in showing that fiscal expenditures and real costs are not equivalents; the former often are transfer payments rather than costs. Taxpayers may be better off if people who consume more in government services than they pay in taxes are denied those services, but society as a whole may be worse off if this taxpayer benefit is bought at the cost of suffering and death.

In succeeding chapters we examine the range of actual and proposed public responses to AIDS, which are basically of three types. The first type, discussed in Chapter 5, consists of regulatory interventions, especially mandatory HIV testing (either of the population at large or, more realistically, of selected subpopulations such as health workers, hospital patients, prison inmates, immigrants, applicants for marriage licenses, and military recruits), which has received the most attention and is the focus of the chapter. Other types of regulation that we discuss are forbid-

---

13. Much of it under the Medicaid program too; Medicaid is jointly financed by the federal government and the states.

ding immigration of HIV carriers; contact tracing (also called "partner notification"); criminalizing the knowing or reckless transmission of the AIDS virus or the exposure of a sexual partner or needle-sharer to the virus; imposing tort liability for careless transmission or exposure; and forbidding employers or health insurers to discriminate against persons having the AIDS virus or AIDS itself.[14] The second type of intervention, the subject of Chapter 6, relies on subsidies rather than restrictions—carrots rather than sticks—to alter behavior, either through education about the danger of AIDS or through the direct provision of AIDS preventives, such as condoms and clean needles. In both chapters we emphasize the paradox that well-intentioned policies, especially those designed to increase information about AIDS, may be ineffectual and may even increase the spread of the disease. Corresponding to "market failure," the failure of a private market to allocate resources efficiently, there is "government failure," the failure of government measures to correct market failures.

The third type of public intervention in the epidemic, examined in Chapter 7, also employs subsidies. But the subsidies discussed in that chapter are for medical research into the causes of AIDS, as well as possible vaccines, meliorative treatments, and cures for the disease, rather than for modifying the behavior of persons at risk of either transmitting or becoming infected with the virus. We ask whether too much or too little is being spent on the various types of medical research on AIDS, and tentatively suggest that too much is being spent on nonbasic research, which could largely be left to the private sector to finance, since it is possible to obtain property rights (via patent and trade-secret law) in the fruits of such research. And we emphasize the different behavioral, fiscal, and policy implications of a vaccine for infectable persons as distinguished from a cure for infected ones.

In Chapter 7 we also begin our inquiry into the causes of the government's policies toward AIDS. Our analysis of the consequences of these policies implies that a theory which supposes them to be economically efficient, disease-minimizing, or preferred by the median voter, will have only limited explanatory success. So we ask who the gainers and the

---

14. The last issue, discrimination by employers or insurers, is also discussed in Chapter 4. Incidentally, the expression "AIDS itself," though convenient, is inaccurate or at least misleading. AIDS is not itself a symptom-manifesting disease; it is a condition of the immune system that lays its victims open to a variety of fatal diseases most of which are either nonexistent or very rare among persons who are not infected by HIV.

losers from the policies, viewed redistributively, might be. In Chapter 8 we systematize the analysis and extend it to other governmental interventions in the epidemic. We argue that the best theory of the government's response to AIDS is an interest-group theory: Articulate, organized high-risk populations (in particular male homosexuals), who have a large, even a life-and-death, stake in AIDS policies, and medical and public health professionals, who have an even larger financial and vocational (and some health) stake, are allied, politically effective interest groups confronting a competing interest group of moral conservatives, who have a weaker but not negligible interest in changing people's behavior. The result of the interaction of these groups is a crazy quilt of AIDS policies that satisfies no one fully, that is not efficient in an economic sense, that may not be effective in reducing the spread of the disease, but that redistributes resources to high-risk individuals and, even more, to members of the health-care industry.

In Chapter 9 we extend our analysis to another risk of sex—that of unwanted pregnancy. We are not interested in pregnancy or birth as such, but rather in the relation between the risk of disease and the risk of conception. We ask how AIDS affects the choice of contraceptive methods and also how that choice affects AIDS, and we explain how restrictions on abortion can affect the incidence of the disease.

The Biology and Epidemiology of AIDS

In this section we present the essential biomedical facts, as they are now understood (many of them will no doubt change as knowledge advances), concerning HIV, AIDS, and the HIV/AIDS epidemic, on which our economic analysis draws.[15]

Biology. Acquired Immune Deficiency Syndrome is the consequence of a viral infection that, by destroying a key component of the body's defenses against disease, exposes the body to cancers, respiratory infections, and other diseases which, with a probability approaching and perhaps equal to 100 percent, eventually kill the infected person. The virus that causes AIDS (HIV-1)[16] enters a type of white blood cell known as the

---

15. On the disease itself, Holmberg et al. (1989), Haseltine (1990), and Mills and Masur (1990) are excellent introductions. For a fuller treatment, see DeVita, Hellman, and Rosenberg (1988). On transmission risks and prevention, Hearst and Hulley (1988) is particularly good.

16. A second human immunosuppressive virus has been discovered, and has been dubbed HIV-2. It is a common form of the virus in West Africa (Pépin et al. 1992), but

T-helper lymphocyte, which contains a specific antigen (disease-fighting agent) called CD4 (so the T-helper lymphocyte is also called the $CD4^+$ cell). The virus binds with the antigen and eventually begins duplicating itself in the cells it has entered. The copies then enter other $CD4^+$ cells and kill them. As the body's $CD4^+$ cell count falls because of the destruction wreaked by the now multiplying, spreading virus, the immune system is depleted of a critical component and thereby weakened. This does not happen immediately upon infection, although a newly infected person will commonly experience an episode of fairly severe sickness, involving symptoms such as swollen glands, fever, diarrhea, and fatigue that resemble those of mononucleosis or flu, within four to twelve weeks after becoming infected, as his immune system tries to fight off the infection. After a short time, he will recover into an asymptomatic state that may last for many years; and he may not realize that he is infected. During this time, following the first appearance of symptoms, the virus is dormant; the immune system has won the first round. Eventually, however, when the virus "wakes up" and begins to replicate itself and to spread, destroying the host cells, the victim's $CD4^+$ cell count will fall to the point at which his immune system is unable to protect him against relatively minor—modulating into serious but nonlethal—ailments characteristic of persons with impaired immune systems (Farizo et al. 1992). The group of diseases that characterizes this intermediate stage in the HIV-caused decay of the immune system was formerly called "AIDS-Related Complex" (ARC). Eventually the characteristic lethal diseases that constitute the Acquired Immune Deficiency Syndrome itself, such as Kaposi's sarcoma, *pneumocystis carinii* pneumonia, AIDS wasting, and esophageal candidiasis, appear, and within another year or two or three the patient is dead. The average interval from diagnosis to death is today 22 months.

Because the weakening of the immune system by the virus and the resulting progression of illness from the asymptomatic initial stage to death are gradual, the determination of the onset of AIDS requires making a dichotomous cut in a continuous phenomenon. It is a determination at once vital to the statistics of the disease and, like specifying the precise moment at which day becomes night, inescapably arbitrary. The

---

not in the United States or Europe. There is recent speculation, related to the concern expressed in the text below concerning undetectable carriers, about the emergence of a third AIDS virus that may be undetectable by current tests for AIDS antibodies. We ignore these complications and use HIV as a synonym for HIV-1.

practice of public health authorities, notably the Centers for Disease Control, has been to date the onset of the disease from the point at which the symptoms of the major diseases associated with a falling $CD4^+$ cell count first appear. The list of those diseases has expanded as more has been learned about the characteristic manifestations of the immunosuppressive action of the virus. This means that some of the growth in AIDS is a statistical artifact (Chang, Katz, and Hernandez 1992). The CDC has gone back and reclassified earlier data in order to produce a consistent time series for the disease. Recently the agency decided that anyone with a $CD4^+$ cell count below 200 (a normal count is 1,000) shall be deemed to have AIDS, even though some of these people are asymptomatic and many are at least free from serious diseases.[17] This reclassification, which we shall ignore, may double the reported number of AIDS cases (American Health Consultants 1992a).

The median time for conversion from the (relatively) inactive or incubation stage to full-blown AIDS is about ten years from the time the patient is infected with the AIDS virus, with about a third converting within seven years (Taylor, Kuo, and Detels 1991; see also Bacchetti and Jewell 1991). A more precise estimate is impossible because most people don't know exactly (and some not even approximately) when they were infected, and many people who have become infected over the course of the epidemic have not yet converted. The range of recent estimates is eight to eleven years (Lemp et al. 1990b; Lui, Darrow, and Rutherford 1988; Mariotto et al. 1992; Muñoz et al. 1989). Incidentally, our use of the word "conversion" to denote the transition from the incubation period to the active state of the disease should be distinguished from "seroconversion," which the medical community uses to denote the point at which the body of an HIV-infected person produces detectable antibodies.

The term "incubation period" also requires explanation. Epidemiologists distinguish the stages of a disease along (at least) two axes. One contrasts the incubation (inactive, asymptomatic) stage with the symptomatic stage. The second contrasts the latent stage, when the disease is not communicable by the person who has it, with the infectious (or infective) stage, when it is. The latent stage of HIV infection is very short; almost as soon as a person is infected with HIV, he is capable of transmit-

---

17. Even a person with a very low $CD4^+$ cell count can be completely asymptomatic, simply because he or she has had the good luck not to have contracted any disease that would require more $CD4^+$ cells to fight off.

ting it, although the degree of infectivity varies over the course of the infection. The fact that HIV has a long infectious incubation period—a long period during which the carrier can infect others without himself being symptomatic—has, as we emphasize throughout this book, profound significance for the control of the disease.

The drug azidothymidine (AZT, formerly known as zidovudine), which has proved successful in extending the life of AIDS victims, is also believed capable, by itself or in conjunction with other drugs, of prolonging the incubation stage by months or even years, especially if treatment with the drug is begun soon after the patient is first infected.[18] The drug is highly toxic, however, and the optimal dose, balancing toxicity against efficacy, has not yet been determined (Collier et al. 1990). Serious doubt has been expressed recently about AZT's efficacy—for ethical reasons, the drug has never been subjected to comprehensive experimental evaluation (Creagh-Kirk et al. 1988)[19]—in postponing the onset of AIDS (Aboulker and Swart 1993; Kolata 1992). Its efficacy in postponing death, once AIDS has set in, is not in question.

Tests for HIV have been available since 1985. But because they test for the presence of HIV antibodies rather than for the presence of the virus itself,[20] and because the production of antibodies is not instantaneous, there is a lag between infection and the detectability of infection. The median time between infection and the production of detectable amounts of HIV antibodies has been estimated at 2.1 months, with 95 percent of infected persons producing detectable amounts of antibodies within 5.8 months (Horsburgh et al. 1989). To test negative, therefore, need mean no more than that six months previously the tested person had not been infected. He may have become infected since, without knowing it. There is speculation, as yet unconfirmed, that some HIV carriers may not test positive for many years after they are infected, sim-

---

18. Volberding et al. (1990); Lemp et al. (1990b); Anderson, Gupta, and May (1991, pp. 356–357). Another benefit of early detection of HIV infection is that vaccines or other preventive therapy are available for some of the characteristic diseases to which the weakening of the immune system by the virus opens a person (Rhame and Maki 1989, p. 1249).

19. A proper study would require withholding the drug from a control group of persons who were HIV-positive. Such persons prefer to have the drug rather than contribute to science for the possible benefit of future infected persons. For a good survey of HIV and AIDS therapies, see Global AIDS Policy Coalition (1992, pp. 233–246).

20. There are now tests for the virus itself, though they are not in common use and are also not foolproof, because a person may be infected and infective even though the virus is in only a few of his cells and is well hidden within them.

ply because the particular strain of the virus with which they are infected does not stimulate an immune reaction.

There is neither a vaccine nor a cure for HIV-AIDS. The tendency of the virus to mutate, so that no two AIDS viruses are quite alike, has retarded progress toward developing either a vaccine or a cure (Waldholz 1992; Chase 1992; Berzovsky 1991), though tests of several vaccines are now under way.[21]

Fortunately the virus is not particularly robust; contact with air, for example, kills it. It is carried in infective form in blood, semen, and vaginal fluids, and can infect a person when the blood, semen, or vaginal fluids of an infected person enter the bloodstream of an uninfected one, as can happen in sexual intercourse when there are cuts or sores in the anus (or rectum), vagina, or penis,[22] in the sharing of an unsterilized hypodermic needle, in a blood transfusion, or even when a splatter of blood (provided it has sufficient volume that not all the virus in the blood is exposed to the air and thus killed) from an infected patient enters an open wound or sore on the skin of a doctor, nurse, dentist, or other health-care worker. The virus will pass the placenta, and therefore a pregnant woman who is infected can infect her fetus; and a nursing mother can infect her child. It cannot be spread by simple touching, as in shaking hands, and almost certainly not by an exchange of saliva, as in kissing, either, even though small quantities of the virus are present in the saliva (Barr et al. 1992). The qualification in "almost" should be borne in mind, however (Woollely 1989). Considerable uncertainty remains concerning the transmission of the AIDS virus. We are told that some doctors advise homosexuals to avoid deep ("French" or "wet") kissing, though we know of no biomedical literature that supports a concern with transmission by kissing.

Even in semen or blood, the virus is not highly virulent, a term we use loosely to refer to the ability of the virus to infect a recipient of bodily fluids containing it. Unless large quantities of blood are injected directly into the bloodstream, as by a blood transfusion, the probability of becoming infected from a single exposure is slight. How slight depends on

---

21. On AIDS vaccine research generally, see the helpful summary in Global AIDS Policy Coalition (1992, pp. 247–257).

22. And, possibly, except in the case of the penis, even when there are not. The virus may be able to enter cells on the surface of the anus, rectum, or vagina (Haseltine 1990, p. 26). Recently, CD4-like receptors have been discovered on rectal epithelial cells, which may explain the ease of HIV transmission in anal intercourse.

the nature of the exposure (for example, a single act of unshielded anal intercourse versus a single act of vaginal intercourse), the condition of the immune system and relevant tissues of the person exposed, and the infectivity of the person transmitting the virus, which varies, apparently widely, across persons, and also at different stages of infection; there appear to be peaks shortly after the carrier is first infected and shortly before he converts to the active status of the disease.

The most dangerous form of exposure is that to which a hemophiliac is subject if he receives unscreened blood solids. Not only is a direct infusion of blood (or an organ transplant) a highly efficient method of transmission, but in the course of a relatively short period of time, a hemophiliac receives the blood of many hundreds or even thousands of people, and if any of them is infected he may become so.

The next most imperiled group, after recipients of unscreened blood, consists of men or women who play the receptive role in unshielded (that is, without a condom) anal intercourse (Detels et al. 1989).[23] The tissues of the anus and rectum are delicate and easily torn in intercourse—and the virus may, as we have pointed out, be able to enter them even when they are intact. Vaginal tissues are delicate too; for this reason, and also because women receive much more fluid in vaginal intercourse than men do, women are considerably more susceptible to infection with the AIDS virus—the range of estimates is 2.9 to 17.5 times—than their male sexual partners (Mantell, Schinke, and Akabas 1988; Padian, Shiboski, and Jewell 1991; Plummer, Moses, and Ndinya-Achola 1991; European Study Group 1992). Nevertheless the risk of HIV infection, even to women, is normally small in vaginal intercourse—on average no more than 1 in 500 exposures and perhaps no more than 1 in 1,000 (Holmberg et al. 1989, p. 116; Fordyce et al. 1991)—compared to the risks posed by anal intercourse (20 to 50 per 1,000 exposures; Holmberg et al. 1989, p. 117 [tab. 2]), needle-sharing, and transfusions of unscreened blood or blood solids. Quantitative estimates of HIV infection risk must, however, be treated with caution. Because of the variety of sexual practices,[24] uncertainties about the mechanisms of transmission

---

23. On the AIDS risk that anal intercourse poses to women, see Voeller (1991, pp. 235–236); Åsard (1992).

24. We have been told, for example, that in the homosexual community today, sex is classified in three risk classes: unsafe (for example, anal sex without condom, water sports, fisting, bruising SM); safer (anal sex with condom, oral sex, wet kissing, lighter SM); safe (mutual masturbation, frottage, dry kissing).

of the virus, and wide variance in susceptibility (depending on such things as the state of one's immune system and the existence of "cofactors" such as having another sexually transmitted disease), the risks associated with various practices are highly uncertain. In particular, rather little is known about the risks associated with unshielded oral sex; they appear to be much smaller than those of unshielded anal or vaginal intercourse but may not be completely negligible (Leonard, Freund, and Platt 1989; Hearst and Hulley 1988, p. 2429). It appears that in the United States and the other wealthy countries, men who confine themselves to vaginal intercourse are in relatively little (though not no) danger of becoming infected.[25] Some evidence for this conjecture is that although many female prostitutes in the United States are HIV-positive, they are not a major source of transmission to men (Rosenberg and Weiner 1988; Cohen, Alexander, and Wofsky 1988).

Sexual promiscuity—sex with many different partners[26]—is a risk factor for AIDS because the more sexual partners one has, the greater is the likelihood that one or more of them is an HIV carrier. (Some qualification is necessary here, however, as we shall see in Chapter 1.) This may be an additional explanation for the much higher incidence of AIDS among homosexuals than among heterosexuals: the former have on average a much higher rate of changing sexual partners (Anderson and May 1991, p. 256), though the rate is declining in response to the risk of AIDS, as we shall see in Chapter 2.

Infection of medical workers, male or female, from accidents involving AIDS patients is possible but rare. Through 1992 there had been only 33 documented and another 69 possible instances in this country (Centers for Disease Control 1993, p. 19 [tab. 15]). These workers are more endangered by the hepatitis B virus, which is also blood-borne. It is true that hepatitis B is much less lethal than AIDS and that there is an effective (though not completely effective) vaccine against it. But the hepatitis B virus is much more easily spread than HIV; more patients are infected with HBV than HIV; and many health workers refuse to be vaccinated. As a result, deaths from hepatitis B among health workers exceed AIDS cases in this group by a hundredfold (U.S. Department of

---

25. If women are 10 times more susceptible to infection from vaginal intercourse than men, this would imply that the transmission rate from female to male is no more than 1 in 5,000 exposures.

26. Consistent with abstracting from ethical issues, we use the terms "promiscuity" and "promiscuous" without pejorative intent.

Labor 1991, p. 64,009). Therefore, policy toward the protection of health workers from patients' blood-borne diseases is, or at least should be, dominated by concern with hepatitis B. Infection of patients by HIV-positive health workers is even rarer than the opposite route (Danila et al. 1991).

Because of HIV's short latency period but long incubation period, and the feasibility of ascertaining one's infection status within six months after exposure to it, many people—primarily, of course, those who have had an HIV test and learned the (positive) result—know that they are infected (and infective) long before they become symptomatic. Have they anything to lose from a medical standpoint if, having discovered that they are doomed, they continue to engage in unprotected sex? This question has significant implications for both private behavior and public policy; unfortunately the answer is unclear. Some biologists and physicians believe that reinfection with a different strain of this highly mutable virus places the body's immune system under additional stress and so accelerates conversion to the active disease state, thus shortening life. We know of no clinical evidence of this effect. One statistical study (van Griensven et al. 1990) concludes that intercourse with a person who has AIDS accelerates conversion, but not intercourse with a person in whom the disease is still in its incubation stage (that is, a person who is HIV-positive but asymptomatic). Phair and colleagues (1992), however, find that unshielded receptive anal intercourse with multiple sex partners accelerates conversion regardless of the partners' infection status.

The risk of infection can be reduced by screening one's sexual partners, by testing blood used in transfusions, by avoiding promiscuous sex, by avoiding unprotected sex with members of subpopulations in which the incidence of infection is high, and so forth. But the only sure method of protecting against transmission of the disease is not to expose one's bloodstream to bodily fluids (other than saliva) that may contain HIV. Hence the centrality of the latex[27] condom in discussions of "safe" sex—sex in which the risk of transmission of HIV is minimized (whether eliminated is another question). Frequently in this book we shall use sex with condoms as a synonym for safe sex, and sex without as a synonym for unsafe sex. But this usage is imprecise. Not only are there are other forms

---

27. The vast majority of condoms are made of latex. A small minority are made from lamb intestine; it is unclear whether these are effective against transmission of the AIDS virus (Cates and Stone 1992, p. 78; Consumer Reports staff 1989). In this book we use "condom" to mean latex condom.

of (more or, often, less) safe sex, including solitary and mutual masturbation and withdrawal before ejaculation (coitus interruptus), and, for
women, lesbian relationships; but condoms are not 100 percent effective
in preventing the emission or reception of semen. They have a limited
shelf life (Nakamura 1990), and they may rip, especially in anal intercourse, for which condoms are not designed,[28] or leak, or spill when
being removed. Moral conservatives, who want people to abstain from
nonmarital sex, emphasize how unsafe condoms are (Bennett 1988, pp.
3–4), arguing for example that repeated intercourse with an HIV carrier
is highly dangerous even with condoms because they have a 10 percent
failure rate. The argument is overstated and imprecise. No one knows
the number of AIDS cases that have resulted either from defective, or
from improper use of, condoms. Ten percent is the most commonly used
estimate for the failure rate of condoms as a *contraceptive*, although some
estimates run as high as 16 percent (Woodard 1991). The failure rate of
condoms as an AIDS preventive, however, has never been measured
(Hearst and Hulley 1988, p. 2430). There is evidence that even sporadic
use of condoms has a substantial effect in protecting female partners of
HIV carriers from infection (Cates and Stone 1992, p. 79 and tab. 2), but
the effect has not been reliably quantified.

The two types of potential condom failure as a prophylactic—defective
condom and improper use—should be kept distinct. Leakage or breakage of condoms is rare. Typical estimates are 1 percent in anal intercourse
and .6 percent in vaginal (Woodard 1991; Consumer Reports staff 1989),
though Golombok, Sketchley, and Rust (1989) report a higher breakage
rate in homosexual anal intercourse, and Cates and Stone (1992, p. 80
[tab. 3]) report a wide range of breakage rates, between .5 and 7 percent
for anal intercourse and between .6 and 2 percent for vaginal. The more
serious problem appears to be improper use, for example failing to put
on the condom before first genital contact or to withdraw before detu-
mescence (Brody 1987). Advocates of condoms as an AIDS preventive
believe that education in the proper use of condoms can make them
an adequately safe method of prevention, given the small probability of
breakage or leakage and the possibility that the spermicidal coating on
many condoms prevents transmission of the virus even if the condom
does break or leak (Rietmeijer et al. 1988). And a condom that leaks

---

28. There are condoms specially designed for anal intercourse, and they have a lower
failure rate (van Griensven et al. 1988b), but as far as we know they are not sold in the
United States.

or breaks may protect the wearer even if it doesn't protect his partner. However, since the probability of condom failure cannot be rated as negligible, repeated intercourse with an HIV carrier can create a substantial cumulative probability of transmission even if a condom is used every time. This suggests that condoms may not be an optimal form of protection for high-risk populations (Perlman et al. 1990; see also Weinstein et al. 1989, pp. 488–489). Moreover, not all sexually active persons are educable in the proper use of condoms.

Epidemiology. AIDS is a worldwide epidemic, but our particular interest is in the United States and other wealthy countries. The AIDS virus spread rapidly in the United States and Europe beginning in the late 1970s, initially among male homosexuals[29] and bisexuals,[30] later among recipients of blood transfusions and blood solids, intravenous drug users, and (via intravenous drug users and bisexuals) women, and from women to some children and heterosexual men. Because of its long latency period, AIDS itself did not begin to show up until the 1980s. First diagnosed in 1981 among homosexual men, within two years the disease had also been diagnosed in intravenous drug users, heterosexuals, recipients of blood and blood products, and the other groups that we now know to be at high risk of HIV infection. By that time the modes of transmission were known, and in the same year (1983) the virus that causes AIDS was discovered (Friedland and Klein 1987).

Among the developed countries, the United States has the highest per capita incidence of AIDS, as shown for a representative set of those countries in Table I-1. As shown in Figure I-1, the incidence of AIDS in the United States has grown rapidly since 1981, though at a decreasing rate, to its 1992 level of 47,000 new cases per year.[31] By the end of 1992,

---

29. "Patient Zero," who is believed to have introduced HIV into the United States, was a homosexual airline steward employed by Air Canada (Shilts 1987).

30. An unfortunately ambiguous term, sometimes used to mean men who are indifferent between having male or female sexual partners, sometimes used to mean men of predominantly homosexual preference who have occasional intercourse with women, but here used simply to mean men who have relations with persons of both sexes, regardless of their preference. Kinsey found a surprisingly high percentage of homosexual acts among predominantly heterosexual men, and subsequent studies confirm this (Rogers and Turner 1991, pp. 505–509; Reinisch, Ziemba-Davis, and Sanders 1990, pp. 69–70; see generally Tielman, Carballo, and Hendriks 1991). There are, of course, female as well as male bisexuals, but, as throughout, we ignore them, since lesbian relations virtually never transmit HIV.

31. This graph, like all the empirical graphs in this book (unless otherwise indicated), is compiled from data in the AIDS Public Information File Data Set as updated in July

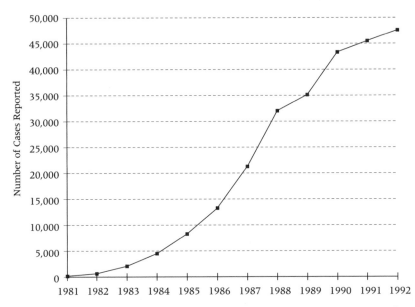

Figure I-1 Number of U.S. AIDS cases reported per year, 1981–1992. (1992 figures are estimates.) *Source:* CDC Public Information Data Set, 7/1/92.

more than 250,000 cases of AIDS had been diagnosed in this country, and there had been more than 170,000 deaths.[32] AIDS is now the second-largest killer of men aged 25 to 44 in the United States, after accidents.

Of current new nonpediatric cases in the United States (that is, cases in which the patient is 13 years old or older), 57 percent are reported

1992 (the latest update available to us when we were preparing our graphs, although complete 1992 data in some categories are published in Centers for Disease Control [1993], and where they are we have updated accordingly). The data set lists cases both by date reported and by date diagnosed. We generally use the former, because as a result of reporting lags complete data for cases diagnosed in the last two years are available only on an estimated basis. We recognize the possibility that changes in reporting lag could distort our statistics on the growth of AIDS, but we point out that the CDC's estimates of new cases, which are designed to correct the distortion in the statistics of diagnosed cases that is induced by reporting lag, generate the same profile as the statistics for reported cases. See Centers for Disease Control (1993, p. 5 [fig. 5]) and Figure 2-1 in Chapter 2; see also Chapter 2 for more on the problem of reporting lag. For a lucid summary of the recent trends in AIDS statistics, see Green, Karon, and Nwanyanwu (1992).

32. The source for the statistics in this and the next paragraph is Centers for Disease Control (1993), passim.

Table I-1   Number of new AIDS cases in 1990[a]

Country	No. of cases	No. of cases per 100,000 population
United States	35,829	13.3
France	3,395	6.0
Spain	2,351	6.0
Italy	2,384	4.2
Australia	568	3.4
Canada	868	2.7
Germany	1,530	2.5
England	932	1.6
Sweden	125	1.5
Israel	27	0.6
Japan	92	0.1

a. The source for these statistics is the World Health Organization. The reason for the lower estimate of the number of 1990 U.S. cases in this table than in Figure I-1 is that the WHO figures were compiled earlier, and thus are more sensitive to reporting lag (see note 31).

to be among male homosexuals, 23 percent among intravenous drug users, 6 percent among male homosexual intravenous drug users, 3 percent among recipients of blood or blood solids, 7 percent from heterosexual intercourse, and 4 percent undetermined. Almost 90 percent of the cases are men, and almost 90 percent of them got AIDS from homosexual sex or intravenous drug use. The principal causes of AIDS in women are intravenous drug use (50 percent) and heterosexual intercourse (36 percent)—these high percentages reflecting, in part, the fact that homosexual sex is not a significant method of transmission among women. Fewer than 2 percent of the total new AIDS cases are among persons under the age of 13. The percentage of cases resulting from homosexual intercourse and needle-sharing, high as it is, is probably underestimated. These are socially stigmatized activities, and the reporting authorities rely for the source of a person's infection primarily on the person's own say-so ("self-reporting"). Since the total number of male homosexuals and intravenous drug users in this country is, though unknown, relatively small (see Chapter 8 for estimates), it is plain that the risk of AIDS is very unevenly distributed across different population groups. Regional variance is also great. Among states, the current annual rate of AIDS cases ranges from .8 per 100,000 persons in North Dakota and 1.1 in

South Dakota to 46 in New York. Among metropolitan areas having a population of at least 500,000, the rate ranges from 4.3 per 100,000 in Grand Rapids, South Carolina (slightly lower than the average rate in all nonmetropolitan areas, which is 5.2 per 100,000 population) to 131.7 in San Francisco.

If relatively few heterosexual men in this country are at high risk of infection with the AIDS virus, it may seem odd that any appreciable number of new cases in women would be attributed to heterosexual intercourse. The number is not large (36 percent of roughly 10 percent), but one reason it is not even smaller is that many men have sexual relations with both men and women (see note 30; see also Carballo, Tawil, and Holmes 1992; Chu et al. 1992). An additional factor is that bisexual men are more likely than exclusively heterosexual ones to engage in anal intercourse with their female sex partners (Voeller 1991, p. 237). And heterosexual men who are infected with HIV as a result of intravenous drug use or blood transfusions transmit the virus to women with whom they have intercourse.[33]

Because of the long incubation period of the disease and the absence of either universal or random-sample testing, the number of persons currently infected with the AIDS virus but not yet afflicted with AIDS is not known. Current statistics on AIDS reflect sexual and other risky activities engaged in years ago, and if those activities have changed, predictions based on the current statistics will prove inaccurate. Estimates of the number of persons infected with HIV today vary widely and are unreliable. The most common range of estimates for the United States is 1 to 1.5 million, but, as we shall note in Chapter 2, this figure probably is too high. Estimates of the number of people infected with HIV are based on extrapolations from the known rate of HIV infection among populations (such as that of military recruits and of patients in certain hospitals) that have been tested, and on the method of "back calculation" described in Chapter 1 (Rosenberg et al. 1991, p. 281).

AIDS in the Third World

The Global AIDS Policy Coalition has estimated that by 1995 more than 17 million people will have become infected by the AIDS virus since the epidemic began and that more than 6 million will have converted to

---

33. Mantell, Schinke, and Akabas (1988) is an excellent discussion of AIDS in women.

AIDS (Global AIDS Policy Coalition 1992, pp. 105, 128 [tabs. 2.8, 3.9]).[34] The vast majority of AIDS and HIV cases are in the nations of the Third World, particularly Africa. A comprehensive economic analysis of AIDS would not ignore the Third World, as we shall largely do. But we have our reasons. The United States and other wealthy countries differ greatly from Third World countries along a variety of the dimensions that are relevant to analysis of the epidemic—and not just in prevalence, which is the difference to be explained. They differ in the availability of good data on HIV and AIDS, in sexual practices (prostitution is much more widespread in many Third World countries, and female circumcision, still practiced in parts of Africa, may facilitate the transmission of HIV to women), in income and education, in the availability of condoms, in HIV strains, and in the prevalence of ulcerative genital diseases, which are endemic in many parts of Africa and which appear to increase HIV infectivity greatly. We have no reason to think the assumption of rationality in sexual practices any less applicable to the Third World than to Europe and North America; but to test the assumption in the Third World setting would require another book.

That book, moreover, would surely be focused heavily on a set of economic consequences of the epidemic that is of minor importance in the United States: the macroeconomic. The current and likely future magnitude of the epidemic here and in the other wealthy countries just is too small to have substantial, or even measurable, implications for such aggregate economic phenomena as economic growth, GNP, and per capita income, although in Chapter 4 we consider the possible consequences for aggregate expenditures on health—and find them to be small. In countries as hard hit by AIDS as some of the African countries are, and as Thailand, India, and some other Asian countries soon may be, the epidemic could have substantial macroeconomic consequences. For example, AIDS could reduce the birth rate in some of these countries, while at the same time (because it is a disease largely of young adults) reducing the fraction of the population that is most productive and the incentive to invest in human capital (Meltzer 1992). The first effect (on birth rate) would tend to reduce poverty, the second to increase it. These effects, the interaction of which poses complex analytic issues, are separate from the impact of AIDS on the costs of health care—an impact that is larger the greater the magnitude of the epidemic, but that is smaller the fewer the resources that a society devotes to health care.

---

34. The HIV estimates are limited to adults.

An econometric literature well illustrated by Gori and Richter (1978) estimates the effect that eliminating major avoidable causes of mortality, such as cigarette smoking and alcohol abuse, would have on economic aggregates in the United States. In this country, however, AIDS is not a major cause of mortality. In countries where it is, the econometric literature is applicable, and should be applied. But that too is a task for a book on the economics of AIDS in the Third World. Our book begins the full-scale economic analysis of AIDS; it does not complete it.

CHAPTER 1

An Economic Model of Risky Sexual Behavior

The AIDS epidemic is primarily, although not exclusively, the consequence of voluntary decisions by persons of different HIV infection status to have unshielded sexual intercourse with each other. Needle-sharing by intravenous drug users, a growing cause of infection, is analytically quite similar to unsafe sex. We explore the relevant differences later. Risky sexual trades, in turn, are analytically similar to conventional market transactions that take place under uncertainty concerning the reliability of the transactors or the quality of the good or service being sold, as in credit markets or the sale of potentially defective goods. In this chapter we develop a model of the propagation of AIDS through voluntary mutual transactions and compare the model's empirical predictions and policy implications with those of epidemiological models of the disease.

The Basic Model

We begin by considering the economic character of the choice between safe and unsafe sex. For simplicity we assume that safe sex means sex with condoms and is completely safe, and that all other forms of sex are equally unsafe. These and other unrealistic assumptions will be relaxed in due course. For expositional clarity only, we denote the representative individuals considering a sexual "trade" with each other as m and f (for "male" and "female"), though of course many risky sexual trades are between persons of the same sex.

If, disease risk to one side, safe sex yielded as much utility as unsafe, the only rational choice, given the low price of condoms, would be safe over unsafe sex, and the scale of the AIDS epidemic would be inexplicable in economic terms. (The scale, but not the epidemic itself. Because many people became infected before the disease was discovered or its methods of transmission understood, the epidemic cannot be entirely ascribed to rational choice.) For most Americans, however, the use of a condom reduces sexual pleasure.[1] This is an example of the distinction mentioned in the Introduction between prices and costs. If evidence is needed for the proposition that condoms are considered by many sexually active persons in this country to impose costs far beyond their price, it is that when they are distributed free of charge on college campuses, many students still engage in unsafe sex.

No iron law of biology or psychology dictates that the use of condoms reduces sexual pleasure; for it retards ejaculation. But for most Americans, particularly men, this advantage of sex with condoms does not fully compensate for the diminished sensation resulting from the presence of a sheath, for the interruption in sexual foreplay, and for the time and bother involved in providing oneself at all relevant times with a supply of condoms. A further disutility of condoms is that an expression of a desire to use one may be taken as evidence of being timid (a particular concern in "macho" cultures, which ours is in part), or of being particularly sensitive to the risk of AIDS by virtue of having engaged in stigmatized activities. So a demand that one's partner use a condom may be taken as an accusation, an offer to use a condom as a confession. Information costs and gender-inequality considerations, discussed in subsequent chapters, further reduce the demand for condoms.

Condoms are more popular in some other countries, notably Japan, though at least part of the reason is that Japan bans the contraceptive pill and so increases the contraceptive value of condoms. Mention of the pill should remind us that condoms reduce the procreative benefits of intercourse for persons wanting to produce children. In Chapter 9 we examine this additional dimension of the choice between sex with condoms and sex without condoms, but for now we assume that their only effect is to reduce the risk of AIDS.

To the extent that safe sex is more costly to the participants than unsafe sex is, the latter may be preferred despite its dangers—or may not. We model the decision to engage in unsafe sex as a problem in rational

---

1. "The much recommended [for homosexuals] use of condoms seems particularly blind. For those for whom sensation and not just will and fantasy is requisite for the transition from arousal to orgasm, condoms fail" (Mohr 1988, p. 232). See also Ekstrand (1992).

decision-making under uncertainty. The expected utility (EU) of unsafe sex for m and for f is equal to the benefits (B) of unsafe sex minus its expected costs, and is given by

(1.1) $EU_m = B - C(1 - P_m)(P_f)$

and

(1.2) $EU_f = B - C(1 - P_f)(P_m)$.

If the special cases of force and fraud are excluded, and attention thus confined to mutually beneficial trades, a risky sexual trade will take place only if both EU_m and EU_f are positive. The equations assume risk neutrality, but that assumption (relaxed later) is inessential to our analysis.

The expected costs of unsafe sex depend on the costs (C) of becoming infected with the AIDS virus and the probability of becoming infected. Equations 1.1 and 1.2 represent that probability as a function of two other probabilities: the probability that m is already infected, denoted by P_m, and the probability that f is already infected, denoted by P_f. A third probability—transmission probability—is introduced later. In the special case in which one's partner, but not oneself, is infected—so that, in equation 1.1, $P_f = 1$ and $P_m = 0$, while in equation 1.2 $P_f = 0$ and $P_m = 1$—both equations reduce to $B - C$.

$B(> 0)$ is the gross benefit of unsafe over safe sex, and is thus, on our assumption that safe sex is sex with condoms, equal to the disutility of using a condom. We assume in our formal analysis that B is the same for both m and f; that is, that both have an equal disutility from using a condom. They might, of course, have different disutilities.[2] They might for that matter have different costs (as well as different risks of infection, which the formal model does take into account). These are potentially important qualifications, given our assumption that a risky sexual trade will occur only if *both EU_m and EU_f* are positive. One might be positive and the other negative even if $P_m = P_f$. If, for example, m had a greater aversion to condoms than f did, the benefit of risky sex for males (B_m)

---

2. In particular, women, unless they want to get pregnant, are apt to have less aversion to the use of a condom than men. The qualification about pregnancy is important, however; in addition we remind the reader that we use "m" and "f" for notational convenience only. In the United States and other wealthy countries, homosexual transmission of the AIDS virus is far more common than heterosexual transmission.

might be high enough to make $EU_m > 0$ while the benefit of risky sex to females (B_f) was so low that $EU_f < 0$. Yet it would not follow that a risky trade would not take place. For m would be willing to offer to compensate f in an effort to overcome f's aversion. In effect, compensation would raise B_f. The compensation would not have to be and ordinarily would not be pecuniary; prostitution is a special case. More often a sexual trade will be embedded in a relationship involving an exchange of multiple services. Suppose that in our simplified formula (in which one partner is infected for sure and the other uninfected for sure) for the expected utility of risky sex B_m is 5 and C_m 2, so that m derives a net expected utility of 3 from risky sex, while B_f is 1 and C_f again 2, so that f derives a net utility of -1 from risky sex. At any price between 1 and 3 for obtaining f's consent to risky sex, both parties will be made better off by having risky sex even though f would, but for compensation, prefer safe sex. We ignore such complications for now, along with alternatives to compensation for overcoming one partner's preference for safe sex (see Chapter 3).

C is the cost—not only medical expenses, loss of earnings, and other pecuniary costs but also and primarily the disutility of a painful and debilitating disease and a premature death, as well as possible social stigma and exclusion from sexual activity or at least some forms thereof—of becoming infected with the AIDS virus. Other sexually transmitted diseases impose other costs, such as sterility, instead or as well. Our analysis could easily be generalized to these other diseases, and we do discuss them from time to time.

For the time being we assume that the cost to one's sexual partner should the latter become infected is not a cost to oneself; that is, we assume that neither m nor f is altruistic toward the other. This assumption is relaxed in the next chapter.

Given the interval, often many years, between infection with HIV and the onset of serious illness, we could interpret C as the *discounted* cost of AIDS. The discount rate presumably is higher for poor people, because discounting the future at a high rate discourages investments in human capital and thus lowers income, and for drug addicts, because addiction to a dangerous drug implies trading future health and income for present satisfaction. These implications are discussed further in the next chapter.

A number of points must be kept in mind in considering the probability terms in equations 1.1 and 1.2. First, in the balance of this chapter we assume—contrary to our earlier discussion of the case where P is either 1 or 0—that neither m nor f can transform the probability that one or the other of them is infected into a certainty of being infected or not infected. In other words, HIV testing is excluded from the model in this chapter although it is the focus of Chapter 3.

P_m and P_f are the simple probabilities that m and f, respectively, are infected. They are not transmission probabilities. To determine the probability of transmitting the AIDS virus and hence the expected cost of risky sex in equations 1.1 and 1.2, P_m and P_f would have to be the joint probabilities (1) that m and f, respectively, are already infected with the virus *and* (2) that if either m or f is infected, unshielded sex between them will cause the other to become infected. For if each probability term denotes merely the probability that m or f is infected, a full cost-benefit analysis of risky sex would require the introduction of another probability—the probability (much lower than 1) that, if one's partner is infected, sex with him or her will result in oneself becoming infected too.

We can make this adjustment by rewriting equations 1.1 and 1.2 as

$$(1.1a) \quad EU_m = B - C[P_{tf}(1 - P_m)P_f]$$

and

$$(1.2a) \quad EU_f = B - C[P_{tm}(1 - P_f)P_m].$$

P_{tf} denotes the fraction of unshielded sexual acts between a positive f and a negative m that result in infection; P_{tm} is defined similarly for the case in which m is positive and f negative. Because infectivity need not be symmetrical—in fact we know that it is easier for a man to infect a woman in vaginal intercourse than vice versa, and for the insertive partner to infect the receptive partner in anal intercourse (homosexual or heterosexual) than vice versa—equations 1.1a and 1.2a distinguish between the fraction of unshielded sexual acts that result in the infection of m by f (P_{tf}) and the fraction of unshielded sexual acts that result in the infection of f by m (P_{tm}). But for purposes of exposition it is simpler to stay with the unrealistic assumption that $P_{tm} = P_{tf} = 1$; and most of our analysis does not depend on asymmetrical transmission probabilities.

P_m and P_f denote subjective probabilities—probabilities as reckoned by each individual—as distinct from frequencies in a population. We assume, however, in part for simplicity and in part to facilitate empirical analysis with available data, that on average, though possibly with great variance, the subjective probabilities correspond to frequencies and hence that P_m and P_f are the fractions of individuals in the two groups who are infected. (Chapters 2 and 6 discuss situations in which infection or transmission probabilities are overestimated or underestimated.) We further assume, as the notation suggests, that the subjective probabilities of each party are the same—that is, that P_m is the same to both m and f and that P_f is also the same to both m and f. Of course they need not be: m for example might think that P_m is high but persuade f that it was low. Fraud would violate our assumption that AIDS is spread by *voluntary* trades. Other involuntary modes of transmission are rape, blood transfusions where the donee has no reason to suspect infected blood, and the infection of a fetus or infant by the mother; but, today at any rate, empirically the most important probably is fraud; we discuss it in — Chapter 3.

One might suppose that $P_f C$ would be the expected cost of risky sex to m (and $P_m C$ the expected cost to f)—the cost if m becomes infected discounted (multiplied) by the probability that f is infected and hence infective—and therefore that the second term on the right-hand side of our equations is unnecessarily complex. One would be wrong. For on the further simplifying assumption that repeated infection with the AIDS virus does not accelerate conversion to the active disease state or otherwise impose an incremental harm on the infected person, unsafe sex with an HIV-positive partner is costly only to a person who is himself uninfected. One's willingness to engage in unsafe sex is thus an increasing function of one's own likelihood of already being infected and a decreasing function of the likelihood that one's partner is already infected. The probability that one is not already infected is given by 1 minus one's own probability of being infected: hence the terms $1 - P_m$ and $1 - P_f$ in equations 1.1 and 1.2. Disregarding as we said we would the difference between being infected and actually transmitting the virus to an uninfected person, we can view $(1 - P_m)P_f$ and $(1 - P_f)P_m$ as probabilities of infecting. This should help to make transparent the character of equations 1.1 and 1.2 as cost-benefit formulas for risky sex, where the net benefit is the disutility of a condom (B) minus the cost of AIDS discounted by the probability of becoming infected as a consequence of risky sex.

The equations implicitly treat P_m and P_f as independent. Yet it is possible to argue that sexual partners are likely to sort themselves by their infection probabilities. Indeed, we shall repeatedly in this book criticize the epidemiological models for assuming random sorting. But this does not invalidate the assumption that P_m and P_f are independent in equations 1.1 and 1.2. One must distinguish between *meeting* and *trading*. Our model assumes random meeting in the sense that potential sex partners are assumed to meet regardless of their respective probabilities of being already infected. A sexual trade, however, which is what can spread the disease, occurs only when potential partners decide to have sex with each other. This sorting, the sorting of actual (trading) sex partners, being guided by incentives, is nonrandom and, as we shall see, may well generate a positive correlation between trading partners' infection probabilities. Emphasis on incentives is in fact the fundamental difference between the economic and the epidemiological models.

Because the cost function in our equations has a probabilistic component, people who prefer an uncertain prospect to its actuarial equivalent (for example, prefer a 1 percent probability of $100 to $1) can be expected to be overrepresented among persons engaging in risky sex. By definition they are more likely, other things being equal, to prefer the uncertain cost (the prospect of AIDS) to the certain cost (the disutility of using a condom). Our formal analysis abstracts from differences among persons in discount rates and attitude toward uncertainty by confining attention to two representative individuals. This simplification is not essential to our results, since, to repeat an earlier point, it is always possible that some form of compensation can be used to effect a mutually beneficial risky sexual trade between persons who differ in the utility they derive from risky sex. This point would be at the forefront of an economic analysis of the effect of the AIDS epidemic on prostitution, whether male or female, but we shall content ourselves with mentioning a few implications of that analysis. Given that male-female transmission of the AIDS virus is more likely than female-male, female prostitutes would, other things being equal, desire safe sex more than their customers did. However, the customers might be able to overcome the prostitutes' desire for safe sex by paying a higher price for prostitutes' risky-sex services. (For evidence, though concerning male rather than female prostitution, see Boulton 1991.) We might expect, therefore, that female prostitution is becoming more expensive, and therefore less common, as a result of the AIDS epidemic, other things held constant. A possibly offsetting factor, however, is that the supply of prostitutes may be increasing because, especially in poor countries, already-infected women both lack good occupational alternatives and incur little or no incremental disutility from engaging in unsafe sex. Notice also that the price effect may be small if safe sex is considered a close substitute for unsafe sex in the market for prostitutes' services.

Male prostitution is even more likely to be a declining industry, because the danger of AIDS to men who patronize male prostitutes is much greater than the danger to the customers, invariably male, of female prostitutes. But again there may be an offset. Men who know they are HIV-positive and have difficulty inducing HIV-negatives to have risky sex with them may turn to HIV-positive male prostitutes, who, having little or nothing to lose from unsafe sex, will not charge a significant premium to engage in it. And again, to the extent that safe sex is a close substitute for risky sex, the impact of an AIDS-driven increase in the price of male prostitutes' services on the demand for those services may be small even if few male prostitutes are willing to engage in risky sex. There is evidence of widespread substitution of safe for risky sex by male prostitutes in response to the epidemic (Pleak and Meyer-Bahlburg 1990).

The two utility functions described by equations 1.1 and 1.2 generate the joint demand for risky sexual trades for all possible infection probabilities (P_m, P_f) of our two representative individuals. That joint demand is depicted in Figure 1-1, which shows how a fatal disease can be spread by voluntary utility-maximizing conduct of rational persons.

The entire box represents all possible pairs of infection probabilities of *m* and *f*. The curve beginning at the left edge of the box and labeled

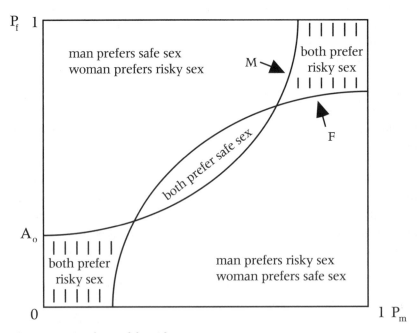

Figure 1-1 Joint demand for risky sex.

M is the locus of probability pairs at which m is indifferent between safe and unsafe sex, while the other curve, labeled F, is the corresponding locus for f.[3] At the left edge of the box, where P_m is zero, it is obvious from equation 1.1 that m will be willing to engage in risky sex provided that B/CP_f, the benefit-cost ratio to him of risky sex under the assumption of $P_m = 0$, is at least 1—that is, if the benefits match or exceed the costs. This condition is more likely to be satisfied the lower P_f is. For example, if B, the disutility of a condom, is 10, C, the cost of becoming infected with the AIDS virus, is 1,000, and P_f, the probability that m's partner will infect one with the virus, is .003, m will prefer risky to safe sex with f, because the benefit (10) will exceed the expected cost (1,000 $\times$ .003 = 3). Notice that at point A_o, P_f, although positive, is low enough to generate a benefit-cost ratio of 1 for m even though $P_m = 0$. But if P_f were any higher, m would refuse to risk unsafe sex with her. As the probability that m is already infected rises, m has less to gain from safe sex. He therefore becomes willing to engage in risky sex with increasingly dangerous f's. This explains the shape of the curve for m. The curve for f is analyzed similarly.

Since we treat risky sex as a mutually beneficial exchange of services, it takes place only in the region in which both m and f derive a positive net expected utility from it. That region consists of the two shaded areas in Figure 1-1. In the lower left-hand segment, where the probability that either m or f is infected is small, the expected cost to each of risky sex is slight and is outweighed by the benefit. In the upper right-hand segment, where the probability that either is infected is great, the expected cost of risky sex is also slight, since risky sex produces only a small increase in the (already high) risk of becoming infected, so again the benefits dominate. In the central region of the diagram, neither m nor f is willing to engage in risky sex, while in the remaining unshaded areas either m or f is unwilling and again risky sex is not chosen, because of the assumption that any transaction is mutually beneficial. Figure 1-1 thus depicts risky sex as an economic transaction that, ex ante, is mutually beneficial to the parties, although ex post it may prove a disaster to one of them.

---

3. The formal definitions of F and M are:

$F \equiv \{(P_m, P_f)$ such that $B = (1 - P_f)P_m C\} = \{(P_m, P_f)$ such that $P_f(P_m) = 1 - B/P_m C\};$

$M \equiv \{(P_m, P_f)$ such that $B = (1 - P_m)P_f C\} = \{(P_m, P_f)$ such that $P_f(P_m) = B/(1 - P_m)C\}.$

Figure 1-1 is not drawn to scale. If it were, A_o would be much closer to the origin. Notice also that the segments enclosed by the curves are not proportional to the distribution of population. In the nation as a whole, the upper-right segment contains only a tiny fraction of the population, and most of the remaining population is in the lower-left corner. This skew may be less, of course, in the case of certain high-risk subgroups.

Another unrealistic feature of the diagram is that the risks of unsafe sex are assumed to be the same to m and to f (that is, $P_{tm} = P_{tf}$), whereas in fact it is considerably more difficult for a female to transmit the virus to a male than vice versa. And remember that we are using "m" and "f" for notational convenience only. We could replace them with a_i and a_r, to denote, respectively, a homosexual who plays the insertive role in anal intercourse and a homosexual who plays the receptive role, and again there would be an asymmetry of risk. If the diagram is modified to reflect asymmetric risk, m's indifference curve will shift upward and to the left, as shown in Figure 1-2. He will be willing to have risky sex at higher levels of P_f since the probability of transmission given that f is positive is now lower. (So here is a case in which the difference between the probability that one's partner is infected, and the joint probability that he or she is infected *and* that intercourse will result in transmission, is vital.) The amount of risky sex will therefore rise; it is the entire shaded

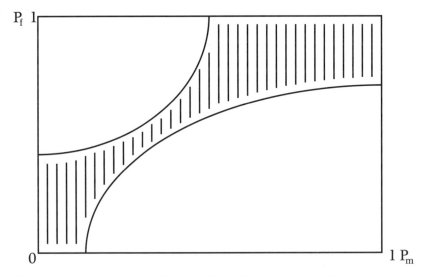

Figure 1-2 Joint demand for risky sex when risk is asymmetrical.

area in Figure 1-2. The incidence of AIDS need not rise, since the rate of transmission from f to m is now assumed to be lower.

Relaxing the assumption of symmetrical risk thus does not change the essential implications of our model. Although Figure 1-2, unlike Figure 1-1, has no region in which both m and f prefer safe sex, that is an artifact of the placement of the lines.

If m and f are both in the lower-left or the upper-right corner of Figure 1-1, risky sex cannot spread AIDS. In every other part of the shaded areas it can. Thus, even though readily preventable, AIDS can spread as a result of purposeful, expected-utility-maximizing behavior. This in turn points up a potential tension between two possible societal goals with respect to AIDS. One, the economic goal emphasized in this book, focuses on social welfare understood in expected-utility terms, though with due regard for the welfare of nonparties to the particular activity (here, risky sex) that is being evaluated. (In Chapter 4 we examine the possibility that behavior that creates a risk of receiving or transmitting AIDS generates external costs—that is, costs to nonparties to a transaction that the parties will not take into account, or costs to a nonconsenting party that the other party does not take into account.) The other possible goal of AIDS policy is minimizing the spread of the disease. This is the epidemiological goal. It is in tension with the economic goal because it assigns no weight to the utility that people derive from risk-creating activities.

The tension between the two goals corresponds to the difference between ex ante optimality, which is implicit in the economist's choice of expected utility as the preference that counts, and ex post optimality, which is implicit in the epidemiologist's goal of minimizing the spread of disease. Every lottery has both winner(s) and losers, but if it is a voluntary lottery and the players know the odds, it is utility-maximizing despite the regret felt by the losers. Mountain climbing maximizes the expected utility of people who derive pleasure from the activity, even though they incur a danger of falling and getting killed. It is the same with fast driving, working at dangerous jobs, and risky sex. The relevance of the ex ante perspective would be obvious if anyone proposed to eliminate mountaineering deaths or driving deaths by forbidding mountaineering or by closing every highway.

The qualification "and the players know the odds" is important in regard to AIDS. Many people, including some who have recently converted from the asymptomatic infection status to full-blown AIDS, were infected before AIDS was discovered or the means of its transmission and prevention understood. They had no way of knowing the odds against them. Their choice to engage in risky sex could not be thought an informed one. This point has both positive and normative implications that are considered in subsequent chapters.

Economic versus Epidemiological Predictions of HIV/AIDS

The basic contrast.[4] Although minimizing the growth of AIDS is not equivalent to maximizing efficiency, our model generates predictions concerning that growth, by in effect embedding the standard epidemiological models in an economic framework. We follow the terminology of epidemiology in distinguishing between "incidence," which denotes the number of new cases in a given period (that is, the flow), and "prevalence," which denotes the overall number of cases at a given time (the stock). As is apparent from Figure 1-1, at the outset of an epidemic subjective probabilities of infection are low, as in the lower left-hand shaded area in that diagram, so risky trades take place. At this stage, the incidence of the epidemic is an increasing function of its prevalence. However, after some point a further increase in prevalence (and hence in both P_m and P_f), by making risky sex more dangerous, induces more and more people to switch to safe sex (as in the unshaded region of the diagram), and so the incidence declines. It does not fall all the way to zero, because some people who are at risk but are in fact negative for the virus continue to trade with other people who are at risk, and some of the latter are positive for the virus. We defer for a moment the possibility, also illustrated by Figure 1-1, that an increase in subjective probabilities of infection can induce switches from safe to risky sex in the upper-right segment of the diagram.

Changes in incidence can be analyzed by modeling a change in incidence among one set of persons (say, m's) as a function of the prevalence of the disease among a set with which it interacts (f's). With random matching between members of the two sets,

(1.3) $I_m(P) = (1 - P_m)P_f D(P_m, P_f),$

$I_m(P)$ denotes the incidence among m's as a function of P. $1 - P_m$ denotes

---

4. For a more technical exposition, see Philipson (1992a, 1992b).

the fraction of males who are uninfected and therefore at risk—the risk denoted by P_f, the fraction of females who are infected. $D(P_m, P_f)$ denotes the joint demand for risky sex of persons in risk classes P_m and P_f. Of D trades, therefore, the fraction $(1 - P_m)P_f$ results in the infection of previously uninfected males.

The effect of an increase in P_f, the prevalence of the disease among f's, on the incidence of the disease among m's is obtained by differentiating I_m with respect to P_f:

(1.4) $\partial I_m(P)/\partial P_f = (1 - P_m)D(P_m, \partial P_f) + (1 - P_m)P_f\partial D(P_m, P_f)/\partial P_f.$

The first term on the right-hand side of this equation is the direct effect (positive) on uninfected m's of an increase in the prevalence of the disease among f's, while the second term is the indirect effect (negative) that results from the effect of that increased prevalence on the demand for risky sex.[5] The first term, which in effect holds behavioral response to the increased risk of disease constant, is a typical epidemiological prediction of the effect of an increase in prevalence on the incidence of a disease. The second term takes account of the economist's typical belief that an increase in relative price (here of risky sex) causes substitution toward cheaper goods (here, safe sex). It is analogous to economists' predictions that the world is unlikely to run out of valuable resources, because as the price of a resource rises the demand for it falls. Substitute risky sex for valuable resource, and the analogy should be plain.

The relation between the epidemiological and economic predictions is depicted in Figure 1-3, which shows how the male incidence (new cases of AIDS among males, per year) is expected to vary with the female prevalence (the stock of female cases at the beginning of the year). This is a cross-sectional prediction; it predicts how the incidence among males would vary across communities in which the prevalence of the disease among females differed. Time-series predictions are considered below.

---

5. The delta expressions in equation 1.4 are the rates of change (first partial derivatives) of I_m and D, respectively, with respect to P_f. Because this equation explores just the effect of an increase in female prevalence on male incidence, other relations between variables in the equation are held constant. So, for example, an increase in female prevalence is assumed to have no effect on male prevalence. In actuality, of course, an increase in female prevalence, by affecting male incidence (that is, the number of new cases among males), will affect the future male prevalence. But equation 1.3 (and therefore 1.4) is a single-period model. We examine multi-period effects later.

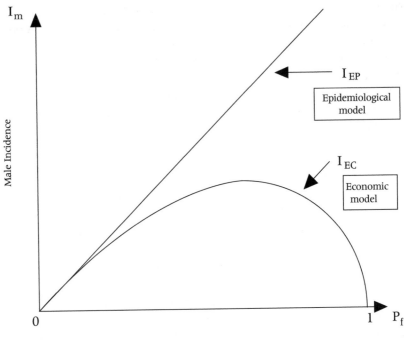

Figure 1-3 Epidemiological versus economic predictions of AIDS incidence (cross-sectional).

The epidemiological prediction, I_{EP}, is generated by the implicit assumption that members of the two groups ignore the actual or probable infection status of their partners, so that the larger the stock of infected females the larger the number of new cases among males because the probability that an uninfected male will encounter an infected female is higher. While some epidemiological models (illustrated by Tan and Hsu 1989) assume a declining number of risky sex acts as a result of growing awareness of AIDS, most assume no change in sexual behavior over the course of the epidemic (May and Anderson 1987; Bongaarts 1989; Colgate et al. 1989; Anderson and May 1991, p. 267). Epidemiologists know, of course, that behavioral changes could slow down the epidemic. But lacking a theory of behavioral change, they rarely try to incorporate the possibility into their models.[6] In contrast, the inverted U

---

6. For a representative treatment, see May, Anderson, and Blower (1990).

shape of the economic forecast, I_{EC}, is generated by the quintessentially economic assumption that persons will avoid risky sex when the relative price becomes too high. In the extreme case in which all females are infected, the economic model predicts no growth in the number of male AIDS cases while the epidemiological model predicts that all uninfected males will become infected.

Together with equation 1.4, Figure 1-3 may explain why epidemiologists have generally overpredicted the spread of the epidemic,[7] notwithstanding the artifactual increase (due to changes in the definition of AIDS) in the number of AIDS cases, which we mentioned in the Introduction. For example, in 1988 the Centers for Disease Control estimated that 365,000 AIDS cases would be diagnosed in the United States through 1992 (Karon, Dondero, and Curran 1988). In fact by the end of 1992 only 253,000 cases had been reported (Centers for Disease Control 1993, p. 6 [tab. 1]), though the total number diagnosed may be somewhat higher as a result of reporting lag. As late as 1989, the consensus prediction of the public health community was that there would be 54,000 new cases of AIDS in 1991 and 61,000 in 1992.[8] The actual total for 1991 was 46,000 and for 1992 47,000 (ibid.). The epidemiological models generate incidence rates higher than those in the economic model because there is no demand for safe sex in the former.

Mathematical epidemiology: the closed-population model. To model incidence within a population over time, as distinct from incidence across populations at a given time,[9] epidemiologists use three basic methods.[10] The first, extrapolation, uses past data on the incidence of AIDS to forecast future incidence without employing any causal model linking the future to the past (Morgan and Curran 1986). The problems with naive extrapolation are well known; used in the early days of an epidemic, it is

---

7. Hellinger (1990); Quinn et al. (1990); Palca (1989); and see Hay (1989, pp. 127–133); Fumento (1990); and Kolata (1991). The extraordinarily high predictions reported in Global AIDS Policy Coalition (1992), to which we referred in the Preface, are based on averages of predictions by public health experts (ibid., pp. 871–874 [app. 2.2]).

8. These are the median projections multiplied by 85 percent to take out the estimate for underreporting (15 percent) and thus produce figures comparable to the unadjusted number of new cases reported in the two years (Centers for Disease Control 1990). See also Buehler, Berkelman, and Stehr-Green (1992).

9. This corresponds to the statistician's distinction between time-series and cross-sectional analysis.

10. Brookmeyer and Gail (1988) compare the accuracy of the three methods of prediction.

bound to generate gross overestimates. The second method, called "back calculation," uses the number of AIDS cases, in conjunction with an incubation distribution (the distribution of intervals, which differ across persons, between infection with HIV and conversion to AIDS), to estimate the future incidence of AIDS (Brookmeyer 1991; Rosenberg et al. 1991a). This method, whether or not supplemented by predictions based on direct estimates of the number of people who are HIV-positive,[11] is good only for short-term predictions. It is also highly sensitive (as acknowledged in Rosenberg et al. 1991a, p. 282, and Gail, Rosenberg, and Goedert 1990) to changes in the incubation period, for example because of widespread use of the drug AZT, which may lengthen that period.

The third method, that of mathematical epidemiology (May and Anderson 1987; Hyman and Stanley 1988; Colgate et al. 1989), is the only one concerned with causal explanation, and we shall therefore pay particular attention to it. A typical epidemiological model of the third type in which the population is "closed"—no infected persons cease being infective, whether because they die or because they recover and become immune, and no noninfected persons are added, whether through birth, in-migration, or recovery—generates increasing rates of growth until half the noninfected population is infected. Growth rates decrease after that but do not fall to zero, so eventually the whole population is infected.[12] The reason for this pattern is that the disease is assumed to spread through random interaction[13] of infected and uninfected persons. As the number of infected persons increases, the epidemic at first grows with increasing rapidity because more and more of the random interactions of uninfected persons are with infected ones. But when the epidemic reaches the point at which half the interactions are between per-

---

11. The problem here is that HIV testing is not random or representative (as emphasized in Lampinen et al. 1992), so statistics of positive test results (as in Centers for Disease Control 1989) do not enable a reliable estimate of the number of persons with HIV to be made. Little credence can be given the widely publicized estimate that between 1 and 1.5 million Americans are infected. See also Chapter 2.

12. This type of epidemic model has been used by economists such as Griliches and Mansfield to model the diffusion of innovations, and by other social scientists to model the spread of rumors! For a review and critique of this literature, see Davies (1979).

13. To repeat an important qualification stated earlier in this chapter, random *meeting* should be distinguished from random *interaction*, or what we call trade. Our economic model assumes random meeting, but not random interaction (in the sense of a potentially infective sexual trade), because the latter is determined in part by perceived risks of infection, both one's own and one's partner's.

sons already infected, and hence "wasted" from the standpoint of spreading the disease further, the rate of growth slows. Another epidemiological reason for eventually falling growth rates is that the most susceptible people are infected first, and growth slows as the remaining noninfected population comes to be dominated by people with high resistance or who are otherwise at low risk. Of course, with no entry of uninfected persons or exit of infected ones (because of the assumption of a closed population), everyone is infected eventually. Indeed, even when growth rates have slowed because so many people are infected already, the risk to the remaining people rises because they are all the more likely to encounter an infected person. The remaining uninfected are a shrinking pool because of the assumption of no entry, while the remaining infected are a growing pool because of the assumption of no exit. In effect, the only thing that happens in the closed-population model is conversion of uninfected to infected.

The assumption of random interaction rules out behavioral responses to changing disease risk. Although epidemiologists do analyze discrete subpopulations having different levels of risky activity, generally they do so under the assumption of "proportionate mixing." This is an abehavioral assumption and does not alter the prediction that the entire population will eventually be infected. The fraction of sexual interactions between one subpopulation (say, females) and each of the subpopulations with which it interacts (say, different groups of men with different levels of sexual activity) is assumed to equal the fraction of sexual activity accounted for by each of those subpopulations (Castillo-Chavez 1988). For example, if there are three equal-sized groups of males engaging in 20, 30, and 50 acts of sexual intercourse per year, respectively, it is assumed that each member of the female subpopulation will have 20 percent of her sexual relations with members of the first group, 30 percent with members of the second, and 50 percent with members of the third. Realistically, however (as recognized in Ramstedt et al. 1991), she might avoid members of the third group, fearing that their higher level of sexual activity would make it more likely that they were disease carriers.

The contrast between the epidemiological and the economic approach to time-series prediction is illustrated in Figure 1-4. A closed population is assumed. The convex region of the curve labeled f_{EP} (the region in which the curve is rising steeply) depicts the increasing growth rates that the epidemiological approach predicts until half the population is infected; the concave region predicts the decreasing growth rates thereafter (Bailey 1975). The curve labeled f_{EC} is the economic prediction: pos-

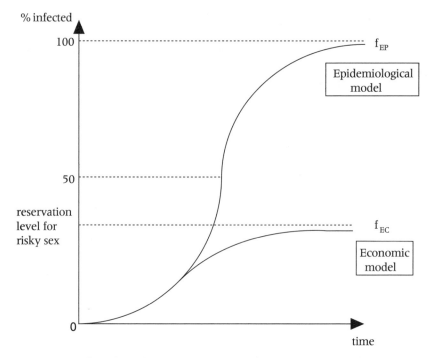

Figure 1-4 Epidemiological versus economic predictions of AIDS incidence (time series).

itive incidence until prevalence reaches the level at which the individual who is most averse to safe sex becomes indifferent between risky and safe sex (so we are relaxing, in the interest of realism, the assumption that B is the same to everyone); above that, no growth, because risky sex is too costly for anyone. The reader can relate this pattern to our model (equations 1.1 and 1.2 and Figure 1-1) by imagining a group of homosexual men who lack good information about the infection status of prospective sexual partners. The expected utility of risky sex to the uninfected is therefore $B - CP$, where P is the prevalence of the disease in the population as a whole. As P rises, a point is reached at which $B - CP$ is negative even for the people most averse to safe sex (people whose B is highest), because C is so much greater than even their B. When that point is reached, the disease ceases to spread.

Thus far we have analyzed the effect of an increasing P (prevalence) on incidence on the assumption that a set of $P = 0$ people interact with a set of $P > 0$ people. It is more realistic to assume that an increase in prevalence will increase P for both sets, given our assumption that no one knows his or her infection status for sure. Then when prevalence increases, every sexually active person will revise upward his estimate of the probability of his being already infected. We know from equations 1.1 and 1.2 that an increase in one's own probability of being already infected increases one's demand for risky sex. In Figure 1-1 this can be seen by noting that once the midpoint of the oval-shaped region in which both sexual partners prefer safe to risky sex is reached, any further increase in P reduces the demand for safe sex and increases the demand for risky sex. How then can we be sure that increases in prevalence reduce rather than increase the demand for risky sex, overall?

To answer in the simplest possible fashion, we assume that $P_m = P_f$ (which, by the way, is plausible for many homosexuals), enabling us to rewrite equations 1.1 and 1.2 as $EU_m = EU_f = B - (1 - P)CP = B - C(P - P^2)$. Differentiating EU with respect to P, we have $dEU/dP = 2P - 1$, meaning that an increase in P will reduce the demand for risky sex and hence the incidence of the disease if but only if $P < \frac{1}{2}$. Otherwise, increases in P will *increase* incidence. The point $P = \frac{1}{2}$ is simply the midpoint of Figure 1-1 when $M = F$, and we have pointed out that above that point further increases in P indeed increase rather than reduce incidence.

This refinement in our analysis of incidence does not upset our basic conclusion. It shows only that if a disease gets completely out of hand, people may have such a high probability of being already infected and hence of having nothing more to lose from risky behavior that they will (rationally) abandon all precautions. Long before this point is reached the incentive to take precautions when the overall prevalence is low may stop the disease from spreading—so one never reaches the devil-may-care high-prevalence region where continued increases in prevalence could indeed result in the entire population becoming infected, as in the closed-population epidemiological model.

The open-population model. Epidemiologists do not, in fact, predict that 100 percent of the U.S. population will eventually become infected by AIDS. They recognize that the assumption of a closed population is unrealistic. The rates at which infected persons exit from the population (primarily through death, in the case of AIDS) and noninfected persons enter the population are vital to epidemiological predictions of the peak prevalence of the epidemic. Specifically, the standard epidemiological models predict that the epidemic will stabilize when the average infected person infects one other person during the former's infective period: there is then one-for-one replacement, and the number of infected persons remains constant (May, Anderson, and Blower 1990, p. 66).

More precisely, let S be the fraction of the population that is at risk, that is, that is infectable but not yet infected. So at the start of an epidemic, if it is assumed that no one is immune, $S = 1$. Let v be the exit rate of infected persons from the population, for example through death; then, under the standard assumption made by epidemiologists concerning the distribution of the incubation period of AIDS, $1/v$ is the average remaining lifetime of an infected person (the interval between when he becomes infected and when he dies). This implies that if, for example, 5 percent of infected persons die each year, the average remaining lifetime of such a person is 20 years. Alternatively, to facilitate computation, average remaining lifetime can be expressed as the number of (potentially infective) encounters per year times the number of years of life that remain. If b is the transmission rate (or per-period transmission probability), that is, the number of infective encounters per year divided by the total number of encounters between infected and uninfected persons, the average infected person will infect b/v other persons before he dies. This is on the assumption that no one else is infected when he begins his infective career. Suppose that some of the population is infected—or immune, but for simplicity we can ignore that possibility, since it is not a feature of HIV. Then $S < 1$. That is, the fraction of our infected person's random encounters that will be with *un*infected persons, and so will have the potential to spread the disease, will be less than one.

More generally, since in each period an infected person meets an uninfected one with probability S and transmits the disease with probability b, the total number of persons whom an infected person will infect during his infective lifetime (T) is given by

$$(1.5) \quad T = 1/v(Sb) = (b/v)S.$$

Thus, for T to exceed 1—that is, for the disease to grow, because the infected person does more than just replace himself before he exits—the ratio of the transmission probability (b) to the exit rate (v) must exceed the fraction uninfected (S). The condition for the disease to enter its steady state, where $T = 1$ (each infected person infects just one other person before exiting), is thus

$$(1.6) \quad S = v/b.$$

So a disease can stop growing because of a saturation effect caused by the shrinkage of the uninfected population. And when T falls below 1, and therefore $S < v/b$, the net flow (new cases minus deaths) will become negative and the prevalence of the disease will therefore diminish, because infected persons will no longer be fully reproducing themselves (that is, creating new infected persons) at the rate at which they are exiting from the population. However, in the special case of a closed population $v = 0$, so $S = 0/b = 0$. That is, no uninfected persons remain.

We have been emphasizing exit; and, given exit, a disease can reach saturation before 100 percent of the population is infected, even if there is no entry, that is, even if the population is closed at one end. Often, indeed, a population is referred to as "closed" provided only that there is no new entry. But the assumption of no new entry is not realistic with respect to HIV. The population at risk of HIV infection is open to entry by persons who are first beginning their sexual activity involving actual or potential exposure to possibly infective bodily fluids, or intravenous drug use. Entry affects S, the percentage of the population that is at present uninfected. The more new entry there is, the higher S is likely to be, because the flow of new uninfected people into the population dilutes the fraction infected. The steady state will be reached later because there is a larger supply of uninfected persons for infected persons to "feed on," as it were, before exiting. However, a communicable disease cannot reach a steady state without entry, although it can either disappear or infect the entire population, depending on the exit rate (which if high enough may drive the infective population to zero while there are still uninfected people). Although the population at risk for AIDS is open to both entry and exit, entry can be disregarded if one is interested merely in the disease experience of a cohort of the population—for example, all men who are between the ages of 20 and 25 today.[14]

We shall see in the next chapter that equations 1.5 and 1.6 imply a higher prevalence of HIV infection than the data will support. Because of the long infective incubation stage—the interval between infection, and infectivity, on the one hand, and exit through death on the other— exit will not check the spread of the epidemic; there will always be plenty of infected persons able to transmit the disease to the remaining uninfected members of the cohort. (In terms of equation 1.5, v will be very low.) Admitting the possibility of new entry requires some but not drastic modification of this conclusion. The annual rate of entry into the sexually active population is not high. If the average person is assumed to have a 40-year sexually active life, the annual rate of new entry would

---

14. A cohort is a group with no new entry into it, though exit (for example, through death) is allowed.

be only 2.5 percent, provided that immigration, different mortality rates for different age groups, and changes in the birth rate are disregarded. Moreover, in the economic though not in the epidemiological model entry is endogenous. Fear of AIDS may induce people to adopt safe sex from the outset of their sexual activity, so that they never become part of the at-risk population; this will further reduce the rate of new entry. At all events, Figure 1-4, though stylized, may capture much of the spirit, if not all the detail, of the epidemiological approach to AIDS—and in doing so may furnish a basis for an assessment of the relative empirical adequacy of the epidemiological and economic approaches. This is one of the tasks of the next chapter.

Although an economic epidemiological approach predicts a slower growth rate of AIDS than a purely biological epidemiological approach, it would be a mistake to suppose that this is a general characteristic of the economic approach to communicable disease. For example, the development of a cure for such a disease may, by reducing the expected cost of the disease, reduce the incentive to make behavioral changes that lower the probability of infection—a consequence (illustrated by the epidemiology of syphilis in this century) that an abehavioral model would miss (see Chapter 2).

We realize that the epidemiological literature contains more general mathematical models of disease transmission than those we have discussed—models for example in which such assumptions as random or proportionate mixing are relaxed (see, for example, Blythe and Castillo-Chavez 1989; Dietz 1988; Sattenspiel and Simon 1988). The critical question from our standpoint, however, is not whether the more general models are more realistic, but whether they contain testable implications different from those of the simple models. We believe not. In particular, as shown in Philipson (1993), the crucial implication of the simple models—that an increase in prevalence in period t will result in a higher infection rate among the noninfected but susceptible population in period $t + 1$—holds in the more general models as well, and, as we shall see in the next chapter, is falsified by the data. We need not, therefore, burden the reader with the complexities of the more general epidemiological models.

The Economic Model Elaborated

The economic model presented in the first section of this chapter was highly simplified, even with the refinements made there. We add more refinements here, and still more in subsequent chapters.

Recall that B in equations 1.1 and 1.2 is the benefit (gross benefit—that is, ignoring costs) of risky sex over safe sex, the latter defined rather confiningly as sex with condoms. Another form of safe sex, "petting to climax," was long a common method of contraceptive sex for American teenagers. Many heterosexuals also engage occasionally or frequently in anal intercourse, for contraceptive and other reasons. We predict that the ratio of petting-to-climax to heterosexual anal intercourse (or, more broadly, the relative shares of less and more risky sexual practices) is a positive function of the prevalence of AIDS. Since oral sex is much safer than anal sex, we also expect a substitution toward the former, as well as a substitution of anal sex with condoms for anal sex without.[15] Because heterosexuals have a closer substitute for anal intercourse than homosexuals do (namely, vaginal intercourse),[16] and because anal intercourse even with condoms is not completely safe, we also predict greater substitution away from anal intercourse by heterosexuals in response to the threat of AIDS than by homosexuals, at least if the risks from heterosexual anal intercourse are comparable to those from homosexual anal intercourse. And because condoms are more effective in preventing the transmission of the virus through vaginal than through anal intercourse,[17] we expect them to be a more commonly used method of safe sex for heterosexuals than for homosexuals. So we predict that heterosexuals who fear risky sex are more likely to use condoms rather than substitute petting to climax or oral sex for vaginal intercourse than homosexuals are to use condoms in anal intercourse rather than substitute other practices for such intercourse. Such predictions

---

15. For some evidence of this last substitution, see Stevens et al. (1990, p. 29).

16. Evidence for this proposition is that anal intercourse appears to be far more common among homosexuals than among heterosexuals (Reinisch, Ziemba-Davis, and Sanders 1990, p. 68), though not uncommon among the latter (Reinisch, Ziemba-Davis, and Sanders 1990, p. 68; Voeller 1991; Pendergrast, DuRant, and Gaillard 1992, p. 138). It is estimated to be engaged in by 50 to 95 percent of homosexuals, but by only 18 to 39 percent of heterosexuals (Reinisch, Ziemba-Davis, and Sanders 1990, p. 68).

17. Using figures presented in the Introduction—2 percent as the probability of transmission by an HIV carrier to the receptive partner in unshielded anal intercourse, .2 percent as the probability of transmission by an HIV carrier to the female partner in unshielded vaginal intercourse, .6 percent as the probability of a condom's breaking or leaking in vaginal intercourse, and 1 percent as the probability of its breaking or leaking in anal intercourse—we estimate the probability of transmission from an HIV carrier in vaginal intercourse in which a condom is used to be 1.2 in 100,000, and the corresponding probability in the case of homosexual anal intercourse to be 20 in 100,000. (This is related to the point that condoms are a less effective AIDS preventive in high-risk activities.) These are extremely rough estimates.

should be empirically testable, because sex surveys frequently inquire about such practices, but we have not attempted to test them. A closely related, and also (in principle anyway) testable prediction is that as the prevalence of AIDS increases, bisexuals (men either indifferent to the sex of their sexual partner or at least more willing than "pure" homosexuals to substitute a female for a male partner) increasingly switch from male to female sexual partners. This trend would accelerate the spread of the AIDS virus to women and may help explain the increasing frequency of cases in women.

Unshielded vaginal or anal intercourse is never "safe" for an uninfected person, in our analysis. But since the degree of danger varies with the probability that one's sexual partner is infected, there is a benefit from estimating correctly a potential sexual partner's probability of being infected, and one's own as well. (We take up this matter in Chapter 3.) There is also a benefit from reducing the *number* of one's sexual partners (that is, from avoiding promiscuity), provided the probability of infection per sexual "trade" with an infected person is not too low. Compare 1,000 unshielded trades with one person who has a 1 percent probability of being HIV-positive with 10 trades with each of 100 persons one of whom is HIV-positive and the others are not. Assume further that 1 percent of trades with an HIV carrier result in transmission of the disease. On these assumptions, the probability of infection is almost ten times greater for the promiscuous than for the monogamous sexual trader. The monogamist will probably get the disease if his partner has it, because the odds on winning all of a thousand .99 bets are low. So his probability of becoming infected is slightly less than .01, the probability that his partner is infected. The promiscuous trader is certain to have ten trades with someone who is infected, each of which has a .01 chance of infecting him, so his odds of becoming infected are about $10 \times .01 = .1$—a little less because of double counting in situations where he gets infected twice. The lower the transmission probability, the closer are the risks to the monogamous and the promiscuous trader,[18] yet we know that for some risky practices the HIV transmission probability exceeds 1 percent.

This is one basis for predictions that an increased number of sexual partners will increase the risk of AIDS (Eisenberg 1989), and there are

---

18. Hence we might expect promiscuous heterosexual males to reduce their promiscuity, in response to the AIDS epidemic, less than promiscuous females would reduce their promiscuity, since the probability of transmission from female to male is so much less than from male to female.

others. First, it appears that some AIDS carriers are much more infective than others (Holmberg et al. 1989, p. 117), and the more sexual partners one has, the more likely one is to encounter such a person. Second, during the period in which the prevalence of a disease is growing, a person who has a monogamous relationship formed early in the epidemic, when the prevalence of the disease and hence the probability of encountering a carrier were lower, will be at less risk than one who engages in the same number of sexual acts with a series of partners acquired over the course of the epidemic (Sandberg and Awerbuch 1989). Third, a person who has many sexual partners is more likely to contract another sexually transmitted disease, which will in turn put him at greater risk of HIV infection (Kirby et al. 1991; Wiley and Herschkorn 1988). Finally, promiscuity will be a good predictor of the likelihood of contracting AIDS if the number of risky sexual trades is positively correlated with the number of sexual partners. That correlation is plausible, especially for prostitutes of both sexes and for male homosexuals generally, because men are more prone to engage in casual sex than women are. A heterosexual Don Juan may encounter substantial costs in finding a partner (other than a prostitute) for casual sex; a homosexual Don Juan is less likely to.

From the standpoint of reducing the risk of AIDS, there would be a benefit in reducing the number of one's sexual partners even if there were no reduction in the number of sexual trades. It is easier to estimate the infection status of one person than of more than one and thus to avoid dangerous partners (Hearst and Hulley 1988, p. 2430). A long-term relationship also facilitates monitoring, by making it more difficult for one person to conceal his true estimate of his probability of infection from the other, or to conceal activities, such as promiscuous sex, that increase that probability. A long-term relationship is also more likely to be altruistic. Altruism, the complete or more commonly the partial incorporation of another person's utility function in one's own, has received considerable attention from economists in recent years (see, for example, G. Becker 1991), with particular emphasis on altruism toward family members. Casual observation suggests that long-term intimate relationships foster altruism; for example, even a person who does not love or even particularly like his or her spouse will often experience a sharp drop in utility if the spouse dies.[19] An altruist is less likely to risk

---

19. Perhaps such a response is not really altruistic, but for our purposes it makes no difference whether the "altruist" has a genuine regard for the well-being of the other

infecting his sexual partner,[20] and therefore more likely to switch to safe sex rather than attempt to conceal that he is infected or has a high probability of being infected, than an egoist. On the other hand, an altruist may be more willing to engage in risky sex if his or her partner derives utility from it. Altruism may thus reduce as well as increase the cost of risky sex. We return to this issue in Chapter 3.

The possibility of altruism shows that an offer of risky sex cannot automatically be taken as a signal that the offerer knows or suspects that he is infected. If he is an altruist, the offer of *safe* sex could just as reasonably be taken as such a signal. Signaling possibilities are further blurred by the fact that people may prefer safe sex for reasons unrelated to disease risk, including fertility risk and considerations of sexual pleasure—some homosexuals, for example, simply prefer oral to anal sex, and oral sex is a form of safe, or at least safer, sex.

---

person or an attitude of guilt or of instrumental dependence. All that matters is that there be some positive interdependence of utilities.

20. Or some of his sexual partners: he may be altruistic toward his spouse or other long-term cohabitor but not toward his casual sexual partners.

CHAPTER 2

Empirical Support for the Economic Approach

In this chapter we investigate whether the economic model of AIDS has sufficient support in the voluminous epidemiological and behavioral data on the epidemic to warrant using the model as a basis for explanation and prediction and for the evaluation of public policy.

Epidemiological Data

First identified in 1981, when HIV infection had already been spread by risky sex uninhibited by any awareness of the HIV-AIDS risk, the AIDS epidemic has grown rapidly, but at a decreasing rate, primarily among male homosexuals and intravenous drug users, who together account for almost 90 percent of the nearly 50,000 new cases per year in the United States today. The number of persons who are carrying the AIDS virus is unknown. But it is estimated—probably overestimated, as we shall see—to be at least 1 million. Although women are far more suscep-tible than men to infection with the virus by heterosexual intercourse, little more than 10 percent of the new cases are among women, of which 50 percent are due to intravenous drug use and 36 percent to heterosex-ual intercourse, primarily with bisexuals or intravenous drug users. We seek to determine whether the economic model can explain these and other data about the growth of the disease better than the competing models, which are drawn from epidemiology.

Such a comparison is difficult for two reasons. First, the more sophisti-cated epidemiological models employ a range of assumptions concern-ing, for example, the unobserved rates of mixing between high-risk and low-risk populations, and thus do not make clear predictions that could be readily falsified by empirical data. Second, it is difficult, at least with only aggregate infection data and without consideration of the kind of micro-behavioral evidence discussed in the next section of this chapter, to distinguish empirically between a decline in the incidence of AIDS, or in the rate of increase of that incidence, that is due to behavioral changes predicted by the economic model and a decline due to the saturation effect predicted by the epidemiological models when the incidence of a disease cannot keep up with exits by the infected. Disentanglement is especially difficult because the economic model has less relevance to HIV infection that occurred before enough was known about the etiology and transmission of the virus to make behavioral change a feasible response.

The fact that epidemiologists have tended to overpredict the growth of AIDS (as discussed in Chapter 1) cannot be decisive in a comparative evaluation of the approaches because there are no economic predictions with which to compare the epidemiologists' predictions. Nor can it be decisive that for a closed population (no entry of noninfected, or exit of infected, persons) the epidemiological models predict increasing growth rates of AIDS until half the population is infected—a prediction, it is interesting to note, that the data falsify. Figure 2-1 and, more clearly,

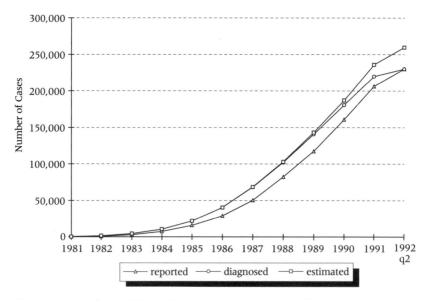

Figure 2-1 Cumulative U.S. AIDS cases: by year reported, diagnosed, and estimated (due to reporting delays), 1/1/1981–7/1/1992. *Source:* CDC Public Information Data Set, 7/1/92.

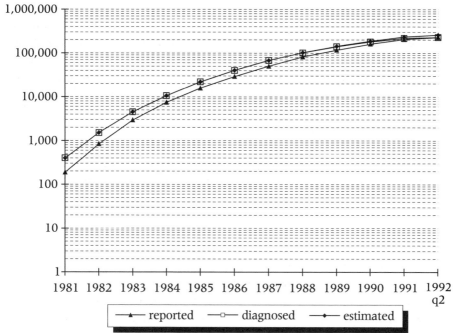

Figure 2-2 Cumulative U.S. AIDS cases: by year reported, diagnosed, and estimated (due to reporting delays), 1/1/1981–7/1/1992: log scale. *Source:* CDC Public Information Data Set, 7/1/92.

Figure 2-2 (which utilizes a logarithmic scale, showing rates of growth) reveal that although AIDS[1] has grown at increasing annual rates, by the end of 1991 the rate of growth was almost flat, even though much less than half the sexually active population had been infected.[2] True, a few subpopulations—for example, homosexual men in San Francisco—may have reached the 50 percent infection level (De Cock et al. 1988; Hessol et al. 1989; Kelly, St. Lawrence, and Brasfield 1991, p. 163). And some epidemiologists believe that the decline in the rate of growth of AIDS cases is an artifact of AZT therapy, which some believe postpones the onset of AIDS as well as death resulting from it (Gale, Rosenberg, and Goedert 1990; Rosenberg et al. 1991b; Stein et al. 1991a; Fife and Mode

---

1. We use AIDS data rather than infection (HIV) data because there is no reliable time series for the latter.

2. On the source of the data for these and other graphs in this chapter, see the Introduction.

1992), or that an increase in reporting lag (see the Introduction) has caused the number of current new cases to be underestimated (Brook-meyer and Liao 1990; Harris 1990), though Figures 2-1 and 2-2 show that our results would not be altered significantly if we used estimated rather than reported cases. Yet with all these qualifications granted, it is apparent that the cumulative total of persons infected through 1991 represented only a tiny fraction of the sexually active population of the United States in that year.

By now the rate of growth of HIV infection may be declining; indeed, Harris (1990, pp. 921–922 and fig. 5), though concerned that increasing reporting lag may have caused the number of new cases of AIDS to be underestimated, nevertheless believes that the incidence of HIV infection among homosexuals who are not intravenous drug users peaked early in 1983. The number of new cases of AIDS can lag behind changes in sexual behavior by many years, not only because of the long incubation period of the disease but also because there is, on average, a lag between engaging in risky sexual behavior and becoming infected. If, as Figures 2-1 and 2-2 suggest, the number of new cases of AIDS in the U.S. population as a whole (and not just in the homosexual subpopulation) has peaked or is peaking, the standard estimate of 1 million[3] HIV carriers probably is exaggerated. For with a median incubation period of 10 years (and ignoring the lag between risky behavior and actual infection), we should expect, if there are that many carriers, that the number of new AIDS cases per year would soon reach 100,000, as now seems highly unlikely. Another reason to doubt the 1 million estimate is that a careful survey of HIV infection in Dallas County, Texas, found that only .42 percent of the county's population was infected (Research Triangle Institute 1990). Although this could be thought to imply 1 million infected nationwide (1 million being .4 percent of 250 million), the incidence of AIDS is 40 percent higher in Dallas than in the United States as a whole (computed from Centers for Disease Control 1993, pp. 7–8 [tab. 2]). A previous estimate of the HIV rate in Dallas County, based on conventional estimating methods, was 2.9 percent—almost seven times as high as the estimate from the survey (Research Triangle Institute 1990).

Although the AIDS data falsify the predictions of the closed-population model, this may be because the population is not closed and we are therefore evaluating the wrong model. There are exits as people

---

3. A suspiciously round number—which underscores the crudeness of the estimate.

with AIDS die (and they usually become sexually inactive sometime before their death), and entries as people become sexually active or take up intravenous drug use for the first time. We can conduct a better test of the epidemiologial approach by focusing on its predictions about the steady-state level of the epidemic. Equation 1.6 showed that saturation effects flatten out the growth of the epidemic when the fraction of the population that is uninfected (S) falls to the ratio of the exit rate $(v,$ which equals 1 divided by the average lifetime of an infected person) and the transmission rate (b).

Since there are estimates for all the variables in the epidemiologists' steady-state formulas, it is possible to test the accuracy of these formulas by plugging in the estimates. Figure 2-3 shows that the stock of AIDS cases (total cases minus deaths) appears to be leveling off at or near 70,000, implying that the infection (that is, the HIV) level has already stabilized in the United States (that is, $T = 1$). This is not widely believed by epidemiologists, but it is the most plausible interpretation of the data. It should make equation 1.6 applicable. We do not know at what level the infection has stabilized, but let us assume that it is at the canonical 1 million figure (a lower and therefore more realistic estimate would

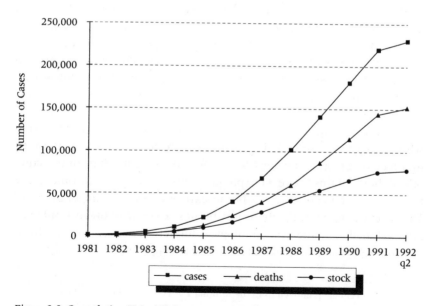

Figure 2-3 Cumulative U.S. AIDS cases, cumulative U.S. AIDS deaths, and stock (prevalence) of AIDS cases, 1/1/81–7/1/92. (Stock = Cumulative Cases − Cumulative Deaths.) *Source:* CDC Public Information Data Set, 7/1/92.

strengthen our conclusions). This is much less than 1 percent of the U.S. population, but some people are sexually inactive because of age or other reasons, so let us assume that $S = .99$. We know that the average remaining lifetime of a person once he becomes infected with the AIDS virus is about 12 years (10 to convert to AIDS, 2 more to die) and that the probability of becoming infected from one episode of unprotected anal intercourse has been estimated at 2 percent, although we repeat our warning that this is an extremely rough estimate.

Most epidemiological models do not distinguish clearly between *meeting* and *transmission*—which is understandable since the models were developed for and are more commonly applied to airborne diseases than to diseases transmitted by voluntary intimate interactions. The models use as their implicit period for measuring v and b the time it takes for one meeting. If one meeting (sexual encounter) per day is assumed, this implies, given a 10-year remaining lifetime for the infected person and a 2-percent transmission probability from each encounter, an absurdly low steady-state fraction of healthy individuals: $S_{day} = (1/4,380)/(2/100) = 1/88$, that is, only 1.1 percent of the population healthy when the disease is in a steady state, as it appears now to be in or approaching.

In the interest of realism, because we are trying to gauge the probability that an infected person will infect others during the period between his becoming infected and his dying, let us annualize v and b. Then $v = .083$, and if the disease is in a steady state and $S = .99$, equation 1.6 ($S = v/b$) implies that b, the transmission probability from unsafe sex with an infected person for a year, is only 8.4 percent. Yet we know that this figure is too low, especially for high-risk subpopulations such as male homosexuals and intravenous drug users, who together account for the bulk of the cases. For example, an infected male homosexual who engages in unshielded anal intercourse 50 times a year with an uninfected person or persons has a 64 percent probability of infecting one of them.[4] If this figure were plugged into equation 1.6 it would imply that only 13 percent of male homosexuals (.083/.64) are uninfected. That is exceedingly unlikely unless homosexuals who practice safe sex are excluded, but the epidemiological models generally abstract from safe sex as part of their general reluctance to consider behavioral changes.

---

4. This percentage is derived from the formula $1 - (1 - p)^n$, where p is the probability of becoming infected in one encounter and is estimated at .02 for unshielded anal intercourse with an infected man; probabilities are assumed to be independent; and n is the number of encounters (= 50).

There may be homosexual subpopulations, such as that of San Francisco, in which HIV infection reached saturation levels before enough was known about the disease for behavioral change to be a feasible response. But we said earlier that purely epidemiological models *should* predict accurately the incidence of a disease that, because of ignorance or other reasons, cannot feasibly be controlled by changes in behavior. AIDS was once such a disease. That phase, however, has ended, except for people who are still converting to AIDS from an infected status acquired before the 1981–1983 period in which it was discovered how to prevent the transmission of the disease through behavioral changes.

Figures 2-4 and 2-5 reinforce our criticisms of the epidemiological models. Figure 2-4 shows that, since 1988, the annual net flow of AIDS cases (new cases minus deaths) resulting from homosexual transmission has been falling. Figure 2-5 graphs similar data but is limited to the western region of the United States, a region whose homosexual population is believed to be heavily concentrated in Los Angeles and San Francisco,

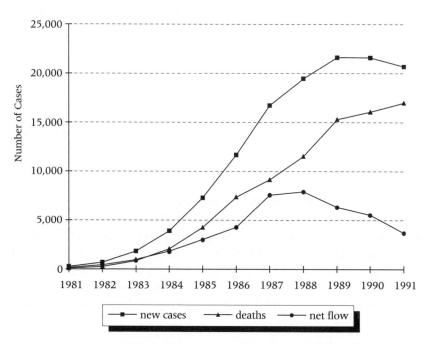

Figure 2-4 New U.S. AIDS cases, new U.S. AIDS deaths, and annual net flow of U.S. AIDS cases, for AIDS transmission via homosexual contact, 1981–1991. (Net Flow = New Cases − New Deaths, per year.) *Source:* CDC Public Information Data Set, 7/1/92.

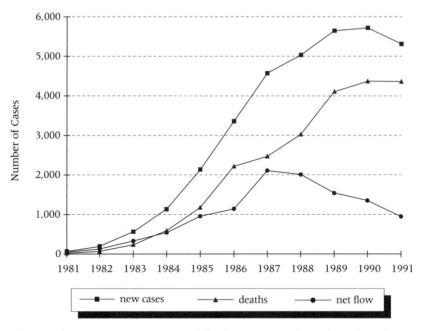

Figure 2-5 New AIDS cases, new AIDS deaths, and annual net flow of AIDS cases, for AIDS transmission via homosexual contact, in the western U.S. only, 1981–1991. Net Flow = New Cases − New Deaths, per year; western U.S. as defined by the CDC as MSA Region 3.) *Source:* CDC Public Information Data Set, 7/1/92.

both high-prevalence cities; in this region the net flow began to fall a year earlier than in the nation as a whole.[5] The net-flow profile is almost identical for another very high-risk group—needle-sharing homosexuals—so we do not include a separate graph for this group.

True, in both graphs the net flow, although declining, is positive— new cases per year exceed deaths per year. But new AIDS cases reflect HIV infections that occurred in a period centered on a decade ago, when knowledge of how to prevent transmission of the virus was first being acquired by scientists and disseminated to the American public. It is entirely possible that the current net flow, properly computed as new HIV infections minus new AIDS deaths, is negative.[6] This would imply (from

5. The AIDS Public Information File Data Set classifies cases (according to method of transmission) by region, but not by city or state.

6. A further reason for this conjecture is that there appears to be greater underreporting of deaths from AIDS than of AIDS cases (Hardy et al. 1991).

equation 1.5) that $T < 1$ and therefore, if the epidemiological models are correct, that *fewer* than 16 percent of homosexuals remain uninfected, which is highly improbable.

We cannot rule out all possibility that saturation effects explain the decline in net flows. Reporting and other measurement errors to one side, the disease may have become saturated in the population subgroups in which it first spread and may now be spreading into other groups only slowly because of limited sexual or needle-sharing contacts across groups, resulting in a decline in aggregate net-flow figures. But this would imply wildfire growth in low-prevalence subgroups in which transmission probability is high, such as homosexuals outside of large cities. While the rate of growth of the disease there is indeed higher, as we shall see, it is not comparable to the rate in the large cities in the earlier years of the disease. It seems that other factors besides S, v, and b are at work—which brings us to the economic model.

Economic analysis provides an account of the data that does not suffer from the infirmities that we have been discussing. At first, with the risk of infection low because there were few carriers, HIV infection, and hence AIDS, grew rapidly, although an even more important factor in the rapid *early* growth of the disease was that many people became infected, but were not symptomatic, before the disease was even discovered and therefore at a time when the expected costs of risky sex were low. Eventually, as both the risk of infection and knowledge of the disease and how to avoid it grew, people began to change their behavior and the rate of growth began to fall. It remains positive for two reasons. First, because of the long incubation period of the disease, today's new AIDS cases reflect the behavior and resulting infection of a number of years ago; a change in behavior takes a long time to show up in the AIDS statistics. Even today, some new victims of AIDS are persons who became infected with HIV before the disease was even discovered, and many before the methods of transmission and avoidance were adequately understood by the relevant population. Second, the overall rate of growth of the disease is a composite of growth rates in distinct subpopulations that have only limited interaction. The economic model implies that growth may be decreasing and may even be negative in one subpopulation, where a high prevalence of the disease has induced substantial changes in behavior, at the same time that it is increasing in another subpopulation, where low prevalence facilitates growth because the risk of infection is not great enough to induce substantial behavioral changes. So, for example, at the same time that the rapid increase in the prevalence of AIDS among homosexual males in cities such as New York and San Francisco where those males are concentrated was causing a fall in incidence (new cases), the spread of the disease (for example by bisexual males, who have female as well as male sexual partners and might even substitute from high-risk male to low-risk female partners) into low-risk heterosexual populations was accompanied by a rapid growth in incidence in those populations (cf. Gardner et al. 1989).

The data in the next two figures provide evidence of this pattern. Figure 2-6 shows that, in males, homosexual and bisexual cases are decreasing as a fraction of all new cases, as homosexuals in high-prevalence areas reduce their involvement in risky sexual activities. Figure 2-7 shows that the composition of new cases due to intravenous drug use is shifting away from the region (the Northeast) where the prevalence of the disease (and presumably of HIV infection) is greatest. Similarly, while the incidence of new homosexual cases has peaked and is now falling in high-prevalence cities, it is still rising in low-prevalence ones (Karon and Berkelman 1991, esp. p. 1182 [fig. 2]; Harris 1990, p. 920 [fig. 4]), where the expected cost of infection is lower.

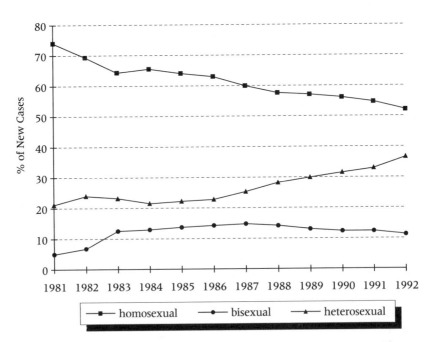

Figure 2-6 Relative frequencies of U.S. male AIDS cases, by patient's sexual orientation, 1981–1992. *Source:* CDC Public Information Data Set, 7/1/92.

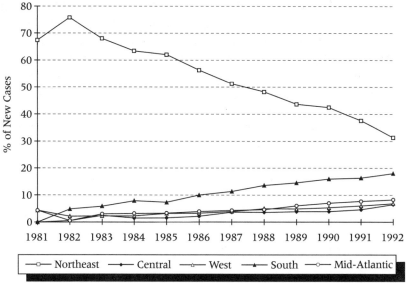

Figure 2-7 Relative frequencies of U.S. AIDS cases, for AIDS transmission via IV drug use, by Metropolitan Statistical Area, 1981–1992. *Source:* CDC Public Information Data Set, 7/1/92.

We cannot exclude the hypothesis that some combination of saturation effects, an artifactual decline in the incidence of AIDS cases induced by AZT therapy, measurement error or other statistical anomalies, and networks of sexual contacts[7] accounts for the patterns in the data that we have discussed. Still, the evidence presented in this section, in particular the leveling out of the infected stock shown in Figure 2-3, exposes serious infirmities in the purely epidemiological models[8] and implies that an economic-epidemiological model may be able to explain and predict the course of the AIDS epidemic more accurately.

Unfortunately, because we are not able with the data available to us to estimate the actual elasticities of demand for safe and risky sex in

7. Gupta, Anderson, and May (1989) show that if persons having a high frequency of sexual activity tend to pair off with other persons having a high frequency of sexual activity, rather than pairing off randomly with respect to frequency of activity, the AIDS epidemic will peak earlier.

8. For evidence that these models, because of their abehavioral character, have failed to predict the spread of other sexually transmitted diseases as well, see Ramstedt et al. (1991).

various subpopulations as a function of the prevalence of HIV infection and other relevant factors, we cannot make our own predictions regarding the course of the epidemic. This will not be the last economic study of AIDS, however; and we have created a theoretical framework that may enable future researchers to make actual estimates of the elasticity of demand for risky sex. As we shall see in the following section, there are abundant though not wholly reliable data on changes in sexual behavior in response to different perceived risks of HIV infection. Elasticity estimates could be derived from these data, although it would be a big job and the estimates would be very approximate. In any event, the value of our analysis does not depend on our being able to make actual predictions of the incidence of HIV/AIDS. We have shown that the epidemiological predictions, which ignore behavior change, are systematically biased. This is an important point even if the size of the necessary correction cannot yet be determined.

Behavioral Data

Responding to risk. A number of empirical studies document the behavioral changes that might account for the data in Figure 2-6. These studies, though not done by economists, provide support for the economic approach. The changes involve the substitution of various forms of safe sex for risky sex as the probability of infection rises, altering the relative prices of the two practices.[9] While the decline in the number of new homosexual cases may be exaggerated because of the possible effect of AZT on the length of the incubation stage of HIV infection, studies of homosexual males consistently show steep reductions in risky behavior through reduced number of sexual partners and reduced frequency of unshielded anal intercourse. The studies are subject to criticism for relying on unobserved, self-reported behavior, but they are corroborated not only by the statistics in Figure 2-6 but also by the well-documented decline in other sexually transmitted diseases among homosexuals,[10] since

---

9. Becker and Joseph (1988), Stall et al. (1988), Turner et al. (1989, pp. 131–136), and Coates (1990) review these studies, which have been conducted mainly in the United States and the United Kingdom. See also Riesenberg (1986). Typical studies are Detels et al. (1989); Ross, Freedman, and Brew (1989); Siegel and Glassman (1989); Chandarara et al. (1990); Ekstrand and Coates (1990); and Stevens et al. (1990). The behavioral changes that might account for the data on transmission by intravenous drug use, shown in Figure 2-7, are discussed later in this section.

10. See Coutinho et al. (1987); Thompson and Robertson (1989); Judson (1990); van de Laar (1990); Quinn et al. (1990); Kingsley et al. (1990, p. 234); and Rolfs and Nakashima (1990, pp. 434–435).

safe sex protects against all such diseases. They are further corroborated by the rapid growth in condom sales during the 1980s (Muirhead 1992a, 1992b; Drug Store News staff 1992). Moran and colleagues (1990) point out that only a small part of this growth can be explained by increased use of condoms as contraceptives.

Additional evidence of rational behavior in the face of risk of AIDS is found in studies showing a positive but smaller switch to safe-sex practices among heterosexuals (Handsfield 1985; DeBuono et al. 1990; Forrest and Singh 1990; Kanouse et al. 1991, pp. 18–31; Samuel et al. 1991; see also Blendon, Donelan, and Knox 1992, p. 982; ACSF Investigators 1992), especially those at greater risk—for instance women with multiple sex partners, or unmarried versus married women (Jurich, Adams, and Schulenberg 1992; McNally and Mosher 1991). Between 1982 and 1988, for example, the fraction of unmarried people using condoms rose, while the fraction of married people using them remained the same (Mosher 1990, p. 201 [tab. 4]). Even the use of condoms by adolescents has been found to be correlated with factors related to rational choice, such as confidence in being able to use a condom correctly (positive correlation), perceived cost of using a condom (negative), and perceived risk of contracting AIDS if a condom is not used (positive) (Catania et al. 1992; DiClemente 1992; Pendergrast, DuRant, and Gaillard 1992; see also Seltzer, Rabin, and Benjamin 1989; Tyden, Norden, and Ruusuvaara 1991). In one survey 78 percent of the respondents who did not use a condom all the time gave as a reason that they were not at high risk for AIDS (Kanouse et al. 1991, p. 28).

Even the increasing rate of "relapses" from safe to risky sexual behavior by homosexuals (van den Hoek, van Haastrecht, and Coutinho 1990; Kelly, St. Lawrence, and Brasfield 1991) is consistent with rationality if the net flow of HIV infection is negative, as by now it may be in high-risk subpopulations. "Because of declining incidence of STD and human immunodeficiency virus (HIV) infections, some homosexually active men may have relaxed behaviors regarding sexual safety" (Centers for Disease Control 1989b). Another interpretation of the relapse phenomenon, but one also consistent with rationality, is that it reflects more careful sorting of HIV-negatives with HIV-negatives and positives with positives—a sorting that can make unsafe sex safe, since transmission requires partners of different infection status. These points are stressed by Hart and colleagues (1992), who point out, correctly in our view, that the very use of the term "relapse" conceals the rational character of much of the behavior so described.

A related phenomenon—the higher incidence of risky sexual behavior among homosexuals in their twenties than among older homosexuals (Stall et al. 1992)—may reflect a tendency for persons to have sex with people of roughly their own age. Young people, having less sexual experience, are less likely to be infected already, hence less likely to infect their sexual partners—so the expected cost of risky sex to the latter is reduced.

Economic theory predicts that the ratio of safe to unsafe sex will be positively correlated with any factor that increases the prevalence of the disease, not only sexual preference but also location (for example, whether it is a high- or a low-incidence area), gender, race, and age. We therefore expect combinations of adverse demographic factors to be associated with a greater demand for safe sex—so that, other things being equal, heterosexual women in New York and San Francisco should be expected to demand safe sex more than heterosexual men in other cities demand it. The qualification "other things being equal" is vital. Particular demographic combinations may be especially dangerous *because* a subpopulation, for exogenous reasons (such as a high cost, due to low levels of general education, of absorbing information about safe sex), does not practice safe sex.

Several studies cast light on the relation between the prevalence of AIDS and the avoidance of risky sex (St. Lawrence et al. 1989; Kelly et al. 1990; Miller 1990; Moran 1990). The Kelly study is illustrative: it found a higher rate of risky behavior among homosexuals in low-prevalence than in high-prevalence cities. The similar but more elaborate study by St. Lawrence and her associates reports the percentage distributions of different homosexual sex practices across cities that have different incidences of AIDS, ranging from 7 to 41 cases per 100,000. The sexual practices of 290 homosexual men were elicited through interviews. Tables 2-1 and 2-2 reveal the large differences in behavior across the two groups of cities. For example, the average number of acts of unshielded anal intercourse during the two-month period studied was almost three times as great in the low-prevalence cities as in the high-prevalence ones (4.6 versus 1.7). Indeed, such intercourse was the most common sexual activity in the low-prevalence cities, while in the high-prevalence ones the most common was the relatively safe activity of mutual masturbation. The major anomaly in the tables is the lower frequency of condom use in the high-prevalence cities, but this may reflect a switch from anal intercourse to less risky forms of sex (for, as discussed in the Introduction, anal intercourse even with condoms is not a completely safe activity).

Table 2-1 Frequencies of high- and low-risk practices among 290 gay men in high- and low-prevalence cities during a two-month period

Variable	High-prevalence city (mean)	Low-prevalence city (mean)	*F* value	*P* value
AIDS risk knowledge test score	36.2	33.2	38.83	.0001
Anal intercourse, no condom				
Insertive partner	0.8	2.4	5.37	.03
Receptive partner	0.8	2.1	NS	NS
Unprotected oral intercourse				
Insertive partner	0.7	1.3	NS	NS
Receptive partner	0.7	1.2	NS	NS
Mutual masturbation, no insertion	4.7	1.9	19.50	.0001
Body rubbing, no insertion	1.6	0.9	4.43	.04
Anal intercourse, condom used				
Insertive partner	0.9	1.4	NS	NS
Receptive partner	0.3	0.4	NS	NS
Number of sexual acts	12.3	12.7	NS	NS
Number of different sexual partners	3.4	2.0	6.90	.01

Source: Janet S. St. Lawrence et al., "Differences in Gay Men's AIDS Risk Knowledge and Behavior Patterns in High and Low AIDS Prevalence Cities." *Public Health Reports* 104 (1989): 391–395. "NS" means not statistically significant.

The St. Lawrence study does not control for the number of (male) homosexuals in the different cities, and it is possible that the percentage of infected homosexuals is lower in the high-incidence cities, in which event the study overestimates the responsiveness of the sample population to the higher probability of infection in those cities. Differences in the number of homosexuals could also explain the greater number of sexual partners of men in the high-incidence cities, another apparent anomaly.

Notice the close agreement between the rates of anal intercourse, both protected and unprotected, and of unprotected oral intercourse, as reported by both the insertive and the receptive partner. This provides some evidence that self-reporting of sexual behavior is a valid research

Table 2-2   Percentage distribution of sexual activities practiced by 290 gay
men during a two-month period in high- and low-prevalence
areas[a]

Activity	High prevalence (%)	Low prevalence (%)
Anal intercourse without condom	13.0	35.4
Oral intercourse without condom	11.4	19.7
Oral-anal contact	14.6	8.7
Mutual masturbation, no insertion	38.2	15.0
Body rubbing, no insertion	13.0	7.0
Anal intercourse, condom used	9.8	14.2

a. Mean number of sexual encounters by men in high-prevalence area = 12.3. Mean
number of sexual encounters by men in low-prevalence area = 12.7 during past two
months.

Source: Janet S. St. Lawrence et al., "Differences in Gay Men's AIDS Risk Knowledge
and Behavior Patterns in High and Low AIDS Prevalence Cities." *Public Health Reports*
104 (1989): 391–395.

procedure. Other evidence is presented in James, Bignell, and Gillies
(1991); see also McCusker, Stoddard, and McCarthy (1992).

Studies of the response of intravenous drug users to the risk of AIDS
have yielded results similar to those of the studies of homosexuals. The
review article by Des Jarlais, Friedman, and Casriel (1990) found dramatic reductions in needle-sharing in high-incidence cities. As early as
1985, intravenous drug users in New York City were sharing needles
less (Selwyn et al. 1987). And in San Francisco, the percentage of intravenous drug addicts reported to use bleach regularly in order to decontaminate their needles (a practice that corresponds to safe sex in the
sexual marketplace) increased from 10 to 67 percent in one study as the
incidence of AIDS rose.[11]

Effects of knowledge, education, and income. Rational sexual choice under uncertainty further implies that knowledge about the transmission
and prevention of AIDS will increase with the probability of infection,
since the benefit from devoting time and other resources to learning
about a disease is greater the higher the risk (as well as the lethality) of
infection. This prediction is supported by the first row of Table 2-1, and

11. See also Colón et al. (1992); Des Jarlais et al. (1992b); Robert et al. (1990); Watters
et al. (1990); and Robertson, Skidmore, and Roberts (1988).

by evidence that ignorance and misconceptions among blacks about AIDS (Mays and Cochran 1990, pp. 104–105, 109; Thomas, Gilliam, and Iwrey 1989) are factors in the disproportionate prevalence of the disease in the black community. Yet we do not expect, or find, that knowledge about the dangers of AIDS *always* produces a substitution of safe for risky sex (Darke et al. 1992; Des Jarlais et al. 1992a). Low-risk persons are not expected to change their behavior substantially even if—perhaps especially if—they are knowledgeable about AIDS.[12] Some high-risk persons, such as drug addicts and members of disadvantaged minority groups, have above-average discount rates or derive relatively little utility from living (see Becker and Kilburn 1992), perhaps reflecting (as well as causing) poverty. They therefore have, irrespective of any knowledge deficits, a more than average likelihood of engaging in an activity that produces a risk of death in the relatively distant future. This may help explain the high level of risky behavior found in a survey of inner-city youths who were quite knowledgeable about the transmission of AIDS, although they underestimated the efficacy of condoms in preventing that transmission (Stiffman et al. 1992). A related point is that if drug addiction impairs life expectancy (which seems plausible, though we have found no statistics), a rational drug addict will discount even more steeply than other poor or disadvantaged persons the risk of contracting a disease that may remain asymptomatic for a decade. A negative relation between discount rates and health has indeed been found (Fuchs 1982b; see also Ehrlich and Chuma 1990, p. 774).

We are led to predict that as knowledge about AIDS has grown, enabling middle-class and upper-class Americans to reduce their risk of infection, the disease has become increasingly one of poor Americans. A study of 3,601 clients of an HIV testing and counseling center in Seattle found a significant negative correlation between income and HIV infection, after correcting for racial and other demographic variables and for risk factors (Krueger et al. 1990). And Figure 2-8 confirms that AIDS is increasingly a disease of black and Hispanic persons, who have on average lower incomes than white and Asian Americans.[13] This is weaker

---

12. For evidence, see Fisher and Misovich (1990) and Tyden, Björkelund, and Olsson (1991); see also Chapter 6 of this book.

13. See also Centers for Disease Control (1993, pp. 10, 15 [tabs. 4, 9]); Mays and Cochran (1987); Marin (1989). And there may be more underreporting of AIDS cases among blacks and Hispanics than among whites (Lindan et al. 1990). The prevalence of AIDS among Asian Americans and American Indians remains very low, and we do not discuss it.

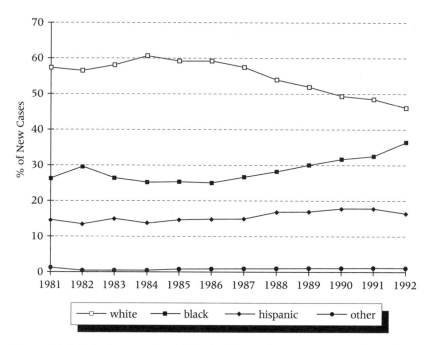

Figure 2-8 Relative frequencies of U.S. AIDS cases, by race, 1981–1992. *Source:* CDC Public Information Data Set, 7/1/92.

evidence for the income hypothesis than the Seattle study, however, because income is not the only factor relevant to AIDS along which blacks and Hispanics differ from other Americans. In particular, blacks and Hispanics are much more likely, even after correction for other factors, to be users of illegal drugs (Sickles and Taubman 1991). Education is still another distinguishing factor, as is the sex ratio; these we discuss next.

Facts that blunt the effect of knowledge on behavior must be distinguished from high costs of absorbing information, which reduce knowledge. On this score we expect a measure of general education, such as years of schooling, to be negatively correlated with probability of being infected with the AIDS virus.[14] We are not aware of any direct studies of this correlation, but a study showing an extremely low prevalence of

---

14. This expectation is supported by evidence that schooling increases health, even after correction for the positive correlation between education and income that is discussed in the next paragraph (Berger and Leigh 1989).

HIV infection among university students provides indirect evidence (Gayle et al. 1990).

Education may have additional significance in predicting HIV and AIDS. Education is positively correlated with income, which in turn is positively correlated with the demand for health (Ehrlich and Chuma 1990, pp. 774–775; Duleep 1986), and therefore negatively with the prevalence of AIDS, as we just noted. And since the pecuniary benefits of education are deferred, while the costs (primarily the forgone income from working) are incurred currently, we predict that university students and other highly educated persons have lower discount rates than otherwise similar persons and therefore a higher expected cost of AIDS. Studies finding an inverse correlation between education and the initiation of cigarette smoking (such as Escobedo et al. 1990) are pertinent here, since smoking too poses a future rather than a present hazard to the smoker's health (see also Viscusi and Moore 1989). We predict and find that safe sex is less common among persons who have a history of other hazardous behavior (Brown, DiClemente, and Beausoleil 1992), implying that they like to gamble with their health, perhaps because they have high discount rates, or that they have difficulty absorbing information about health hazards.

Race and gender. Factors not yet mentioned, but relevant to economic analysis, lead us to expect AIDS to be disproportionately prevalent among blacks, especially black women, even if education and income are held constant across racial groups. The unusually low effective sex ratio (that is, ratio of males in the market for sexual relationships to females in that market) among blacks[15] reduces both the demand for monogamy by black men and the leverage of black women in bargaining for the use of a condom—in fact condoms are much more rarely used by blacks than by whites—while the greater hostility to homosexuality in the black than in the white community is likely to lead homosexuals to substitute bisexual for purely homosexual behavior in order to conceal their homosexuality.[16]

Figures 2-9 and 2-10 support these conjectures concerning race and

---

15. The reasons include poor neonatal care (female infants are more robust than male), the very high homicide rate among young black males, their very high imprisonment rate, and the fact that black males are far more likely to date or marry white females than white males are to date or marry black females (see Posner 1992, pp. 137–138, and references cited there).

16. See Mosher (1988); Mays and Cochran (1990); Doll et al. (1991b, pp. 33–37); Posner (1992, pp. 136–141); cf. Boulton, Hart, and Fitzpatrick (1992); Ross (1988).

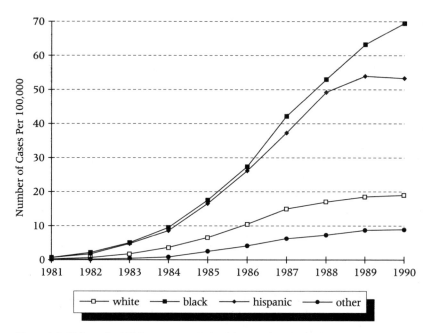

Figure 2-9 U.S. male AIDS cases per 100,000 men, by race, 1981–1990. *Sources:* U.S. Bureau of the Census, Current Population Reports, Series P-25; CDC Public Information Data Set, 7/1/92.

gender. Figure 2-9 shows that the rate of new AIDS cases among black males is more than three times the rate among white males—and Figure 2-10 that the rate for black females is ten times that of white females. The figures for Hispanics are in between, which is not surprising because while drug usage is also high and education and income low in the Hispanic community, there is not the same imbalance of males and females—gender inequality in a literal sense—in the market for marriage and other heterosexual relationships.

The issue of gender inequality can be further elucidated with the help of the model in Chapter 1. Since it is plausible that men have a stronger aversion to condoms than women do even without regard to disease risk, and since in addition the AIDS virus is much more easily transmitted from male to female than the reverse, we would expect B_m (the benefit of risky sex to the male) to exceed B_f by a wide margin, implying that women would often derive a negative net expected utility from engaging in risky sex and men a positive one. Alternatively, in the more complex model summarized in equations 1.1a and 1.2a, B_m exceeds B_f merely to

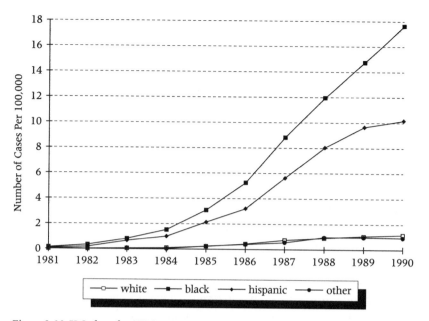

Figure 2-10 U.S. female AIDS cases per 100,000 women, by race, 1981–1990.
Sources: U.S. Bureau of the Census, Current Population Reports, Series P-25; CDC Public Information Data Set, 7/1/92.

the extent that males have a greater aversion to condoms than females, unrelated to disease risk, but P_{tm} exceeds P_{tf}, which makes C (the cost of infection), discounted by the probability of infection, greater for f than for m, even if $C_m = C_f$. In fact C_f may well exceed C_m—further reinforcing the asymmetry between male and female demand for safe sex—because an additional cost of HIV infection to a woman is the 30 percent probability that any child she conceives after she becomes infected will be infected also (see Chapter 9). This is a potential cost to the father also, but probably a smaller one on average.

We expect the relative preference for safe sex by women compared to men to be greater among blacks than among whites, since black men, constituting the pool from which black women choose the vast majority of their sexual partners, have a higher infection rate than white men. If, however, a woman has few alternatives in the market for sexual relationships, a man may be able to compensate her at very low cost to himself—perhaps just by being willing to have a relationship with her—for her acceding to his request for risky sex. Because black women have poorer options in the dating and marriage markets than white women, we expect black women to be more willing to accept such compensation.[17]

Still another factor is that safe sex is contraceptive. Women who want to have children, but whose sexual opportunities are limited to men among whom the prevalence of HIV infection is high—say because they are intravenous drug users, as a disproportionate number of black men are—will perforce run a significant risk of becoming infected. All things considered, it is not surprising that the ratio of female to male AIDS cases is so much higher in the black than in the white community.

The low effective sex ratio in the black community also is helpful in explaining the higher rate of AIDS among black men than among white men. The scarcity of black males results in an increase in the average number of their sexual partners, and number of sexual partners is a risk factor for AIDS. This, as well as the lower demand for condom use that we expect among men who have a favorable position in the market for sexual relations,[18] leads us to predict that the rate of AIDS would be higher among black men and women than among white men and women of the same income and education.

We should not ignore the vastly greater incidence of other sexually transmitted diseases among blacks compared to whites. The rate of syphilis, for example, among black men and black women is more than 50 times that among white men and women, and we know that being already infected with a sexually transmitted disease is a risk factor for HIV/ AIDS (Centers for Disease Control 1990a, p. 144 [tab. 4]). However, this may just mean that the same factors that, by reducing condom use among blacks, increase the prevalence of HIV in the black community directly may do so indirectly by increasing the spread of other sexually transmitted diseases and thus making blacks more susceptible to infection by HIV.

Evidence from Other Sexually Transmitted Diseases

If people are rational about AIDS, we would expect them to be rational about other sexually transmitted diseases, and vice versa. Hence another

---

17. For evidence, see Fullilove et al. (1990).

18. For evidence that black men in fact have a far more negative attitude toward condoms than black women, see Johnson et al. (1992).

empirical implication of our analysis is that, other things being equal, sexually transmitted diseases will be more common the less deadly they are, because the benefits of safe sex are fewer the less costly the disease that it avoids. The qualification "other things being equal" is critical. The expected cost of a communicable disease is a function of its contagiousness or virulence as well as of its lethality, and contagiousness varies widely across diseases. For example, the risk of transmission of gonorrhea from a single exposure has been estimated at 22 to 25 percent, compared to ≤ 0.2 percent for male to female transmission of HIV per exposure.[19] Moreover, the risk of sexually transmitted disease differs dramatically across persons and groups. Obviously, sexually inactive persons are not at risk of sexually transmitted disease, and we know that male homosexuals, for example, are more at risk from such diseases than male heterosexuals are (Posner 1992, p. 163). So the prevalence of a disease in the general population cannot be used as a proxy for the risk of infection.

The World Health Organization has estimated that in 1990 there were (worldwide) 25 million new cases of gonorrhea, 20 million of genital herpes, 3.5 million of syphilis, and 1 million of AIDS (Dicsfalusy 1992; see also De Schryver and Meheus 1990, and Global AIDS Policy Coalition 1992, ch. 5). Prevalence thus was negatively correlated with lethality. Without information about probability of infection, this correlation has little if any significance. We do know, however, that both gonorrhea and hepatitis B are at once less serious, and more easily transmittable, sexually transmitted diseases than AIDS—and both are more prevalent than AIDS among homosexuals.[20]

Table 2-3 summarizes the relevant data for seven sexually transmitted diseases, including HIV. The table is useful for evaluating two other differences in prediction between the economic and the epidemiological models. First, epidemiologists generally assume that prevalence will be proportionate to the likelihood of infection given an unsafe sexual contact. So if, for example, as is the case for gonorrhea, an infected man is two or three times as likely to transmit the disease to an uninfected woman as an infected woman is to an uninfected man, the epidemiological models predict that two or three times as many women as men will

---

19. This is average risk. Actual risk depends on the infectivity of the carrier, the particular sex act, the condition of the immune system and genital tissues of the exposed person, and possibly other factors.

20. On hepatitis B in homosexuals, see Kingsley et al. (1990).

Table 2-3 Characteristics of sexually transmitted diseases[a]

Disease	Period of infectiousness	Incubation period	Transmission probabilities (per encounter, unless otherwise noted)	Incidence (average 1980–1991)	Gravity
AIDS/HIV	Lifetime	Mean 7–9 years	Male to female: ≤ 0.2% Female to male: 2.9 to 17.5 × m/f	Male: 13,078 Female: 1,402	Fatal for m, f
Chancroid	About 30 days	3–10 days	Male to female: 63%	Male: 3,802 Female: 655	Mild for m, f
Chlamydia	Untreated: < 1 year	Men: 7–10 days Women: 7–? days	Male to female: 15.4% Female to male: 12.2%	Male: 50,250 Female: 173,906 (most screening done on females)	Mild for m, grave for f
Gonorrhea	Untreated: variable	Men: 3–7 days Women: 7–60 days	Male to female: 50–70% Female to male: 20%	Male: 487,579 Female: 350,103	Mild for m, grave for f
Herpes	Potentially lifetime	7–14 days	Male to female: 18.9% Female to male: 4.5%	Estimated: 500,000 total cases	Grave to mild for m, f
Papilloma virus	Potentially lifetime	2–5 months	60% (within 3 months)	Estimated: 750,000 total cases	Grave: f only
Syphilis	2–4 years	21 days	Both directions: 20–25%	Male: 23,522 Female: 12,437	Grave to mild for m, f

a. The sources for the data in this table are: Centers for Disease Control, Center for Prevention Services, Division of STD/HIV Prevention, Surveillance and Information Systems Branch (unpublished data on incidence); miscellaneous "Backgrounders" disseminated in mimeograph form by the Office of Communications, National Institute of Allergy and Infectious Diseases, National Institutes of Health, Bethesda, Maryland, in January and February 1992; Aral and Holmes (1990); Csonka and Oates (1990b); Goldsmith (1989); Hart (1975); Holle (1986); Holmberg et al. (1989); Hooper et al. (1978); Jones and Wasserheit (1991); Katz (1992); Mertz et al. (1992); Oriel and Walker (1990); Padian, Shiboski, and Jewell (1991); Potterat, Dukes, and Rothenberg (1987); Robertson, McMillan, and Young (1989); Schmid et al. (1987). All data are for the United States.

have gonorrhea (Hethcote and Yorke 1984; Bailey 1975, ch. 11; Anderson and May 1991, ch. 11), when in truth, as Table 2-3 shows, the prevalence is markedly higher among men. This is not surprising to an economist. The higher cost of risky sex to the woman[21] causes her to screen her sexual partners more carefully than a man screens his partners, though how much more carefully may depend on the effective sex ratio and other factors affecting bargaining power between men and women, as we noted in discussing the high rate of AIDS among black women.

Although male to female and female to male transmission probabilities for syphilis are approximately the same, the costs of syphilis to women are higher, in part because it can be transmitted to the fetus (Aral and Holmes 1990, p. 24). So again we are not surprised that the incidence is higher among men than among women. Chlamydia, the least serious and (not unexpectedly) one of the most prevalent sexually transmitted diseases in the United States, is slightly more easily transmitted from male to female than from female to male, so it is not entirely surprising that the female incidence is higher; it is somewhat surprising, though, because women are more likely to experience complications in the form of pelvic inflammatory disease. Genital herpes presents a similar though not identical picture: easier transmittability from male to female than vice versa, complications evenly divided by gender, and (weak) evidence of a higher incidence among women (ibid., p. 26).[22]

Second, the typical epidemiological model abstracts from the relative lethality (cost) of different sexually transmitted diseases. Recall that the percentage of uninfected persons (S) in an epidemic's steady state is equal to v/b, where b is the probability of transmission from an infected to an uninfected person and v is the exit rate, that is, the fraction of the population that was in the infected (and infective) class in the previous period but has been removed from it by death, out-migration, or recovery followed by immunity. In the formula, the predicted percentage of healthy people is the same whether infected persons are removed from the infected roll by dying, or by recovering and becoming immune, or by other methods of exit such as emigration. Yet rational people will

---

21. Not only is the probability of transmission from male to female higher than the reverse, but women are much more likely to experience serious complications from gonorrhea, notably pelvic inflammatory disease.

22. The 500,000 figure in Table 2-3 for the number of cases of genital herpes probably is grossly underestimated, but the CDC does not track this disease and no better estimate is available.

take more precautions against infection with HIV than infection with a nonfatal disease such as herpes. For this (economic) reason alone, AIDS would be less prevalent than herpes even if AIDS were as easily spread. Hence the statistics on the pre-AIDS prevalence of herpes place an upper bound on the likely prevalence of HIV and AIDS.

Similarly, the economist is not surprised that although the discovery of a cheap, painless, and effective cure for syphilis in the 1940s (penicillin) initially caused a drop in the prevalence of the disease as cured persons left the ranks of the infected, prevalence later rose when the invention of the contraceptive pill, first approved for sale in the United States in 1960, lowered the fertility risk of sex—penicillin having already lowered the disease risk by making syphilis curable. When AIDS raised the perceived disease risk, beginning in the early 1980s, syphilis again declined.[23] The time series of syphilis, shown graphically in Figure 2-11,[24] suggests that behavioral response can dominate changes in prevalence that are due to purely epidemiological factors, such as a cure that reduces the prevalence of the disease by removing infected (and infective) persons from the relevant population.

Despite the evidence marshaled in this chapter of rational behavior toward the risk of AIDS and of other sexually transmitted diseases, we do not claim that everyone in the United States is behaving optimally with regard to such risk. Several multivariate studies have found, for example, that a person is more likely to adopt safe sex if he knows someone who has AIDS (Ekstrand and Coates 1990, p. 975; Hingson, Strunin, and Berlin 1990, p. 26; Klein et al. 1987, p. 744); yet a rational person doesn't have to know someone with AIDS to assess the risks of unsafe sex. Nor do we deny the significance of studies which find that addiction and intoxication interfere with people's ability to make a rational choice between safe and risky sex (Butcher, Manning, and Neal 1991; Penkower et al. 1991; Schleifer et al. 1990). Ericksen and Trocki (1992) note the high positive correlation between alcohol abuse and having a sexually transmitted disease, and Aral and colleagues (1991), for example, emphasize "chemical foreplay" as a factor in the spread of AIDS: drug addicts often use drugs in conjunction with sex. We consider the

---

23. The surge in syphilis among blacks that began in 1986 remains unexplained (Rolfs and Nakashima 1990). The rate among whites has continued to decline (Centers for Disease Control 1990a, p. 11 [fig. 8]).

24. Based on Aral and Holmes (1990, p. 22). See also De Schryver and Meheus (1990, pp. 640–641); Felman (1989); and Brandt (1985, ch. 5, and 1988, pp. 368–369).

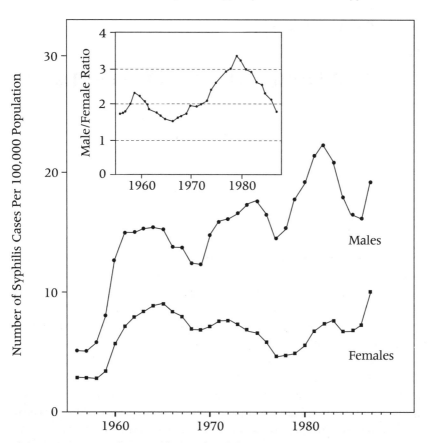

Figure 2-11 U.S. per capita incidence of syphilis, 1956–1988. *Source:* Sevgi O. Aral and King K. Holmes, "Epidemiology of Sexual Behavior and Sexually Transmitted Diseases." In King K. Holmes et al., eds., *Sexually Transmitted Diseases,* 2nd ed. (New York: McGraw-Hill Information Services, 1990): 23.

policy implications of this point in Chapter 5. Doll and colleagues (1991a) find a positive correlation between drug abuse and unprotected anal sex between men, although one possible interpretation is that drug abusers have high discount rates or low utility of living. A subtle but potentially important point, though not one necessarily inconsistent with a rational model of human behavior, is that consumption of heroin reduces penile sensitivity and so increases the disutility of condoms to heroin addicts (Rhodes et al. 1990). Alcohol abuse may also have a multiple effect on AIDS, since there is evidence that it weakens the immune system and thus makes the abuser more susceptible to HIV infection (Molgaard et al. 1988).

CHAPTER 3

The Demand for HIV Testing

Policymakers and public health scholars alike believe that widespread testing for HIV is essential to reducing the incidence of AIDS (see, for example, Presidential Commission 1988, ch. 6; Coates et al. 1988; Rhame and Maki 1989). In this chapter we discuss the demand for, and the effects of, HIV testing and show that a simple economic model which works well in explaining the pattern of demand for HIV testing implies that such testing may increase the incidence of AIDS rather than being sure to decrease it. Consistent with the economic emphasis on choice and incentives, we ask *why* people choose to test or not to test. This inquiry, which is missing from most epidemiological analyses because epidemiologists are generally not interested in issues of choice, incentive, and information, can reverse the implications of those analyses. We acknowledge the shortcomings of our simple model and spend a good deal of time qualifying and refining it. But even duly qualified and refined, it seriously undermines the case for HIV testing as a method of controlling the epidemic by showing that testing can encourage risky sex.

The economic model developed in Chapter 1 implies that risky sex will usually be avoided when sexual partners have substantially different subjective probabilities of infection; the one with the much lower probability will generally be unwilling to have risky sex with the one with the much higher probability.[1] Avoiding risky sex imposes a cost, however,

---

1. See especially Figure 1-1. The analysis of needle-sharing by intravenous drug users is parallel and does not require separate consideration. The qualifications in the text ("usually," "generally") are to allow for the possibility of compensating the low-probability partner for assuming the risk of becoming infected.

given the disutility of condoms and other methods of safe sex. This opens up the possibility that measures which reduce subjective probabilities that prospective sexual partners are infected may increase expected utility by inducing risky sex, the preferred form provided the risks are not great. One possibility is to establish one's noninfected status, with certainty, by testing negative for the virus. Granted, "with certainty" is an exaggeration. Apart from false positives and false negatives, both of which occur, and the difficulty of proving to another that one's infection status is as represented, there can be a lag of as much as six months between becoming infected with the virus and testing positive for it. We shall ignore these complications for now and assume that an HIV test enables a probability of being infected to be converted into a certainty that, at the time of taking the test, one was either infected or not infected. Another simplifying assumption to be relaxed later is that both persons involved in an actual or potential sexual relationship are selfish rather than altruistic.

A critical question is, who gets the test results? Just the person tested? His employer? Insurers? Most important, as far as the spread of the disease is concerned, his potential sexual partners? We focus on two situations. In one, which we call "partner-observed" testing, the result of one's test becomes known to one's potential sexual partner before the next act of sexual intercourse. In the other, "partner-unobserved" testing, the person tested keeps the result of the test to himself. In both cases we are interested in predicting who will be likely to test and what effect, if any, testing will have on the growth of the disease and on economic efficiency.

"Partner-Observed" Testing: Welfare and Epidemiological Implications

It might seem that partner observation would occur only under governmental compulsion, and at this point we are considering not the government's but the sexual market's response to the AIDS epidemic. As we noted in Chapter 1, however, if two persons are in a long-term relationship it may be impossible for one to conceal a positive result of his HIV test from the other—and there is no incentive to conceal a negative result. Moreover, a person who has either tested negative or knows himself to have a very low probability of being infected may be unwilling to have risky sex with another person unless the latter agrees to be tested and to reveal the result. In both cases the test is in effect observed by the potential sexual partner of the person being tested.

The effect would, it is true, be more direct if there were "partner-administered" rather than just "partner-observed" tests and if they cost no more. Such tests, if feasible, would be more efficient, because the partner of the person testing has more to gain from learning of a positive result than the person who is tested. A partner-administered test would eliminate the danger that a person who tests positive will try to conceal the result from his partner. Later we consider the effect on the demand for testing and on the spread of the disease should such a test come on the market.

A model of the private demand for HIV testing. In Chapter 1 we showed that the demand for risky sex is negatively related to your partner's probability of being already infected. If you thought that that probability was high, you might refuse to have risky sex with him, although he might be willing to have it with you because he (and perhaps you also) thought that your probability of being already infected was very low. He might therefore decide to be tested in the hope that if he tested negative you would consent to have risky sex with him—and you would.

To be more precise, let $V_m(P_m, P_f)$ denote the expected utility to m of the type of sex with f that is chosen under probabilities of infection P_m, P_f.[2] Then m will test if and only if

$$(3.1) \quad P_m V_m(1, P_f) + (1 - P_m) V_m(0, P_f) \geq V_m(P_m, P_f).$$

The parallel condition for f to test is

$$(3.2) \quad P_f V_f(1, P_m) + (1 - P_f) V_f(0, P_m) \geq V_f(P_m, P_f),$$

but we can confine discussion to inequality 3.1. The first term on the left-hand side is the expected utility of a trade with f if m tests positive ($P_m = 1$) and the result is revealed to f. We assume that such a trade would be some form of safe sex because f would not consent to risky sex with a person whom she knew to be infected unless she knew herself to be infected too. This simplifies reality. Since the probability of infection from one or for that matter many acts of risky sex with an infected

---

2. Since we are modeling a consensual transaction, $V_m(P_m, P_f)$ and $V_f(P_m, P_f)$ are positive only if $U_m(P)$ and $U_f(P)$ are both positive. That is, both partners must derive positive utility from the transaction. V is thus, in economic jargon, an indirect utility function.

person is less than 1, uninfected persons who like to gamble with their life or health or who set a low value on living may engage in risky sex with a person whom they know to be infected. (For evidence, see Dublin, Rosenberg, and Goedert 1992.)

Discounting by the probability of m's testing positive, P_m, is necessary to determine the *expected* utility of the (safe) sexual trade that will ensue should m test positive. The second term on the left-hand side of inequality 3.1 is the expected utility of a sexual trade if m tests negative, so in that term P_m is replaced by 0. If the sum of the two expected utilities exceeds that of whatever trade (the right-hand side of the inequality) with f is available to m on the basis of neither person's knowing m's infection status, m will test. This condition is most likely to be satisfied, given the preference for risky over safe sex, if the only sexual trade available to m if he does not test is safe sex. Therefore, m's demand for testing is more likely to be positive the higher his probability of being infected (more precisely, the higher f's estimate of his probability of being infected; but we ignore that complication for now by assuming, as in Chapter 1, that both partners agree on the probability that each is infected). For the higher that probability is, the more difficult it will be for m to find an f who is willing to have risky sex with him without insisting that he agree to test and that he test negative.

This point can be seen more clearly with the aid of Figure 3-1, which

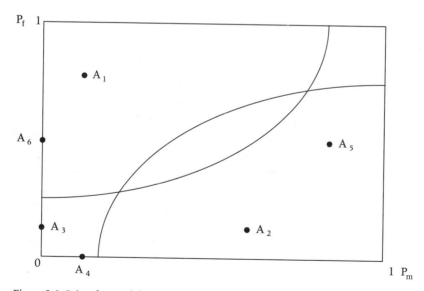

Figure 3-1 Joint demand for risky sex: effect of partner-observed HIV testing.

is Figure 1-1 with the shading and labels deleted and additional points inserted. Let's begin with A_2. This is a combination of P_m and P_f at which m would be willing to have risky sex with f but f would be unwilling to have risky sex with m. If, however, m tested, and tested negative, f would reclassify m from A_2 to A_3 and would therefore be willing to have risky sex with him. A_1 and A_4 are the corresponding points for the case in which m but not f refuses to have risky sex unless the other tests.

What about a point like A_5? Here, as before, m is willing to have risky sex without testing but f is not. However, if m tested negative, thus repositioning him at A_6, although f would now be willing to have risky sex with him he would no longer be willing to have risky sex with her, because, now that he knows he's negative, he has a greater expected loss from engaging in risky sex with someone who has as high a probability of already being infected as f does. At this second stage he will demand that she test, and if she does and tests negative, both will move to the origin (0). They will engage in unprotected sex with each other, but there will be no risk because intercourse between a negative and a negative cannot transmit the disease.

What happens to a person who tests positive? He (or she) moves to the top (if it is f who is positive) or right (if it is m) edge of Figure 3-1, where the opportunity to engage in unsafe sex is limited to persons who either are themselves positive or, though negative in fact, have a very high probability of being positive. In the latter case, our positive tester may infect them. Thus, in the model that we are expounding here, HIV testing increases the demand for potentially infective behavior whether or not the person tested tests negative or positive. Before testing, he could not obtain risky sex from low-probability persons and did not want risky sex from high-probability ones; so the only sex for him was safe sex. After testing, if he tested negative he obtains risky sex with a preferred sexual partner who may be positive, and as a result he may become infected, while if he tested positive his preferences shift and he obtains risky sex with a person who may not be infected and therefore whom he may infect. In either case he substitutes potentially infective sex for safe sex.

Epidemiologists typically assume that screening (for example by testing) for a communicable disease results in the elimination from the infective pool of anyone who tests positive. This assumption seems unwarranted, for reasons discussed later in this chapter and also in Chapter 5. But the point to be emphasized here is that even if the assumption is accepted, partner-observed HIV testing may increase the demand for risky sex and hence the likelihood that the disease will spread. For we are focusing on the case in which a person who tests was unable, before he tested, to obtain the risky sexual trade that he desired. If he tests negative, he obtains the trade. If he tests positive, and if, contrary to the assumption in the preceding paragraph, all persons who test positive are excluded from the infective pool (that is, do not engage in risky sex), there is no increase in risky sex as a result of his learning his infection status. (Indeed, in the formal model *all* the increase in risky sex as a result of testing comes from the increased demand for risky sex by persons who test negative.) But neither is there any decrease, since our positive tester did not engage in risky sex before. Because the increase in potentially infective behavior in our model is consistent with the basic assumption that epidemiologists make about screening, the model should encourage them to reexamine their views on the benefits of screening.

Notice that the demand, in the economic sense of the word, as opposed to the request,[3] for partner-observed testing comes from people who prefer risky sex but, because they have a high probability of being infected, cannot obtain the risky sex that they desire without producing a negative test result to their prospective partner. It might appear that people with a low probability of being already infected might want to test also, so that if they tested negative they would know it was worthwhile to avoid taking risks.[4] But they would have relatively little to gain from the test. By assumption, their probability of being already infected is low; it may be only slightly greater than zero; therefore pushing it all the way to zero will not markedly increase the gains to them from safe, or safer, sex. To see this, suppose they do test. Should they test negative, then by the assumption that they are testing for the purpose of deciding whether they would benefit from safe sex (as they would not if they are already infected), they will adopt some form of safe sex in order to protect themselves from infection. Should they test positive, their partner will force them to adopt safe sex unless the partner is either positive or, at least, has a very high probability of being positive. The gain to a low-risk person from the test, therefore, is the prospect of risky sex with

---

3. Which need not be explicit. A high-P person who wishes to improve his prospects in the market for risky sex may test before any of his prospective sexual partners asks him to do so. The only problem is that a negative test result is a rapidly depreciating asset in that market, since a person can, of course, become infected after taking the test.

4. This incentive for testing is discussed further in the next section of this chapter.

positive or high-risk sexual partners should the test be positive and thus establish, on our assumptions, that there is no incremental risk to him. This prospect, small because the person testing is very unlikely to test positive, is unlikely to induce a great deal of voluntary testing; for testing is, as we shall see, more costly than its price alone implies. Given that cost, a low-risk person who is so relatively indifferent between safe and risky sex that he will prefer the former if he tests negative will probably adopt safe sex without bothering to incur the cost of the test.

This analysis ignores, it is true, the continuous rather than dichoto-mous character of the safe-risky choice when viewed realistically. One point along the continuum is to continue engaging in risky sex, in the sense of sex without condoms, but to switch to sexual partners with a lower probability of being carriers. We can therefore imagine a person testing so that he could use the result to guide his choice of sexual part-ners. If he tested positive he would have risky sex with anyone, while if he tested negative he would have risky sex only with persons who had themselves tested negative or were otherwise believed to have a low probability of being infected. Still, these are both forms of risky, that is, potentially infective, sex. The low-risk person to whom the person who tests negative switches may be infected and infect him; the higher-risk person from whom he switches may now return to the sexual mar-ket for a new partner and infect (or be infected by) that person. If our hypothetical tester tests positive rather than negative, he may infect a high-risk (but in fact uninfected) person to whom he turns when ex-pelled as it were from the low-risk market. The essential point remains: the principal gain from testing in our model accrues to the high-risk person who, by testing negative, gains access to risky sex previously de-nied him.

"Previously denied him" may be too strong a phrase. It may be that without testing, the high-risk person was able to obtain risky sex by compensating low-risk prospective sexual partners. He will test if testing is a lower-cost method of obtaining such partners, as it may well be, since compensation for a *substantial* risk of becoming infected with HIV may well exceed the cost of testing even when the expected cost of flunking the test and being spurned is reckoned into the equation. Our essential point is unaffected: The availability of testing, to the extent that it is utilized voluntarily, reduces the cost of risky sex.

We have now shown that even without any government intervention, recruitment to participate in research studies, or insistence by employers or insurers, there will be a demand, motivated by desire for risky sex, for partner-observed HIV testing. Since HIV tests are not expensive,[5] demand and supply will intersect, resulting in a positive amount of voluntary testing. The analysis further implies that the demand will be concentrated, and hence the amount of partner-observed testing will be greater, in areas or subpopulations in which there is an above-average prevalence of the disease.[6]

Effect on the epidemic. If partner-observed tests enable risky sexual trades between persons of different infection status that would not have occurred in the absence of testing, the availability of testing may increase the spread of the disease. In our model, the principal demand for testing comes from persons who wish to engage in risky sex but cannot find a willing partner because of the high probability that they are infected. If these persons therefore test, and test negative, they will be able to find a sexual partner willing to engage in risky sex, and if that partner happens to be HIV-positive, the stage is set for the disease to spread.

This assumes that the person who tests negative does not, on the basis of that test result, demand that his partner test. Although there are no data on the number of cases in which one partner, at the demand of the other, tests, and the other does not, the wealth of anecdotal references to the practice (illustrative discussions are *Newsday* staff 1991; Dubin and Kelleher 1991; Koehl 1991; Duckett 1992) suggests that it is empirically significant and not merely a logical possibility. But we must also consider the case, apparently common as well (Miller 1991; Adler 1991), though again we do not know how common, in which each partner demands that the other test; and we must consider more fully than before the significance, under either one-sided or two-sided partner-observed testing, of a positive test result.

The case of two-sided partner-observed testing with both testing negative is important under conditions of monogamy, which we define as any long-term sexual relationship, heterosexual or homosexual, that is exclusive during that term. Partners both of whom test negative will have an increased incentive to remain with each other and not reenter

---

5. The cost of the test (including a retest for checking a positive result), in 1987 dollars, ranged from $4.40 to $35, depending on the quantity purchased (Bloom and Glied 1991, p. 1800 [tab. 2]). A more recent estimate is $20 (Henry and Campbell 1992, p. 139). Persons who, to maximize confidentiality, decide to be tested by their private physician may pay $75 or more for the test.

6. Government intervention to compel or encourage testing is a special case, discussed in Chapter 5. We consider later in the present chapter other sources of private demand besides a desire to obtain additional risky (or less risky) sexual trades.

the risky-sex market. They will not transmit the disease, but by the same token their removal from the market will leave a higher percentage of HIV carriers in it. This will increase the danger to the uninfected persons who remain in the market by removing from it two uninfected persons with whom they might have had risk-free unprotected sex. Yet the increase in danger may not translate into an increase in the prevalence of the disease. For as risk rises as a consequence of the withdrawal of uninfected pairs, there will be some substitution of safe for risky sex, and after this adjustment the remaining uninfected persons may face no greater average risk than before the withdrawals.[7] A further complication, examined at greater length below, is that an increase in the danger of infection may lead to an increase in testing, since the demand for testing, we have said, is concentrated among persons having a high probability of being already infected.

Two-sided partner-observed testing with both testing negative is related to what we are calling monogamy in another way. Two persons may each have a low probability of being HIV carriers, implying little risk of transmission in a one-night stand, because the transmission probability is substantially less than one even if one sexual partner is infected and the other is not. But if they contemplate a long-term sexual relationship, the cumulative probability of transmission is of course higher—as are the aggregate expected costs of safe sex. So they will have an incentive to test, and are likely to test negative. However, monogamously inclined persons are not important sources of transmission of AIDS. Therefore, as suggested earlier, the likeliest effect of their both testing, and testing negative, is their withdrawal from the market for (new) sexual partnering—increasing the risk of that market to the uninfected persons who remain in it, but, because the higher risk will induce substitution toward safer sex in that market, not necessarily increasing the incidence of the disease.

Earlier we suggested that while persons who test positive may be frozen out of the risky-sex market altogether, they would have been frozen out without the test—that is why they took it. We now must qualify this conclusion in recognition of the possibility that the test was taken to induce risky sex with a particular person and that other persons would have been willing to have risky sex with the tester even if he had not

---

7. Notice, though, that in this example testing still imposes an external cost—that of the safe sex adopted in defense against the added disease risk created by testing. More on this point in the next chapter.

tested. Then, if the result of his testing positive is to make him a pariah, unable to obtain any risky trades, the spread of the disease will be retarded. But that result is improbable. Partner-observed testing means that the outcome of the test is observed by a particular partner, not by the whole world.

The possibility that persons who test positive will engage in risky sex either with other HIV-positives or with high-risk persons who are in fact negative suggests a tendency consequent upon widespread HIV testing to a form of positive assortative mating (that is, like mating with like). This phenomenon has been emphasized in economic analysis of the marriage market (G. Becker 1991, pp. 109–119). In the closely related market for sex, low-risk persons (the "high quality" sexual transactors) will tend to pair off with other low-risk persons, and high-risk persons with other high-risk persons, just as persons with high IQs tend to marry other persons with high IQs, and persons with low IQs tend to marry other persons with low IQs. Contrast the random pairing assumed in most epidemiological models,[8] in which a low-risk person is as likely to have sex with a high-risk person as with another low-risk person.

As low-risk persons, or high-risk persons who had tested and discovered they were negative, paired off and withdrew from the sexual sorting market, the incentive of the untested to test would grow. At the limit represented by universal, frequently repeated, partner-observed HIV testing, P_m or P_f would take a value of either 1 or 0 for every person. The result—if, with some exaggeration, we assume that no person who does not know that he is infected will knowingly engage in risky sex with a person whom he knows to be infected—is that noninfected persons would have risky sex only with other noninfected persons, while infected persons would have risky sex only with other infected persons. The growth rate of the disease would be zero. The corresponding oversimplified epidemiological model, that of the spread of infection in a closed population, predicts, we recall, the infection of the entire population. That model is oversimplified in assuming random matching. The assortative-matching model oversimplifies in the opposite direction by assuming a perfect positive correlation between sexual partners' infection status. The assumption is unrealistic because, as we shall see, the private market in HIV testing will not in fact generate a demand for universal testing.

---

8. Though not all. See Castillo-Chavez (1988); Gupta, Anderson, and May (1989); and Ramstedt et al. (1991).

With many people not testing, voluntary partner-observed testing is unlikely to reduce and may well increase the spread of AIDS. This does not make testing necessarily a bad thing. We distinguished in the Introduction between utility and incidence as criteria of public policy in regard to AIDS. Voluntary testing can increase, ex ante, the utility of persons trading in the sexual marketplace, even if at the same time it increases the incidence of AIDS by increasing the volume of unprotected sexual trades between persons of different infection status. A similar paradox has been observed with automobile liability insurance (Shavell 1987, p. 212). Such insurance reduces the expected cost of accidents to drivers and therefore can be expected to increase the number of accidents, since many forms of risky driving, such as driving fast in order to save time, confer utility. However, provided that liability insurance is sold at market rates that cover all expected costs of automobile accidents to victims, so that there is no external cost imposed on them, and provided also that the insurance company is able to assess the liability risk of each insured, so that there is no systematic redistribution within the risk pool, a market in liability insurance will increase utility ex ante. Indeed, if the utility gains are sufficient it will do this even though there are some externalities. But our point is that a market can increase both expected utility and the accident rate—or, as here, the disease rate— without imposing any external costs.

There are external costs of AIDS, as we shall see in the next chapter, so that voluntary HIV testing may not bring about a net increase in utility ex ante—may in fact reduce total utility ex ante (as well as ex post). This would mean that the market would produce too much testing even without a subsidy! It is unlikely, at least on the basis of our simple model, that it would produce too little and therefore that it should be subsidized.

"Partner-Unobserved" Testing and Altruists versus Egoists

The feasibility of confidential testing. We now relax the assumption that one's sexual partner (actual or potential) observes the result of one's test. Suppose he can't. We shall see that this is not the same as assuming that a person who tests positive can conceal this fact from his sexual partners, but for the moment let us assume that he can—that test results are really and not just formally confidential. We know from equations 1.1 and 1.2 that the demand for risky sex is positively related to one's own infection status and negatively related to the infection status of one's partner. Hence under confidential testing, if m tests positive his demand for risky sex will increase, but f's demand will not decrease, since P_m, in its aspect as f's subjective probability that m is infected, is unchanged by the test if f does not know whether m has been tested.

The assumption that confidentiality is possible may be questioned, notwithstanding the elaborate efforts that are made to maintain the confidentiality of HIV test results. Anyone who tests negative has an incentive to disclose this fact, together with whatever proof is regarded as convincing, to his sexual partners. If he does not disclose a negative status, there are two possible inferences that potential sexual partners might draw. One is that he has not tested; the other is that he has tested positive. The larger the fraction of persons who test, the likelier it is that nondisclosure of a negative result will be interpreted as a signal that the nondiscloser has tested positive. In the limit, if everyone tests and everyone who tests negative discloses this fact to his sexual partners, anyone who does not disclose a negative status will be assumed to be positive, and the set of partner-unobserved tests will be empty.

This assumes, of course, that a person who tests positive cannot fake a negative result. The assumption is false. People lie about such things, and the lies are sometimes believed (Goleman 1988; Cochran and Mays 1990). Hence the strategic analysis sketched above is weakened, and we begin to understand why the existence of a market in testing has not resulted in most, let alone in all, people being tested. The possibility of fraud is but one reason. Another is that a person's request to test may be taken as a signal of having engaged in socially stigmatized behavior[9] and thus of having become sensitized to the dangers of risky sex and being likely therefore to be infected. Other reasons are fear of learning that one is doomed (Archer 1988); legal sanctions for *knowingly* exposing another to the risk of AIDS (see Chapter 5); the fact that many people are frightened of even the least painful and intrusive medical procedures;[10] the risk of a false negative or false positive; the lag between infection and testing positive, which reduces the utility of testing nega-

9. Especially when the test is taken at a clinic for sexually transmitted diseases or other publicly supported AIDS testing site—just visiting such a site could be thought stigmatizing.

10. Almost half the population believes that there is some likelihood that one can get AIDS from *giving* blood (see, for example, Kanouse et al. 1991, p. 38 [tab. 11]). A person who believes this may equally believe that any test which involves drawing blood—such as the HIV test—is potentially infective.

tive as a means of inducing risky sexual trades that may be preferred, even if there is no fraud; and the fact that most people (correctly) believe themselves to be at only slight risk of being HIV carriers. For all these reasons the fraction of all Americans who have been tested apparently is small. Stated differently, in real though not in money terms HIV testing is expensive.[11] This provides a reason, independent of fear of what the test will reveal to a prospective sexual partner, for not being tested.

There are no reliable statistics on the fraction of the sexually active population that has been tested. Estimation is complicated by the unknown number of tests performed by private physicians and by repeat testing of the same individuals. We should expect repeat testing to be especially common among persons who, consistent with the analysis in the first section of this chapter, use a negative test result to obtain risky sex, since with each risky encounter with an untested sexual partner, their probability of infection, and hence demand for a retest, rises from the zero level implied by their having tested negative.[12] The Centers for Disease Control has calculated that between 1985 and 1991, 3.25 million different persons—an average of fewer than 600,000 a year—were tested under programs that it finances at public clinics throughout the United States (Centers for Disease Control 1991b), and "a large [but unknown] number of persons not reported here are tested for HIV antibody in hospitals, outpatient medical facilities, physicians' offices, blood-donation centers, military facilities, and other settings" (ibid., p. 2196). A careful telephone survey conducted in 1989 found that 23 percent of the entire adult population of Los Angeles had been tested for HIV (Kanouse et al. 1991, p. 61). Even though we would expect a high rate of testing in this high-prevalence area, the 23 percent figure is, nevertheless, surprisingly high. For California as a whole, the figure was only 6 percent (ibid., pp. 61–62). Because of aversion to learning that one is doomed, skepticism about the accuracy of the test, and possible sanctions for concealing a positive test result, a smaller percentage know their actual HIV status (Lyter et al. 1987; Coates et al. 1988; Catania et al. 1990). With (it appears) relatively few even high-risk people having been tested

---

11. Corroborative evidence for this is that subsidizing HIV testing appears not to increase the amount of testing (Phillips n.d.). This suggests that the price of the test is only a small part of the test's total cost.

12. We exaggerate, of course; because of the possibility of a false negative and the lag between infection and the production of detectable antibodies, a person who tests negative never can truthfully claim to have a zero probability of being HIV-positive.

(and fewer having been tested recently) and, if they have been tested, knowing the result of the test, failure to produce proof of a negative result does not convey a great deal of information to a potential sexual partner. An additional reason is that there is no accepted method of proving that one's test status is as one has represented it to be. Therefore, confidential HIV testing is feasible.

It might not be if the full cost of testing—not the price, but the price plus every other source of disutility—were much lower than it is today. Imagine a simple saliva test: you lick a piece of paper, and if it turns red (which it will do in one second) you're HIV-positive and if green you're negative. The test is 100 percent accurate no matter how recently you were infected; it cannot be tampered with; its price is one cent; and it is sold everywhere, including through the mail in a brown paper wrapper. Then most costs of HIV testing would be eliminated, and demand would rise. It might rise to the point where refusal to take the test would be interpreted as a strong signal that a person knew or believed himself to be an HIV carrier. And then we would be far along the road to positive assortative mating with respect to infection status, and zero growth of the disease.

This point can be clarified with the help of game theory. Suppose the law provides that a student's grades cannot be disclosed to a prospective employer without the student's permission. If no students give their permission, an employer will treat each applicant as an average student, that is, as being in the 50th percentile of his class. This assumption will hurt all applicants who are between the 50th and the 100th percentile, so they will give permission to disclose their grades to prospective employers. When this is done, the employer will revise his assumption about the remaining applicants, those who have not given permission: now he will assume that an applicant who has withheld consent for the disclosure of his grades is in the 25th percentile, the midpoint of the refusers' distribution. Then all applicants between the 25th and 50th percentile will be hurt, and so they will give permission for disclosure. This process will continue until only the person at the bottom of the class refuses permission—and his refusal will signal that he is indeed at the bottom.

The reason for this pattern is that each student learns his grades at zero cost. Were it as costly to learn one's grades as it is to learn one's HIV status, prospective employers could not infer, with progressively greater and ultimately perfect accuracy, a student's grades from the student's refusal to disclose them.

The bearing of altruism. The day of the costless HIV test that would generate an equilibrium in which everyone's HIV status would become known is not yet come. But in the meantime our conclusion that confidential HIV testing is feasible depends on an additional assumption—that the relevant population consists of egoists, in the sense of persons indifferent to infecting their sexual partners, rather than of altruists, who would perceive such a consequence of risky sex as a cost to themselves. Altruists, we may assume (though this depends on *how* altruistic they are), will not engage in risky sex if they test positive.[13] Hence, in effect, altruists will not engage in confidential testing. But when they test negative this may lead by our earlier analysis to their obtaining more risky trades, resulting in the spread of the disease to these altruists. The net effect of voluntary testing by altruists on the spread of the disease is therefore uncertain.

Studies which find that many persons who discover that they are HIV-positive continue having risky sex with persons whom they do not know to be also HIV-positive imply that not all persons who are tested for the AIDS virus are altruists.[14] Lyter and colleagues (1987, p. 471 [tab. 3]) report for example that one reason men give for not wanting to know their test result is that "they would not change their sexual practices no matter what the test showed." An egoist who tests in the hope of obtaining additional risky sexual trades if he tests negative will, if he tests positive, attempt to conceal this information—and will increase his efforts to obtain risky sex since the cost of risky sex to him is now lower. He may not encounter much difficulty in his quest for risky sex. There is a distribution in the sexually active population of information about the risk of contracting AIDS from particular sexual practices and the likelihood that a prospective sexual partner is a carrier. In one tail of the distribution are people who underestimate both risks. They are prime prospects for the egoistic carrier who knows he is a carrier to have risky sex with, even if he doesn't resort to misrepresentation. Recall from Chapter 1 that an offer to engage in risky sex is not a reliable signal that

---

13. We similarly assume that they will not engage in risky sex if they have AIDS. So, were it not for the fact that persons carrying the AIDS virus are infective before they have symptoms and therefore before they know they are infective (unless they have tested), altruists would not spread the disease at all.

14. See Fox et al. (1987); Coates et al. (1988); Frazer et al. (1988); Kegeles, Catania, and Coates (1988); Krajick (1988); van Griensven et al. (1988a); Cleary et al. (1991); Higgins et al. (1991, p. 2426); Burgess and Baker (1992); Marks et al. (1992); and van den Hoek, van Haastrecht, and Coutinho (1992). For a striking case study of such an egoist, see Kelly (1991). And see Poku (1992) for four other case studies.

the offerer probably is infected—that in fact an offer to engage in safe sex may signal the same thing just as strongly.

The literature on charitable gifts finds that altruistic behavior is a positive function of income (Clotfelter 1985; Kingma 1989). Because learning that one has the AIDS virus reduces one's expected income, one might think that few persons who knew they were carrying the virus would be strongly altruistic. We doubt this. Although the propensity to make an altruistic *transfer* is a positive function of one's income or wealth, altruistic behavior that takes the form of forgoing risky sex does not involve any monetary outlay and is therefore only analogous to a charitable gift. Once altruism as an argument in a person's utility function is distinguished from altruistic transfer payments, it becomes possible to argue that knowledge that one is infected may induce *more* altruistic behavior. The HIV carrier who knows himself to be such can make a nonmonetary gift—almost literally a gift of life—by refraining from risky sex. As perceived by him it is a bigger gift than before he knew that he was infected (for then the value of the gift had to be discounted by the probability that he was infected), yet it is made at the same cost. So testing may actually elicit some altruistic behavior; but it is safe to assume that some, perhaps a great many, persons who learn they are HIV-positive remain egoists in the relevant sense.

A further complication is found in evidence that drug abusers respond to discovering that they are HIV-positive by increasing their consumption of drugs, as a "coping" strategy (Heckmann 1991). And we saw in Chapter 2 that drug use increases the incidence of risky sex.

An arithmetical example will help clarify the effect on the epidemic of encouraging egoists to be tested. Consider a group of egoists who have not been tested, and assume that 10 percent in fact are carrying the virus and that 50 percent, randomly distributed with respect to their AIDS status, engage in safe sex—to protect themselves from infection, not, of course, their sexual partners. Then 5 percent will be potential sources of contagion. Suppose now that all are induced, perhaps by a heavy subsidy or even legal compulsion, to be tested, and they are told the result of the test, so that 90 percent discover that they are negative and 10 percent that they are positive. To those who tested negative, the benefits of safe sex are now greater. Before, each faced a 10 percent probability that safe sex was not benefiting him because he already had the virus; now (for those in the negative group) that probability has fallen to zero.[15]

---

15. Recall from Chapter 1 that one's demand for risky sex is positively related to one's own probability of being infected. (That is, $\partial EU_m(P)/\partial P_m > 0$, $\partial EU_f(P)/\partial P_f > 0$.) A different

If the *net* benefits of safe sex were greater, we could expect a higher usage of condoms in this group, and this would be a social benefit even though none of the persons in it was infected now, because some might otherwise have become infected in the future and then would have spread the virus to still other people (here safe sex is like vaccination). An offsetting consideration, however, is that proof of a negative status will enable the persons in this group to obtain risky sex with persons having a low probability that they are infected, and the existence of this new option makes safe sex less valuable.

The principal social cost of testing our hypothetical group of egoists is that the ones who test positive will abandon safe for risky sex. Granted, not all of them will do so. Since there is some basis for believing that reinfection may accelerate conversion to the active disease status (see the Introduction), an HIV carrier may derive a benefit from safe sex. And discovering that one is a carrier may have a depressive effect on sexual desire (Brown and Pace 1989). If nevertheless we assume, admittedly with exaggeration, that no egoists will engage in safe sex once they learn they are infected, the number of HIV-positive egoists who are engaging in unsafe sex will double. But even if the number increases by only, say, 25 percent, the resulting cost of testing in increased infection (always assuming that HIV-positive egoists can find partners for risky sex among the uninfected) will probably exceed the benefit. For against the increase in the number of infected persons actually engaging in unsafe sex and thus spreading the disease, there is only the deferred benefit from the fact that those who are not infected *may* use condoms somewhat more frequently, in which event they will become infected less and so will spread the disease less. And they may not use condoms any more frequently, for the reason stated earlier.

Since voluntary testing by egoists is more likely to increase the spread of the disease than voluntary testing by altruists (because most altruists who test positive will switch to safe sex, while most egoists who test positive will switch to risky sex), we must consider which group will have the greater demand for testing. Probably the altruists. The members

---

consequence, psychological rather than economic in character, of testing negative has been suggested: "Taking the test would heighten the sense of vulnerability that is a necessary part of decisions to adopt more healthful behavior" (Rhame and Maki 1989, p. 1250)—that is, would scare the test taker into switching to safe sex even if he tested negative, by making him more conscious of AIDS. The opposite could be argued as plausibly: that a negative test result would heighten one's sense of invulnerability. The relevant evidence is reviewed in the last section of this chapter.

of both groups gain from learning that they are negative, since they can use this information to obtain risky sex. Both also gain, though in different ways, from learning they are positive. The altruist gains because he incurs disutility from infecting others; the egoist gains because the information enables him to increase his expected utility by switching to risky sex. However, the egoist obtains this gain only if he can conceal his positive status. To the extent that he cannot—to the extent, that is, that he is in a situation of partner-observed testing—knowledge of his positive status reduces his welfare because he is compelled by his partner to practice safe sex.

Equations 3.3 and 3.4 formalize (though incompletely, as we shall see) male and female altruists' utility functions for risky sex:

$$(3.3) \quad EU_m(P) = B - C_s(1 - P_m)P_f - C_a(1 - P_f)P_m,$$

$$(3.4) \quad EU_f(P) = B - C_s(1 - P_f)P_m - C_a(1 - P_m)P_f.$$

C_s and C_a denote respectively the selfish cost of becoming infected oneself and the altruistic cost of infecting one's partner. If C_a is greater than zero, individuals who would engage in risky sex if testing were infeasible may not engage in risky sex if testing is feasible.

To see this, let $V(P_m, P_f)$ be, as before, the indirect utility of a risky trade. To determine the benefit of testing for an altruistic male who would (in the absence of testing) prefer, and obtain, risky sex (that is, for whom $V_m(P) = U_m(P) > 0$), we must subtract (1) the utility of risky sex to him without testing from (2) the utility of risky sex to him with testing. Utility (1) is given by $V(P)$. Utility (2) is given by $P_m V_m(1, P_f) + (1 - P_m)V(0, P_f)$—the utility of risky sex to him if he tests positive, discounted by the probability of his testing positive, plus the utility of risky sex to him if he tests negative, discounted by the probability of that test outcome. This is cumbersome, but is easily simplified. $V_m(1, P_f) = 0$ because of the assumption that f will not knowingly engage in risky sex with an infected m—and anyway we are assuming that an altruistic m who knows he is infected will not knowingly engage in risky sex with an f whom he does not know also to be infected. $V_m(0, P_f) = B - C_s P_f$ because, if m is uninfected, risky sex cannot impose an altruistic cost on him. Thus the expression for the difference between the utility of risky sex with testing and without testing simplifies to $B - C_s P_f - V(P)$. By substituting into this from equation 3.3 (which we can do because $V =$

U under conditions satisfied here), we obtain the intuitively appealing result that the net benefit from testing for an altruistic male is

(3.5) $C_a(1 - P_f) - B.$

So an individual who because of altruistic cost would not engage in risky sex if he knew he were HIV-positive, because he would, if he knew this, derive a benefit—$C_a(1 - P_f)$—from avoiding risky sex that would exceed the disutility of safe sex (B),[16] may (depending on the cost of the test) decide to test in order to discover whether he is HIV-positive and therefore whether avoiding risky sex would in fact increase his utility.[17] Should he test negative he will continue to engage in risky sex (thus putting himself at risk)—and indeed, by our earlier analysis, will be more likely to obtain such trades. However, there is an additional effect: with altruism, testing results in the withdrawal from the market for risky sex of some persons who, in the absence of testing, would participate in that market because they did not know they were HIV-positive. Some—but perhaps few. The demand for safe sex is higher among altruists anyway, because the cost to them of risky sex is higher than it is to an egoist, who does not incur an altruistic cost of risky sex. The low rate of voluntary testing implies that the full cost of testing is high to many people, presumably including altruists. The cost of the test may exceed the cost of safe sex, leading the altruist, for whom risky sex is on average more costly than it is to the egoist, to switch to safe sex without bothering to ascertain his infection status.

So there will be, we expect, fewer altruists in the risky-sex market to begin with. Even if a higher percentage of the smaller group (the altruists) test, there is no reason to expect the absolute number of altruists who test to be greater than the absolute number of egoists who test.

Thus far we have assumed a kind of global altruism—an altruist is someone who will not have risky sex with anyone whom he does not know to be HIV-positive. The assumption is unrealistic, especially if we were correct in suggesting in Chapter 1 that altruism is fostered by a close relationship. It is possible, indeed extremely common, for a person to be altruistic toward people with whom he has a close relationship, familial or otherwise, and egoistic toward the rest of the world. An altruist who tests positive for HIV, therefore, may substitute risky sex with

---

16. That is, $EU_m(1, P_f) = B - C_a(1 - P_f) < 0.$

17. The benefit of avoiding risky sex is of course larger, the less likely his partner is to be infected already; that is why $1 - P_f$ enters into the calculation of the benefit.

strangers for risky sex with a person whom he loves—in which event HIV testing of altruists could increase the spread of the disease. Perry and colleagues (1990, p. 551) give the example of a man who "disclosed his infection to a current live-in partner, then terminated the relationship and had unsafe sex with anonymous partners to whom he did not disclose his seropositivity."[18]

Another unrealistic assumption is that altruism affects only the cost side of the safe sex/risky sex trade-off. It can also affect the benefit side. B will be larger for the altruist if his or her partner prefers risky sex, and the larger B is, other things being equal (which they are not, since C is also larger under altruism, as we have seen), the greater the demand for risky sex. This may explain the finding by Doll and colleagues (1991a, p. 174) that homosexual men are more likely to engage in unprotected anal sex with steady partners than "one-night stands" even if they do not know the infection status of the steady partners and are not in a monogamous relationship with them. Similarly, male prostitutes are more likely to engage in unprotected anal sex with their boyfriends than with their customers (Pleak and Meyer-Bahlburg 1990, p. 579). The inconsistency with the example given by Perry (above) is thus superficial: altruism toward steady partners can result in more *or* less risky sex with them.

The foregoing point is related to the discussion of compensation in Chapter 1. Recall that m might compensate an f for whom the utility of risky sex was negative, if $B_m > B_f$. Given altruism, m might not have to compensate f, or might have to compensate her less, because the effect of altruism would be to raise B_f. Particularly ominous for the spread of the disease is the case of one-sided altruism. Suppose f is altruistic but m is not. Then B_f will rise, for the reason just explained, but there will be no offsetting increase in C, because C_a will be zero (for m, and presumably for f as well, provided f respects m's preference for risky sex).[19] In sum, one-sided altruism reduces the cost of risky sex. Thus, if women are assumed to be more altruistic than men, and given that women are more easily infected by the AIDS virus than men are, altruism might actually increase the spread of the disease.

Another simplifying assumption that we now drop is that HIV testing

---

18. For statistical evidence that HIV status is more likely to be disclosed to a steady than to a nonsteady partner, see Doll et al. (1991a, p. 172).

19. The qualification is important, because one can imagine a case in which f is motivated by "paternalistic" altruism to refuse to engage in risky sex with m, even though m is perfectly willing to take his chances on being infected.

produces an error-free determination of the tested person's infection status at the moment of testing. Even if we ignore the interval between the test and the disclosure of the result to the tested person's sexual partner—an interval during which the tested person may have become infected—it is apparent that HIV testing produces false negatives. Not only is the test itself not perfectly accurate, but there is the possible six-month lag between becoming infected and showing up positive on an HIV test. False negatives amplify the effect of testing in increasing the spread of AIDS. False positives are also possible, but are unlikely to have an offsetting effect; and this for three reasons. First, if the six-month lag is treated as a source of false negatives, there are more false negatives than false positives. Second, anyone who tests positive is likely to take a second test to lessen the possibility that the first result was false. With a retest, the rate of false positives is less than one-tenth of 1 percent (.08 percent, to be precise). The fraction of negatives is much higher: .6 percent (Bloom and Glied 1990, p. 1800 [tab. 2]). Third, false positives do not necessarily leave the risky-sex market, even if testing is always partner-observed. They may simply move to the high-risk part of the distribution—and become infected by having sex with a person who really is infected.

The Effect of Voluntary Testing on the Incidence of AIDS

Our task is now to estimate the likely effect of the adjustments proposed in the preceding section of this chapter, and of other relevant factors, on our suggestion stated in the first section that the availability of HIV testing may increase rather than, as generally believed, reduce the spread of AIDS. The adjustments are critical because we did not estimate the *magnitude* of the epidemic-increasing effect in the first section. Suppose, to recur to our discussion of positive assortative mating, that the probability of being already infected with HIV is highly correlated positively with other characteristics by which people sort themselves into sexual pairs (cf. Ramstedt 1991, p. 430). Then demand for partner-observed testing based on asymmetry in probabilities of infection—the demand identified in the first section of this chapter—might be weak, resulting in few one-sided tests. And our assumption of random dating (random with respect to probable infection status) may seem uneasily reminiscent of the epidemiologists' assumption of random mixing. The difference is that we assume that the random daters make rational choices between safe and risky sex. That is, we distinguish between meeting (random) and trade (nonrandom).

It is plain that *some* dating occurs between people of significantly different infection status. Apart from the anecdotal evidence cited earlier, it is noteworthy that out of almost 1.4 million HIV tests administered in 1990 under voluntary-testing programs supported by the Centers for Disease Control, 3.7 percent were positive (Centers for Disease Control 1991b). This is almost ten times higher than the estimated prevalence of HIV in the population as a whole (.4 percent, assuming, generously, that there are 1 million HIV carriers in the nation). And more than 60 percent of the people who took the test and furnished information about their self-perceived risk category had one or more acknowledged risk factors, such as homosexuality, hemophilia, or intravenous drug use.[20] This is a vastly higher percentage than in the adult population as a whole. These disparities suggest that the demand for the test may indeed be concentrated among persons who believe (or whose partners believe) that they have a substantial probability of being positive. The large majority—more than 95 percent—who test negative thereby obtain additional prospects of being able to find partners for risky sex among persons who have not tested. We do not know how many of those prospects are good ones, however. High and low probabilities of already being infected may be correlated with other personal characteristics that are important in sorting in the market for sexual relationships. A further consideration is that an increase in prevalence in period t, brought about by testing, may lead to a substitution of safe for risky sex in period $t + 1$ in response to the increased probability of infection brought about by the increase in prevalence.

The analysis in the second section of this chapter brought to light another source of demand for testing besides the desire to obtain risky sex—altruists concerned with the risk of infecting their sexual partners. And we saw that testing positive might actually stimulate an altruistic response by increasing the donative value of safe sex. But we also saw that a possibly offsetting demand for testing comes from egoists who want to know their infection status so that they can discontinue safe sex in the event that they are already infected and therefore have less to lose from engaging in risky sex than if they thought they were negative for the virus.

---

20. A multivariate analysis finds, consistent with the analysis in the text, that persons at high risk for HIV are more likely to test than persons at low risk (Phillips n.d.).

Some of the demand for HIV testing is unrelated to sexual strategies, whether altruistic or egoistic. A person may decide to be tested because it is a condition of obtaining life insurance or medical insurance or a job that he wants.[21] Or because he wants to conduct his life with a realistic view to its likely duration.[22] Or because he suspects that he is infected and believes that treatment with AZT, or other therapies, will be more effective the sooner treatment is begun (see the Introduction). Or because his physician suspects that he may have ARC or AIDS but is not sure (Stein et al. 1991b). Or because he wants to give (or sell) blood. A woman may want to be tested in order to know whether she is likely to bear children who are infected with HIV and doomed to die prematurely—or may want to learn whether she is doomed so that she can have children before it is too late. How a person having one or more of these motivations to test will react to testing positive or negative will depend in part on whether he or she is altruistic or egoistic. Finally, as we shall see in Chapter 5, contact tracing,[23] which presupposes testing, may reduce the spread of the disease by warning off persons from risky sexual encounters, although this effect is, as we explain there, likely to be small.

When all relevant considerations are factored into the analysis, there is no longer a clean theoretical prediction of the net effect of voluntary testing on the spread of AIDS. The issue is an empirical one, and, unfortunately, there is little usable empirical evidence that bears directly on

---

21. These examples are analyzed in Chapter 5 as cases of "mandatory testing." As we explain there, the line between voluntary and mandatory testing is blurred.

22. Yet most people very much do *not* want to know the day of their death, despite all the benefits that such knowledge would confer in the form of more accurate decision-making concerning consumption, savings, marriage, procreation, retirement, medical care, education, and choice of jobs. This preference for uncertainty is not easy to square with the economist's assumption of rational behavior, but that is true of many preferences. People may be rational in the actions they take to satisfy their preferences even if the preferences themselves are nonrational. The preference for uncertainty about one's health may be related to the phenomenon that decision theorists discuss under the rubric of "intrinsic risk aversion" (Bell 1988; Bell and Raiffa 1988), to distinguish it from the risk aversion that is a consequence of diminishing marginal utility of income. Taking a test to find out whether or not one is doomed is like a high-stakes gamble, which some people are timid about apart from the possible income consequences. Whether this is "rational" timidity is an open question, but not one we need try to answer in this book.

23. HIV contact tracing is the practice whereby public health officers or other medical professionals try to track down the current and former sexual partners of a person whom they know to be HIV-positive and urge them to be tested and to avoid risky sex.

it.[24] People who are tested as part of research programs or contact tracing tend (though not in all the studies)[25] to report afterward a modest reduction in risky behavior, which is inconsistent with the model in the first section of this chapter—but the reported reduction is primarily by those who test positive (Crystal et al. 1990, p. 293; McCusker et al. 1988; Wykoff et al. 1988; Rutherford and Woo 1988; Wiktor et al. 1990), which is consistent with it.[26] No one knows how representative these subpopulations are of the entire population of voluntary testers. And because knowing transmission of or even, in some states, just knowingly exposing someone to the AIDS virus is criminal conduct, one would expect persons who test positive to underreport subsequent risky sex with persons who may be negative and hence infectable, especially to public officers and health professionals—it would be confessing to a crime. Furthermore, the studies are concerned with the effects not just of testing but of the accompanying counseling aimed at inducing people to change their behavior. Finally, and most important, since most people who test voluntarily are at high risk for HIV infection, and since as pointed out in Chapter 2 high-risk persons have been substituting toward safe sex, there is a potentially spurious positive correlation between test-taking and risk reduction (cf. Higgins et al. 1991).

The underlying problem is that the dynamics of the process modeled in the first section of this chapter are highly complex. It is relatively clear that the availability of testing enables some people to obtain risky sex that they could not obtain were testing unavailable, but it is uncertain what happens next, when the market rearranges itself in response to the outcome of the test results. Hence, were it proposed to forbid HIV testing[27] in order to reduce the spread of the disease, we would empha-

---

24. For a recent review of the evidence, see Higgins et al. (1991).

25. Doll et al. (1990) is illustrative of studies finding no effect on risky behavior of knowledge of infection status.

26. Wykoff and colleagues (1991, p. 220) find a decrease in number of sexual partners after testing (the decrease is greater among HIV-positives than HIV-negatives) but do not report the number or fraction of HIV-positives who switched from risky to safe (or safe to risky) sex with their remaining partners.

27. And rely on involuntary testing of a sample of the population, without disclosure of the results to the persons tested (so-called "blinded seroprevalence surveys"), to monitor the epidemic ("Special Section" 1990). Truly random sampling of people's blood would be very difficult to effectuate, however, because it would mean forcing people to take a blood test regardless of their conduct, occupation, or health status. It would thus be an unconventional (and highly unpopular) form of conscription—the health analogue to the draft and to jury selection. And it would raise serious questions under the Fourth Amendment (search and seizure).

size the lack of firm proof that such testing has in fact increased that spread. But since the thrust of policy is to encourage—and some would require—such testing, we are entitled to emphasize instead the reasons for believing that testing is unlikely to reduce, and may increase, the spread of the disease. If it is unknown whether a practice is on balance harmful, beneficial, or neutral, the best estimate of the net expected benefits of government intervention, whether to subsidize, mandate, or forbid the practice, is apt to be negative, because intervention is costly. This would imply that for now the amount of HIV testing should be left to the market to determine, but this conclusion must be regarded as highly tentative until we evaluate the case for mandatory testing in Chapter 5.

CHAPTER 4

Social versus Fiscal Costs of AIDS

The previous chapters have shown that AIDS can be spread by voluntary transactions. The fact that, ex post, some of these transactions turn out disastrously for one of the participants no more establishes a "market failure"—a failure of the free market to allocate resources efficiently—than the fact that some business ventures end in bankruptcy, or some automobile trips in head-on collisions, signifies market failure. However, transactions that maximize the expected utility of the parties to them may also impose costs on other persons that the transacting parties will not take into account—"external costs"—because the costs of transacting with those third parties are too high.[1] A standard example is pollution. The sale of a polluting firm's output may maximize the utility of the parties to the sale, but the costs imposed on the victims of the pollution may exceed the gain to the transacting parties, so that from the standpoint of society as a whole, which includes pollution victims as well as transacting parties, it would be better if the firm produced less.[2] External costs thus provide a conventional, although not always a compelling, economic rationale for public intervention. So does the use of force or fraud to induce a transaction that is not in fact mutually advantageous.

Voluntary transactions can alter the distribution of income and wealth even when they impose no (other) externalities.[3] A person afflicted with

---

1. If transaction costs are low, the market will generate optimal results through voluntary transactions among all affected parties (Coase 1960).

2. The example assumes that the cost of avoidance is greater to the victim of pollution than to the injurer. It may not be, as Coase (1960) stresses.

3. Transactions that merely alter that distribution are sometimes said to impose purely "pecuniary" externalities, as opposed to "technological" externalities, which are pure social costs, as in the pollution example. We discuss both sorts.

AIDS will incur medical expenses and lost earnings, and may seek to shift these costs to others through private or social insurance. Conversely, government may take steps to reduce the expense of programs such as Medicaid, for example by forbidding HIV carriers to immigrate to the United States. We argue in Chapter 8 that the effects of AIDS on the distribution of income and wealth are particularly important to an understanding of the policies that have been adopted to deal with the disease and its consequences.

The External Costs of AIDS

Contracting a communicable disease imposes medical and other costs, both pecuniary and nonpecuniary, on (1) the infected person (or his insurer, employer, the government, and so on), and (2) persons who may catch the disease from the infected person, discounted by the probability of their catching it. Not only are the costs under (2) not borne by the infected person directly (they may be borne by him indirectly if he is an altruist), but it may not be feasible for the members of the exposed class to negotiate with him in advance—to pay him not to expose them or to demand compensation for exposing them. He may therefore take insufficient care, from an overall social standpoint, to prevent himself from catching or spreading the disease.

It is therefore not surprising that compulsory vaccination is generally considered an economically efficient form of governmental intervention.[4] Vaccination protects not only the person vaccinated but also those to whom he might transmit the disease were he not prevented by the vaccine from catching it in the first place. In deciding whether to be vaccinated, a nonaltruistic person will not weigh the benefit to other persons, and this means that in deciding whether to engage in an activity that might spread the disease from himself to them he will not take into account the cost to the other persons (Phelps 1992, ch. 15).

However, the traditional economic view of compulsory vaccination is incomplete in several respects. To begin with, in the situation where, as with AIDS, the disease is invariably fatal, persons at risk of contracting

---

4. Efficient or not, there is no denying the extent of government intervention in the vaccine market. The federal government alone purchases half the doses of vaccines distributed in the United States, and all states have laws requiring all or most schoolchildren to be vaccinated against common childhood illnesses (U.S. Congress 1979; Comptroller General 1980; see generally Institute of Medicine 1985).

it have powerful incentives to protect themselves against becoming infected. Were there an effective vaccine against HIV, governmental compulsion would not be necessary to induce sexually active persons to be vaccinated. It is true that some people have religious objections to vaccination, and others fear possible side effects. But AIDS differs from many other contagious diseases, including typhoid, gonorrhea, influenza, and hepatitis B, in that there are no carriers who are not themselves doomed. If pollution invariably killed the executives of a polluting enterprise, the need for public regulation of pollution would be weakened, even though pollution would still be a source of external costs.

Second, when a completely effective vaccine is available at zero cost, a person who fails to be vaccinated will not impose any cost on anyone else, since anyone desiring to avoid the costs of the disease can do so at zero cost by having himself vaccinated (Brito, Sheshinski, and Intriligator 1991).[5] The standard argument of moral conservatives against public subsidization of efforts to develop an AIDS vaccine or otherwise reduce the spread of the disease has, implicitly, the same structure as the economic analysis of the costless vaccine. AIDS can be avoided by abstinence before marriage followed by monogamous marriage to a similarly abstinent person. Since, these conservatives believe, abstinence and marital fidelity are independently desirable goods,[6] their social costs are actually negative. Thus AIDS can be prevented at no social cost without public intervention, just as in the case of the hypothetical costless vaccine.

The economic objections to the conservative position are twofold. First, it is arbitrary, at least as a matter of economics, to assume that abstinence and marital fidelity have no social costs. They plainly have private costs—otherwise it would be very difficult to explain the continued existence of sexually transmitted disease. To give these costs a zero weight in the design of social policy is to treat the observer's ethical preferences as the determinants of social value. Many people, for example those who have a strong homosexual orientation, derive utility from engaging in practices that happen to violate the tenets of the traditional Judeo-Christian-Muslim sexual morality, and there is no economic basis

---

5. If the vaccine is not completely effective, however, people who are vaccinated will benefit if others are vaccinated; so vaccination will in that case confer an external benefit (Brito, Sheshinski, and Intriligator 1991, pp. 84–85).

6. In the words of the Reverend Jerry Falwell, "AIDS is God's judgment on a society that does not live by His rules." Quoted in Horn (1989). For a secular version of the moral conservative view, see Bennett (1988, pp. 2–4).

for valuing that utility at zero from a social standpoint. Second, even if all departures from traditional morality impose net social costs, there probably is no feasible way of restoring that morality, the decline of which in the United States and other wealthy countries appears rooted in economic and demographic trends unlikely to reverse themselves in the near future (Posner 1992, ch. 6). To argue that AIDS could be prevented without public intervention if only people returned to the traditional morality is like arguing that AIDS could be prevented without public intervention if there were a vaccine against AIDS available at zero (rather than, at the moment, infinite) cost.

A better argument against public intervention is that AIDS can be prevented without such intervention, and at much lower cost than by abstinence, by the simple and relatively inexpensive private expedient of substituting safe for risky sex. In this respect it differs from the traditional airborne and waterborne epidemics, such as the medieval Black Death. Although the spread of the Black Death could have been retarded by relatively simple methods such as killing rats, quarantining infected people, and fleeing cities during plague seasons (in fact many of the wealthy followed the last course), ignorance and poverty made these methods largely infeasible (see generally Ziegler 1969; Gottfried 1983). The analogy to AIDS is not totally inapt, however. Many people were infected with the AIDS virus before AIDS was discovered or the methods of its transmission and prevention were well understood, and some of these people are just now converting to the full-blown disease state. They cannot be said to have knowingly forgone safe sex. However, they are victims of unavoidable accident rather than of markets distorted by externalities. As victims of unavoidable accident, they are appealing claimants for social insurance to the extent that private insurance markets fail to protect such victims. But the issue of the merits of social insurance, here or generally, raises complex ethical questions that we do not address.

It might seem that with safe sex now a feasible option because the risk and prevention of AIDS have become well understood, the external costs of AIDS would be zero, just as in the case of the costless vaccine. But, *pace* the moral conservatives, safe sex is not costless. Nor is the cost always trivial. Aversion to the use of a condom may be very great—and not only for a heterosexual couple wanting children. One might be tempted to argue that since safe sex does not transmit the AIDS virus (ignoring, for the moment, the occasional condom failure), it is not a cost *of the disease*. Two persons who engage in risky sex have by doing so made a decision that the cost of a condom exceeds the expected benefit, and so they do not incur the cost of a condom. In avoiding that cost, however, they impose a cost on third parties who, fearing the disease more, will switch to safe sex. The higher the prevalence of the disease, the more likely people are to substitute safe for risky sex. The added cost (in reduced pleasure, and so forth) of safe compared to risky sex is an external cost of risky sex. And it is not the only such cost. Our original couple, by dispensing with a condom, incurs an expected disease cost created by earlier sexual activities of other people. This shows that risky sex imposes not only an external cost of safe sex but also a smaller external cost of risky sex in the case in which the risk is too small to warrant switching to safe sex. It is smaller because if the cost of risky sex were higher than that of safe sex, the couple would switch to safe sex.

Notice that the more costly an avoidable disease is to its sufferers, the lower its prevalence will be and therefore the larger the fraction of the total costs of the disease (including avoidance costs) that will be borne by noninfected, but susceptible, people. AIDS is both fatal and avoidable, so it is plausible that a large part of the current costs of the epidemic is borne by persons who are avoiding exposure by practicing safe sex.

Another reason why AIDS is not costlessly avoidable by behavioral change is that it can be spread by involuntary contacts, such as that between a pregnant woman who is HIV-positive and her fetus, or an HIV-positive rapist and his HIV-negative victim. It can also be transmitted by methods that cannot be neutralized by a condom (or its equivalent for intravenous drug users, a clean needle), such as by a health worker's accidentally sticking herself with a needle that contains infected blood. The "universal precautions" that the Centers for Disease Control has recommended, and the Occupational Safety and Health Administration now requires (U.S. Department of Labor 1991), for health care workers who are apt to be splattered by patients' blood are estimated by OSHA to cost the health care industry $813 million a year (ibid., p. 64,039).[7] This is analogous to the cost of safe sex, but may greatly overstate the expected cost of HIV infection to health care workers. The precautions are equally efficacious against infection with the hepatitis B virus—a greater hazard to health care workers than HIV, as we noted in the Intro-

---

7. They are called "universal" precautions because they are not confined to situations in which the health care worker is treating a patient believed to be an HIV carrier or to be likely to be a carrier.

duction—and would in all likelihood be required on that account alone, even if HIV and AIDS had never been heard of. The *incremental* cost of the precautions for health workers that is imposed by the AIDS epidemic may be zero.

Persons who are or suspect that they may be HIV-positive will often have an incentive to conceal the information from their sexual partners in order to induce the latter to engage in risky sex.[8] Sometimes they will succeed. Resources spent on deception and on unmasking deception are social costs of the AIDS epidemic, as are the infections that result because the deception has been successful. Suppose a married man is bisexual but, as is common, keeps his wife ignorant of his double life (Doll et al. 1991b, p. 31; Boulton, Hart, and Fitzpatrick 1992). As a result she does not insist on safe sex, and he infects her with the AIDS virus, which he contracted in a homosexual encounter. The cost of the disease to her is an external cost of risky sex, just as the cost of heterosexual adultery to the deceived spouse is an external cost of adultery (Posner 1992, pp. 184–186). So fraud as well as force (in the form of rape) is at work in the AIDS "marketplace." And while even fraud and force can often be avoided, or at least the probability of becoming a victim of them reduced, the costs of self-protection against deliberate impositions are often very high. Those costs are external costs of the AIDS epidemic, just like the costs of safe sex. Indeed, just as in the case of safe sex, the costs of self-protection against force and fraud cap the external costs that those wrongs impose.

Feminists will want to go further and argue that many ostensibly "voluntary" transactions in the sexual market are products of subtle forms of coercion. Our suggestion in Chapter 2 that gender inequality in the black community may be a cause of the greater prevalence of AIDS among black than among white women could be taken as support for the feminist position. However, to argue that the low effective sex ratio among blacks "coerces" women to engage in unprotected sex would be tantamount to regarding all market transactions as coerced, since their terms are determined by (among other things) the relative number of suppliers and demanders. In any event it would be a mistake to place too much weight on gender inequality as a factor in the AIDS epidemic; women who contracted the AIDS virus in sexual intercourse account

---

8. Or any sex: because safe sex is not perfectly safe, very cautious people may refuse to have sex on any terms with someone they know to be HIV-positive.

for only 5 percent of new AIDS cases and 4 percent of the cumulative number.[9]

Despite these considerations, the earlier example of the costless vaccine remains relevant. Suppose the perfectly effective vaccine were not costless, but it cost only a penny. Then the external cost from not vaccinating oneself would be positive, but small. Similarly, if we set to one side the AIDS cases that cannot be prevented by safe sex or its intravenous drug equivalent, a new or decontaminated needle, the cost of safe sex or a clean needle places a ceiling on the external costs of AIDS. This is an important point. It is natural to think that the entire disutility incurred by people who get AIDS is an external cost of risky sex and of other unsafe practices such as needle sharing by intravenous drug users. Actually, little of that disutility is an external cost. For the most part it is the expected consequence of playing a lottery of risky sex. Most of the *external* cost is not borne by AIDS sufferers at all, but by persons who substitute safe sex and avoid AIDS; the extra cost of safe compared to risky sex is the external cost. That extra cost places an upper bound on the cost that these persons incur as a result of risky sex by other persons. The aggregate cost of safe sex is not trivial, because it is incurred by all who fear AIDS enough to practice safe sex, rather than by the smaller number who actually get AIDS (indeed, most of those have not incurred the cost of safe sex at all), and because it is high for some people. It may well be higher than the costs of avoiding many contagious diseases by simple self-protective measures, such as boiling water (cholera) or avoiding oysters (hepatitis A). But it is less than the ex post cost of AIDS itself.

An analogy may be helpful. Suppose you were in the path of a speeding car, and you could avoid being run down simply by stepping back onto the curb. Instead you decide to take a chance and sprint across the street in front of the car, and you are hit. The external cost of the driver's negligence is not the cost of your injury, but the much smaller cost that you would have borne had you stepped back. Similarly, the social costs of thefts that are easily prevented by taking inexpensive precautions

---

9. Computed from Centers for Disease Control (1993, pp. 9, 11 [figs. 3, 5]). For other criticisms of explanations that tie AIDS-risky behavior to gender inequality, see Kline, Kline, and Oken (1992). Note, however, that the percentage of the infected population that is female is higher in a number of other countries, approaching 50 percent in Africa and Haiti (Mantell, Schinke, and Akabas 1988, p. 19; Brettle and Leen 1991).

such as locking one's car doors are capped by the costs of the precautions, including the cost of attentiveness—which has a direct counterpart in the use of condoms against sexual transmission of the AIDS virus.

If safe sex is so cheap, the reader may be tempted to ask, why are there 50,000 new AIDS cases a year? Part of the answer is that many of these cases are the result of infections that occurred before the modes of transmission of the disease were understood. Those infections are not sources of external costs in any sense relevant to public policy; they are unavoidable accidents, like injuries caused by storms of such unprecedented severity as to be rationally unanticipated and unprotected against. But the main answer is that most of the new cases result from deliberate risk taking by persons who could have avoided the risk at modest cost.

It might seem that the best way of estimating the costs of safe sex, and hence the (main) external costs of AIDS, would be to work backward from estimates of the ex post costs of AIDS to its victims. Suppose that of the 50,000 new cases of AIDS in the United States in 1992, 25,000 could have been avoided by substituting safe for risky activities. And suppose the cost of each such case—primarily the disutility to the victim of suffering and death—is reckoned at the relatively modest sum of $1 million. Does this not imply that the minimum cost of safe sex is $25 billion—the amount that victims of AIDS could have saved by switching to safe sex? It does not. It is apparent from observing the behavior of pedestrians that people assume nontrivial risks of injury and death for trivial benefits in time saved. Should we tote up the costs of avoidable pedestrian deaths and use that figure as a basis for evaluating public policies aimed at reducing pedestrian accidents? We think not. The cheapest way to avoid such accidents is pedestrian care. If pedestrians fail to take care, this tells us that they set a lower cost on small risks of injury and death than we might suppose if we worked backward from an ex post estimate of the value of life. This inference assumes, plausibly however in this example and also for most current HIV-risky behavior, that people have both an adequate, though not necessarily a precise, comprehension of the risks and the physical and mental ability to take adequate precautions against them. On this assumption, public intervention to give people more protection than they want would be paternalistic. Paternalistic regulations may sometimes be justifiable on ethical grounds, but they are difficult to justify on grounds of economic efficiency.

Not only are the external costs of AIDS probably lower, though we do not know how much lower, than usually believed, but there may be external benefits. The argument of social conservatives may have a kernel of validity. Irregular sexual practices, such as nonmarital sex that produces children born out of wedlock (many of them unwanted), may be a source of external costs. Those costs are diminished when fear of contracting AIDS induces people to substitute marital for nonmarital sex because the former is safer. Yet many sexual activities of which most moral conservatives disapprove—lesbian relations, monogamous sexual relations between homosexual men, monogamous but nonmarital sexual relations between heterosexuals, homosexual safe-sex activities more generally, and indeed nonmarital safe-sex activities—create little risk of spreading AIDS.

As we suggested in discussing unavoidable accident, the use of the concept of external cost to guide policy presupposes that public intervention to eliminate or reduce an externality has reasonable prospects for success. Market forces limit the potential effectiveness of public efforts to reduce the external costs of AIDS. Recall the discussion of vaccination, and now assume that some but not all members of the relevant population are vaccinated. This will reduce the danger of infection to the unvaccinated and, at least in the case of a disease such as AIDS that is spread by conduct that is valued by the participants (unsafe sex), will induce them to engage in that conduct more.[10] Thus a vaccine or cure might not lower the nation's total bill for health services and might actually raise it. A reduction in expected disease cost will increase the prevalence of the disease, and while the cost per patient will be lower, total cost will be higher if the reduction in cost per patient is proportionately less than the increase in the number of patients. Only if the vaccine or cure were at once completely effective and costless could we be certain that it would lower the total costs of AIDS. The point is parallel to the suggestion made in Chapter 3 that the effect of HIV testing in increasing the prevalence of AIDS by increasing the demand for risky sex may be offset by the feedback effect of prevalence on the demand for safe sex. The general point is that the self-regulating character of a disease that is avoidable by behavioral change may blunt the effect of public intervention to control the disease.

A complete analysis, moreover, must consider the external costs not only of the disease but also of the measures for controlling it. If it is true that HIV testing increases the spread of AIDS—or even if it merely

---

10. This may depend, however, on the precise form of the vaccine. See Chapter 7.

increases the defensive recourse to safe sex (as when the withdrawal of a couple that has tested negative from the risky sexual market increases the disease risk of unsafe sex to the persons who remain in it and thereby induces them to switch to safe sex)—then subsidizing that testing, ostensibly in order to reduce the external costs of the disease, may itself be a source of external costs.

To summarize, despite the great suffering that AIDS has engendered, the *net* external costs of the disease—the focus of the *economic* case for public intervention—might be relatively modest were the disease left to run its course without public intervention. Important as this point is to the evaluation of existing and proposed public programs, none cheap, for reducing the incidence or lethality of AIDS, previous analyses of the epidemic have ignored it. Studies measure the gross costs of the disease and assume implicitly that these are its net social costs. In fact, a substantial though unquantified fraction of them are offset by the benefits that many individuals derive from engaging in risky sex with full awareness of the possible consequences. Since few people derive utility from the risk of death itself, society would be better off if AIDS could be cured or prevented at low cost. But the same would be true if the word "cancer" were substituted for "AIDS." What is thought to make AIDS different, from an economic standpoint, is that it is infectious, and therefore a source of external costs. We are suggesting that the *magnitude* of this difference—the portion of the costs of AIDS that is external—is smaller than usually assumed.

The Effects of AIDS on Expenditures on Health

The major cost of contracting AIDS is the disutility of a painful and debilitating illness and of a premature death. This is not a monetary cost. But the withdrawal of the AIDS sufferer from the employment market can impose monetary costs, to which must be added the monetary costs of medical treatment during the course of the disease—more precisely the diseases, mild at first but progressively more serious and ultimately fatal, that strike a person whose immune system is being destroyed by the AIDS virus. Some fraction of these costs is paid for by the AIDS patient himself, his family or friends, or charities, and therefore presents no special issue of policy; for this fraction of the costs is borne voluntarily. Another fraction, however, is paid for by the patient's private insurance carrier, and hence by the members of his risk pool; and another by federal and state government through Medicaid and other public health

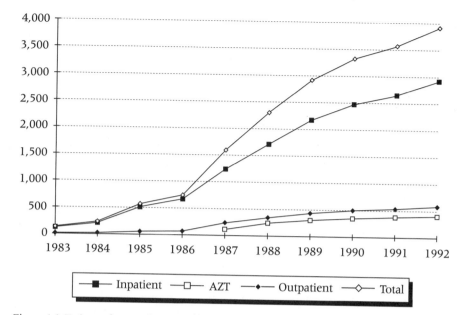

Figure 4-1 Estimated annual medical cost of AIDS, by major cost component, 1983–1992. (Figures are in millions of 1992 dollars.) *Source:* The sources of these estimates and the details of their derivation are available from the authors.

programs, either because the AIDS sufferer is indigent from the start or because his assets get depleted over the course of the disease.[11] The aggregate medical-treatment costs of AIDS and HIV are not known for sure, but in Figure 4-1 we attempt to estimate them. The attempts that have been made to shift these costs in whole or part to insurance carriers and government raise the principal issues of policy discussed in this section.

It might appear that the externalization of medical-treatment costs through purely private insurance would be transient—that as soon as the risks of AIDS were fully understood, premiums would adjust accordingly. But they may not. If an insurance company cannot determine at reasonable cost which persons are engaging in risky sex, those persons will be able to shift a portion of the expected medical costs of risky sex to the other policyholders. This point suggests that insurance companies should not be forbidden, as they are in several states (Faden and Kass

---

11. It has been estimated that Medicaid pays 23 percent of the medical costs of treating persons with AIDS (Baily et al. 1990).

1988), to take measures designed to identify and exclude persons who have a high risk of contracting AIDS. Such measures reduce the externalization of the costs of AIDS, and such a reduction is economically efficient. The argument is incomplete, however, in three respects. First, we saw in the preceding chapter that measures which increase people's knowledge of their HIV status by encouraging them to be tested for the virus may accelerate the spread of the epidemic. Second, since medical costs are a small fraction of the total costs, pecuniary and nonpecuniary, of becoming afflicted by AIDS, it is unlikely that allowing AIDS patients to shift some of their medical costs to the shoulders of other ratepayers or taxpayers will have a significant effect on the incidence of the disease.

Third, and most interesting, the medical-cost externality created when AIDS patients are enabled to shift their medical expenses to other persons may be offset by an external benefit. The reason is the fatal character of AIDS, in consequence of which the medical expenses that the AIDS victim would have incurred in later life had he not died from AIDS are averted. Suppose that a person's expected remaining lifetime is t years, and for each of these years he has some probability of having wealth W below the level w that is the cut-off for public assistance and of having an illness requiring medical attention at cost c. C, his total expected lifetime public-assistance cost discounted to a present sum, will be higher the more years he is expected to live, the lower his wealth, the lower the public-assistance eligibility threshold, and the more costly the diseases he is likely to get. AIDS affects two of these variables: it increases c in the year in which the individual is stricken with AIDS, which has the partial effect of raising C, and it reduces t by shortening the patient's life, which has the partial effect of lowering C.

The first effect is the one that people point to when they discuss the medical costs of AIDS and predict a disastrous impact on the nation's health budget, though often the costs are exaggerated. The most thorough studies that we have found estimate the lifetime cost of medical care per AIDS patient to be between $80,000 and $85,000 (Sisk 1987; Bloom and Carliner 1988; Hellinger 1991; see generally Fox and Thomas 1989), which is comparable to the medical costs of other fatal diseases (Hellinger 1991, p. 607). Some other competent estimates are lower—$30,000 to $60,000 (Bennett, Cvitanic, and Pascal 1991; Ohsfeldt and Gohmann 1992); on the other hand, the most recent estimate is $102,000 (Chase 1992b).[12] These estimates ignore expenditures on

---

12. Our own estimate, presented in Chapter 7, is $75,000 in 1990 dollars.

AIDS research and education, but, as we shall see in Chapter 7, this omission may be justified by uncertainty about their impact on medical costs. Also ignored is the fraction of medical costs that is paid for by the AIDS victim out of his own pocket rather than by an insurance company or (via Medicaid) the government. Whether the lifetime medical costs of treating AIDS are rising or falling is another question examined in Chapter 7.

The *total* medical costs of AIDS, of course, are not the costs per case but those costs multiplied by the number of cases. Insofar as economics provides a more realistic basis for predicting the incidence of the disease than epidemiological models that take no account of behavioral change, its contribution to dealing with the epidemic goes beyond estimating the average cost of treatment, which has been the emphasis of the previous economic studies. Our particular interest here, however, is in the second effect of AIDS on medical costs, the reduction of *future* costs, which has been ignored in previous discussions of AIDS.[13] (This is parallel to ignoring the consumption that is saved when a person dies.) The greater t is (that is, the younger the AIDS patient is), and hence the greater the reduction in t as a result of AIDS; the lower W is (the poorer the patient); the higher future c is (the likelier the person would have been to incur expensive diseases had he not contracted AIDS); and the lower w is (and therefore the more generous public assistance is), the smaller will be the net medical costs of AIDS. This suggests that as AIDS becomes increasingly a disease of poor (low W) young (high t) people, the net medical-costs externality, already smaller than the public, most health professionals, and even many economists believe, will become smaller still.

The cost savings from AIDS are, however, incurred in the future. AIDS is a recent phenomenon and no respecter of age. Most of the persons whom it has eliminated from the demand side of the medical-services market would not, had they lived, yet have reached an age at which they were a big drain on the public health budget. In a sensible system of public accounting, the future cost savings would be discounted to present value and subtracted from the public medical bill for AIDS in order to even out consumption between present and future. The necessary calculation would be straightforward, although we have not done it. The future cost savings can be estimated from Medicaid expenditures

---

13. Though not in the literature of health economics generally. See, for example, Fuchs and Zeckhauser (1987) and Gori and Richter (1978).

on persons who have the same characteristics as AIDS patients other than HIV status.

The net present value of the health expenditures (other than by AIDS victims themselves) associated with AIDS is thus given by

$$(4.1) \qquad NP = c_{a0}[1 - p_a(W_0, w_0)] - \sum_{t=1}^{\infty} (c_{ot}[1 - p_{ot}(W_t, w_t)](1 + i)^{-t}).$$

c_{a0} denotes the cost (assumed for simplicity to be incurred wholly in year zero) of the average AIDS victim's medical treatment for AIDS and its satellite diseases, and p_a the fraction of the cost paid for by the AIDS victim himself. c_{ot} and p_{ot} are the corresponding cost and fraction for the other diseases that the AIDS victim would have suffered in year t but for his dying from AIDS. $\sum_{t=1}^{\infty}$ denotes the summation of the victim's averted future disease experience over his remaining lifetime, had he not been stricken by AIDS, and i is an interest rate for discounting future costs to present values. The first term on the right-hand side of the equation is thus the medical expenditure on treating AIDS, which is the current focus of policy discussions, and the second term is the present value of the future medical expenditures that are saved by AIDS, which is the focus of our discussion.

In addition to its effect on medical costs, AIDS eliminates the earnings that its victims would have had if they had not been disabled and eventually killed by the disease. Some studies therefore add to the medical costs imposed by AIDS the earnings lost as a result of disability and death due to the disease (for example, Scitovsky and Rice 1987, pp. 11–15). The addition of earnings lost as a result of death, a much larger figure than earnings lost because of disability (ibid., p. 15 [tab. 9]), is questionable. Since people consume in the form of private and public goods and services most of what they earn, a death need not impose significant monetary costs on the rest of society even if, as in the case of most AIDS victims, the person dies during his working years. Moreover, because after retirement people consume more than they produce, a disease that reduces longevity can reduce consumption as well as production—and depending on the structure of retirement benefits, the former more than the latter. Disability is different because the disabled person continues to consume resources that may have to be paid for by other persons if his income and wealth are inadequate, and the disability may not reduce his longevity.

Particularly in the case of publicly provided services, the fit between expenditure and consumption is often loose. People are taxed to pay for programs such as social security, Medicaid, and Medicare in which ordinarily they are not yet eligible to participate. If these people die before they become entitled to benefits under these programs, they get no refund, and thus are net contributors to the public fisc. The loss of their contribution because they die prematurely as a result of AIDS is a cost to the government that should be factored into equation 4.1 as an offset to the benefit they confer because their death removes them as potential recipients of government benefits. Some people, moreover, are abnormally productive. They receive wages equal to their marginal product, but their total product is larger; a plausible example is the great French philosopher and intellectual historian Michel Foucault, a victim of AIDS. Or, to recur to our point about the loose linkage between expenditures on and consumption of public services, they pay taxes that vastly exceed a fair valuation of the benefits they receive from government; an example is the actor Rock Hudson, another victim of the disease.

Despite these points, the large (and growing) fraction of AIDS victims who are drug abusers or otherwise economically marginal members of society makes it uncertain that the net public costs of the epidemic in lost output received by other members of society are significantly greater than zero. This is not to say, nor do we believe, that the lives of drug addicts, prostitutes, homosexuals who engage in risky sex, or any other persons at high risk of HIV infection are less valuable in an ethical sense than those of any other persons. Indeed, we are about to show that even from a narrowly economic standpoint their lives may be valuable even if their income is very low or for that matter zero. Our point is only that the looseness of fit between expenditures on public services and the consumption of those services has brought into being a class of net recipients of such services as well as net payors, and that a reduction in the longevity of the net recipients may reduce the costs of government.

This analysis bears on the evaluation of laws that forbid insurers to exclude or otherwise discriminate against persons infected by the AIDS virus. Such a prohibition is bound to raise the insurance premiums of the other policyholders, but the aggregate increase would probably not be large (Vogel 1989, p. 991). More to the present point, these policyholders (or their children) might benefit as taxpayers, or as owners of medical insurance policies, from the effect of AIDS in eliminating the medical costs that the infected persons would have incurred in the future had they not been killed by AIDS now. The burdened policyholders would also benefit as taxpayers from the reduction in the expenses of

Medicaid for AIDS victims if private insurers were forced to insure HIV carriers (cf. Green and Arno 1990).

Yet if AIDS victims are assumed to be of average productivity, or even perhaps of below-average productivity, it may seem obvious that their removal from the society through death will harm the other members of society, if not by increasing tax burdens then by reducing opportunities to achieve economies of scale or by weakening the country militarily. It is far from obvious. It is as likely that the United States is overpopulated as that it is underpopulated (see Posner 1992, pp. 192–196, and references cited there). Congestion externalities may be great, and they would be reduced by thinning the population. It is true that homosexuals, who have on average fewer children than heterosexuals, contribute less to overpopulation and place fewer burdens on publicly financed services for children, including education. When they are killed by AIDS in their working prime (the median age of death for victims of AIDS in the United States is 38), society loses a taxpayer whose expected contribution to public revenues, net of contribution to public expenditures, may well be positive. But the balance may be reversed in the case of the second-largest victim class, the intravenous drug users. This is just our loose-fit point again.

However all this may net out, it would be a mistake to suppose that AIDS has a "silver lining" because it kills off people who might, had they lived, have someday imposed heavy medical or other costs on the rest of the population not offset by the taxes they would pay or other benefits they would confer. The welfare of the victims of AIDS is part of the aggregate social welfare with which the economist is concerned; and the suffering and death of those victims represent a greater cost to them and their families, in economic although not pecuniary terms, than the savings in their future medical costs represent to others. People do not value their lives merely at the difference between their earnings, or their total or marginal social product, and their consumption (although the rest of society might value them that way), since that consumption, and indeed life itself, yields them utility over and above the cost of the things they consume.[14] Our point is only that it would be a mistake to suppose that AIDS is likely to cause a fiscal crisis. And, to return to the first section of this chapter, insofar as the efficient scale of public inter-

---

14. There is an extensive economic literature on the value of life. A pertinent summary is Hay (1989, pp. 140–143). In Chapter 7 we investigate whether value-of-life considerations support public funding of research into possible vaccines or cures for HIV-AIDS.

vention in the sexual market is a function of the *external* costs imposed by the AIDS epidemic, rather than of the total costs, one must be careful not to exaggerate the external costs, lest the economic case for public intervention be exaggerated. The suffering of a person who knowingly assumed the risk of it for a greater expected gain is not an external cost; and if he is altruistic toward the members of his family, he will internalize their suffering, or at least a great part of it, as well.

CHAPTER 5

Regulatory Interventions

The fact that AIDS is a source of negative externalities creates a potential case for public intervention to reduce the incidence of the disease. Two qualifications must be borne in mind, however. The first is that the negative externalities do not appear to be as large as generally believed (as discussed in Chapter 4), so any proposals for costly public programs should be received with caution. The second qualification (stressed in Coase 1960) is that the existence of an externality or any other source of market failure is a necessary rather than a sufficient condition for public intervention. Intervention is warranted on economic grounds only when it will produce a net increase in social welfare. To try to correct even a serious market failure would be a mistake if the only feasible corrective cost more than the costs it would eliminate. This is a pertinent observation because, as we shall see, a number of actual and proposed AIDS programs are very costly or even counterproductive.

The programs, both existing and proposed, are of two types.[1] The first type, the subject of this chapter, is regulatory, and consists of programs, such as mandatory testing, punishment for recklessly transmitting the virus, and immigration controls, that place restrictions on people's freedom of action. The second type, examined in the following two chapters, employs subsidies rather than restrictions—for example, subsidies for AIDS education and medical research, for HIV testing and counseling,

---

1. For helpful surveys of governmental intervention in the AIDS crisis in developed countries, see Hook (1991) and especially Kirp and Bayer (1992). Intervention worldwide is well surveyed in Global AIDS Policy Coalition (1992, ch. 13). Legal interventions are surveyed in a variety of works, including Wiley Law Publications Editorial Staff (1992); Jarvis et al. (1991); and Curran, Gostin, and Clark (1988).

and for condoms or clean hypodermic needles. As techniques for providing public goods, regulation and subsidization may appear to differ profoundly: regulatory programs often entail only small public expenditures but impose allocative costs by altering relative prices, while subsidies often entail large public expenditures but may not appear to alter relative prices and thus impose social costs—may appear to be, in short, purely distributive.

The appearance is misleading, the contrast overdrawn. Public subsidies must be financed by taxes (including indirect taxes such as inflation or interest on public debt); and taxes, even income taxes, have misallocative effects similar to those of regulation (Friedman 1966; Posner 1971). Thus the difference between regulation and subsidization is not fundamental, at least if fiscal consequences are ignored. This is easily seen by imagining that voluntary testing were subsidized so generously that everyone tested. The effect of the subsidy on the amount of testing and hence on the spread of the disease would be the same as that of universal mandatory testing. The subsidy might not have to be so generous to induce universal testing. As our analysis of low-cost testing in Chapter 3 implied, if the subsidy were large enough either to make refusal to be tested difficult to explain on grounds other than fear of being found positive or (for this or other reasons) to induce a substantial fraction of the population to be tested, refusals to test would become an increasingly strong signal of positive status, thus putting pressure on the holdouts to test as well, or, stated otherwise, reducing the net cost of testing to them.

Epidemiological versus Economic Approaches

The perspective from which we examine the regulatory programs that have been adopted or suggested for controlling AIDS differs from that of epidemiologists. They typically make two assumptions that are uncongenial to economic thinking. The first, which is implicit rather than explicit, is that there is no private demand for, and there are therefore no private markets in, measures related to public health—tests, vaccines, contact tracing, and so forth—so that the adoption of these measures requires public intervention. The second assumption, which is explicit, is that any regulatory intervention in an epidemic results in the removal of the target of the intervention from the infectious or potentially infectious pool and, as a consequence, in an unambiguous decline in the incidence of the disease (Wickwire 1977; Hethcote, Yorke, and Nold 1982; Anderson and May 1991, pp. 230–231). The assumptions are related in ignoring the incentives that the disease, and measures for controlling the disease, respectively, create for people to change their behavior and by doing so affect the further spread of the disease.

Epidemiologists assume, for example, that vaccination, even if incomplete either because the vaccine is not a hundred percent effective or because not everyone in the population at risk is vaccinated, reduces the prevalence of a disease because the random encounters of infected with uninfected persons are "wasted" from a contagion standpoint on the fraction of the uninfected population that is immune. In an economic model, prevalence may fall much less as a consequence of incomplete vaccination of the potentially susceptible population, because the reduction brought about by the vaccine in the probability of infection may increase the demand for risky activity by lowering its relative price. And, unless a cure increases the exit rate from the infective population to a level at which the disease peters out, it may actually increase prevalence by reducing the expected cost of the disease to its victims. For example, the development of a cure for syphilis seems to have been a factor in the later resurgence of the disease. As another analogy, consider the probable effect of a cure for lung cancer or heart disease on the level of cigarette smoking: the level would rise because the cost of the diseases would fall, and the higher level would increase the incidence of the diseases.

Contact tracing. Similarly, epidemiologists model "contact tracing"—the practice, long standard in the public-health response to sexually transmitted disease, of asking a disease carrier to name his contacts in order to identify asymptomatic carriers (Rutherford and Woo 1988)—as automatically removing the carriers from the infectious pool.[2] But unless joined with additional measures, such as quarantining, it need have no such effect; and even if it does, the resulting fall in the probability of infection can, as before, increase risky behavior. In the case of AIDS, moreover, insofar as contact tracing may result in additional HIV testing (that is, by the contacts), it may increase the spread of the disease, as discussed in Chapter 3. This cost of contact tracing would have to be compared with the benefit in warning the unsuspecting sexual partners

---

2. Under the name "partner notification," contact tracing is a feature of most HIV testing programs in this country (Crystal et al. 1190; Fox, Day, and Klein 1989, p. 106; Centers for Disease Control 1988; Giesecke 1991; Roper 1991), in part because the Centers for Disease Control requires all states that receive federal funds for HIV prevention and surveillance to adopt procedures for partner notification. For an excellent introduction to the problems of contact tracing in the HIV-AIDS setting, see Bayer and Toomey (1992).

of an infected person to desist from unprotected sex with that person (provided they are not yet infected themselves) because he is HIV-positive. That benefit may be small. Because the people most likely to spread the disease are those with the most sexual partners, and because, as we have seen, the level of voluntary testing is low, so that most HIV-positives do not enter contact-tracing programs until years after they started infecting their sexual partners, it is difficult for the contact tracer to find the names and addresses of the carrier's (mostly former) sexual partners (Brandt 1990)—some of whom, indeed, may have been anonymous.[3] Contact tracing is more likely to be effective with diseases such as syphilis and gonorrhea that have short incubation periods. Another difference is that in the case of a curable disease, contact tracing should result in the cure of any infected contacts that are found, and once cured they are no longer infective. HIV/AIDS is incurable; an infected contact is rendered harmless to others only if he ceases engaging in risky sex.

The efficacy of contact tracing is further limited because no one supposes that it is feasible to *compel* a person found to be HIV-positive to name his sexual contacts. The question therefore arises why the government or the medical profession should be involved in contact tracing at all. If the infected person wants to notify his contacts, he will; if he doesn't want to, he won't give the government or his doctor their names.[4] More precisely, we should distinguish among persons (1) from whom the infected person may have gotten the disease, (2) whom he may have infected already, or (3) with whom he is currently having risky sex. If altruistic, he will have some incentive to notify the last group, or at least those in it who are not already infected, but may decide, as an alternative, to switch to safe sex with them. He will also have an incentive to notify members of the second group who do not know they are infected, if he believes they will benefit from that knowledge (see the Introduction). He will have little or no incentive, altruistic or egoistic,

---

3. Wykoff and colleagues (1991, p. 221), however, report that the HIV contact-tracing program that they studied managed to locate 58 percent of the sexual partners (within the previous two years) of the persons whose contacts the program attempted to trace. But the program was in a rural area, and the authors caution that its results may not be generalizable to the urban settings in which the epidemic is concentrated. The Landis study cited in the text below had a 50 percent success rate, but again in a low-prevalence, predominantly nonurban region (North Carolina).

4. There is some notification by infected persons of their previous or current sexual partners that is unrelated to any contact-tracing program (Marks et al. 1992; Perry et al. 1990). We call this "private tracing."

to notify the persons who may have infected him, but neither is he likely to have any reluctance to give their names to the authorities. Here the only thing that deters notification is an excess of private costs over private benefits (the latter being zero), so if the government assumes the costs, this should tip the balance in favor of notification. Even in the case of notification of actual or potential sexual partners to whom the infected person is altruistically disposed and whom he may have infected, the private costs (including the cost involved in being identified as an injurer) may exceed the private benefits. So once again, if the government or the medical profession assumes or eliminates the costs of partner notification—and it can eliminate some of them simply by not identifying the infected person to his contacts—the balance may be tipped in favor of notification. A recent study found that even where a state law made it a crime for a person who knows he is HIV-positive not to notify his sexual partners, only a small percentage of HIV carriers were willing to do so, whereas notification by the public health department reached 50 percent of the carriers' sexual partners (Landis et al. 1992). The authors acknowledged, however, that since HIV carriers might have enrolled in the study because they wanted help in notifying their sexual partners, the study may have underestimated the amount of private tracing (ibid., p. 104).

Nothing we have said warrants a conclusion that publicly financed or publicly conducted or administered contact tracing is socially cost-justified. Most of the costs of private tracing are not eliminated, but merely shifted to the government. The aggregate costs may even be higher, because private tracing does not require an intermediary between the sexual partners, as public tracing does. And the benefits may be slight. The potential benefits are to not-yet-infected sexual partners of the infected person and to their noninfected partners, but they are only potential benefits, because notification may not lead the notified to change their behavior. If, moreover, the infected person is altruistic toward his sexual partners, he probably will take steps (such as switching to safe sex) to protect them, whereas if he is not altruistic toward them he may not disclose their names to the contact tracer, because he wants to continue having risky sex with them. He may not have a similar reluctance with respect to notification of former sexual partners (the results of the Landis study are consistent with this conjecture), but notifying them will come too late to protect them against him.

A related issue in contact tracing concerns notification of infection status, without the consent of the infected person, to his current sexual partners, some or all of whom may be endangered by him. There is judicial authority for requiring a health professional who knows that his patient poses a danger to another to warn the endangered person, on pain of tort sanctions if he does not do so.[5] The usual approach of state AIDS statutes is to permit rather than to require such warnings if the professional has reason to believe that the HIV carrier will not notify, or avoid risky sex with, his sexual partners. It is hard to quarrel with requiring, let alone permitting, such warnings; and if the effect is to reduce the amount of voluntary testing,[6] this need not entail any social cost, as we have been at pains to stress. The efficacy of such a requirement may be doubted, however. The issue arises only if the infected person names his sexual partners, and, once again, if he doesn't want them warned he won't name them.

Screening and surveillance. If the assumption made by most epidemiologists that contact tracing will significantly reduce the further spread of HIV infection is questionable, equally so is their assumption that screening, as through voluntary or mandatory testing, automatically removes persons who test positive from the infectious pool. (Even if it does, we saw in Chapter 3 that screening may still result in an increase rather than a decrease in the incidence of the disease.) Although most epidemiologists oppose mandatory HIV testing, they want to encourage voluntary testing, through generous subsidies if need be. We shall argue that subsidization and coercion are not sharply different, that mandatory testing therefore has similar properties to subsidized voluntary testing, and, consistent with our analysis in Chapter 3, that neither practice seems very likely to reduce the spread of the disease.

Screening blood donors for HIV is much more likely to be a sound policy, both because infected blood discovered by HIV testing is easily prevented from infecting the blood supply, by being destroyed (Eisenstaedt and Getzen 1988), and because people who need a blood transfusion cannot protect themselves by behavioral change. Yet even HIV testing of donated blood may have a cost from the standpoint of disease control, if the donors learn the result of the test on their blood. And they are bound to do so, because the blood bank will want to caution donors who test positive not to try to donate blood in the future.

In each of the cases discussed in this section, other than that of blood

---

5. The leading case is *Tarasoff v. Regents of University of California,* 17 Cal. 3d 425, 551 P.2d 334 (1976).

6. Which may well be a consequence of contact tracing generally (Ohi et al. 1988).

screening, the epidemiologist predicts different consequences of intervention from the economist by assuming that individuals do not change their behavior in response to the altered incentives created by the intervention—or by the disease itself. The contrary assumption—that people do respond to incentives, and hence that there is a private demand for possible responses to disease risk, such as HIV testing and partner notification, and private decision-making with respect to compliance or non-compliance with public-heath measures—is fundamental to the economic approach.

We should not ignore noninterventionist public-health measures. The most important is surveillance—that is, tracking the spread of a disease. Economists have long studied the responses of stock prices to public releases of information. The public release of information about the incidence of AIDS by the Centers for Disease Control, which monitors the occurrence of diseases in the U.S. population, can be expected to have the same type of effect on "sexual exchanges" as the public release of information about unemployment or inflation by other federal agencies has on the stock exchanges. This is different from expensive subsidy pro-

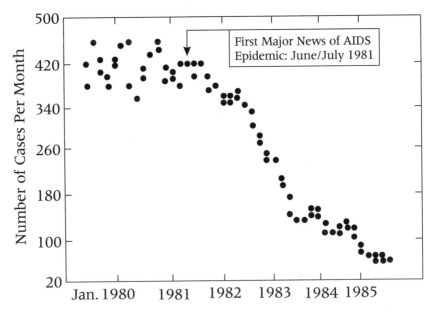

Figure 5-1 Number of cases of anal gonorrhea in a San Francisco gay men's health clinic, 1980–1985. *Source:* Based on unpublished data collected by Dr. James Wiley, Survey Research Center, University of California at Berkeley.

grams that aim to educate the public about the danger of AIDS and the methods of prevention, which we discuss in the following chapter. Here our point is simply that the surveillance of a communicable disease can operate as a form of preventive health care, provided that the agency which conducts the surveillance releases the results from time to time to the mass media, which will then disseminate those results to the public at large. Empirical support for this idea is provided in Figure 5-1, which indicates that the male homosexual community in San Francisco reacted with dramatic swiftness to the first news of the AIDS epidemic.

We add that surveillance is more effective as a method of preventive health care the more readily the disease is preventable at low cost by behavioral change, and less effective the more prone the public would be to exaggerate the risk of the disease in the absence of accurate surveillance. The latter is a possible problem in the case of AIDS, as we shall see in Chapter 6.

Mandatory Testing

Mandatory testing for a disease, followed by isolation of all persons who test positive, is a conventional, and often a highly successful, method of controlling an infectious disease.[7] Although our analysis emphasizes the behavioral consequences of mandatory testing, the practice has the additional value, which we do not discuss, of enabling more accurate short-term predictions of the spread of the disease. In the short term, the incidence of the disease can be predicted from the number of persons who are HIV-positive, information on when they became infected, and the distribution of the incubation period. For this purpose, however, mandatory testing of random samples of the population would be sufficient.

Although mandatory testing has been a focus of the debate over public policy toward AIDS,[8] the term, at least as used in connection with AIDS, is vague. No responsible person proposes that everybody in the United States be required to undergo an AIDS test. Proposals are limited to specific subpopulations, such as health workers, hospital patients, applicants for marriage licenses, applicants for life or health insurance, prison inmates, applicants for the Job Corps and the foreign service, applicants for and members of the armed forces, and, of course, blood donors. Man-

---

7. See Kleinman (1992); Mockler and Kleiman (1988); and for a description and analysis of state HIV mandatory-testing statutes, Eisenstat (1991).

8. For a representative discussion, see Field (1990).

datory testing is already in effect for some of these groups; and the state of Illinois experimented for a time with requiring applicants for marriage licenses to submit proof of having taken an HIV test.[9] We shall therefore distinguish between *local* (that is, partial) and *universal* (population-wide throughout the nation) mandatory testing.

Another useful distinction is between *avoidable* and *unavoidable* mandatory testing. Universal mandatory testing is by definition avoidable only by emigration—for most people a prohibitively costly option. Unavoidability is also a characteristic of some local mandatory testing, as of prison inmates, rape suspects, and many hospital patients,[10] but not, for example, of mandatory testing that is merely a condition of some benefit, such as a desired job, or life or medical insurance. What we are calling unavoidable mandatory testing is, when imposed by government, deemed a "search and seizure" within the meaning of the Fourth Amendment to the U.S. Constitution, and hence requires special justification.[11] But we shall disregard this limitation on the use of the device.

Another relevant distinction that is obscured by the blanket use of the term "mandatory testing" is that between *publicly* and *privately* imposed requirements of undergoing HIV testing. A private program is more likely to be optimal, because it is more likely to be constrained by competitive pressures in the employment, insurance, or other relevant market. But any program, public or private, can generate external costs. If testing is likely to increase the spread of AIDS, a private employer who creates an incentive to test by making the test a condition of employment may increase the extent and hence the costs of the epidemic, although we have emphasized that not all those costs are external.

There are other uncertainties about what is meant or implied by mandatory testing for AIDS. Who would get the test result? Just the person tested, or, as is more common, the authority that required the test as well (such as the person's employer)? If someone other than the person tested gets the result, what follows? Isolation? Cuba has an extensive program of mandatory testing—by 1989, 40 percent of the population

---

9. So did Louisiana, but we are aware of no studies of the effects of the Louisiana statute, which was repealed after only six months.

10. The clearest example would be a person who has a stroke and is taken unconscious to the nearest hospital emergency room. Of course a rapist could avoid the test by refraining from rape, and prison inmates by refraining from whatever crimes caused them to be imprisoned, but we shall ignore these qualifications to "unavoidability."

11. *Glover v. Eastern Nebraska Community Office of Retardation*, 867 F.2d 461, 463 (8th Cir. 1989); cf. *Dimeo v. Griffin*, 943 F.2d 679 (7th Cir. 1991) (en banc).

had been tested—and it quarantines the people who test positive (Bayer and Healton 1989; see also Pérez-Stable 1991).[12] Finally, how often should persons who test negative be required to retest?

Local mandatory testing. We can simplify our analysis by assuming to begin with that mandatory testing is imposed on the employees or job applicants of some employer or class of employers, that the test is administered only once, that the test results are given both to the persons tested and to their employer(s), and that persons who test positive are expelled from or forbidden entry into the job in question but that no effort is made to notify their actual or potential sexual partners. This is essentially the situation in the U.S. armed forces. The use of HIV status as a criterion of eligibility for life or health insurance is a close nonoccupational parallel.

Mandatory testing can change the behavior only of persons who would not test unless required to do so. Therefore, to estimate the effects of mandatory testing we must first consider who the nonvolunteers are likely to be. Since the demand for testing is various, this is difficult to say. But they are likely to be people who have a below-average probability of already being infected. Such people have less difficulty inducing others to have risky sex with them (remember that risky sex is preferred if the risk is not too great) without testing, and therefore have a lower demand for testing. In addition, persons who either know they are infected or believe there is a high probability that they are will be less likely to enter, or apply to enter, an occupation in which there is mandatory testing than persons who have a low probability of being already infected, or to apply for life or health insurance if the insurer requires an HIV test and rejects applicants who test positive.

Our prediction that the pool affected by mandatory testing is likely to be dominated by persons who have a very low probability of testing positive is given support by the fact that, in the first four months in which the state of Illinois required applicants for a marriage license to provide proof of having been tested for HIV, only 5 HIV carriers were discovered among the 44,726 applicants—while at the same time applications by Illinois residents for marriage licenses in states that did not require proof of an HIV test soared (Belongia 1988; Turnock and Kelley 1989; McKillip 1991). The Illinois law, which was repealed after being

---

12. This figure was said to have risen to 89 percent by 1991 (O'Connor 1991). O'Connor's article reports, almost certainly inaccurately (see Bazell 1992; Pérez-Stable 1991), that HIV carriers are free to leave Cuba's AIDS sanitariums.

in effect for only 20 months, is estimated to have reduced the marriage rate in the state by 14 percent (McKillip 1991, p. 652).[13] Although the overall rate of HIV infection in marrying couples is unlikely to exceed the nationwide prevalence of the disease and may well be lower, it is almost certainly higher than the prevalence among the Illinois applicants. The estimated number of persons in the United States who are HIV-positive is 1 million, which is .4 percent of the total population. The percentage of Illinois marriage applicants who tested positive was only .01 percent—one-fortieth of the national average (though the latter is probably overestimated, as we noted in Chapter 2). Similarly, blood donors, who know they will be tested, have an HIV-positive rate far below the national average (Gayle et al. 1990, p. 1540). It is consistent with our analysis of the Illinois experience that in another state (New Jersey), when premarital blood specimens submitted for a syphilis test were tested for HIV *without the knowledge of the marriage applicants,* the infection rate was much higher (Altman et al. 1992).

The steep decline in the fraction of Army and Navy personnel, as well as blood donors, testing positive for HIV after mandatory testing for these groups was instituted (Centers for Disease Control 1989a, pp. 18–19, figs. 10-13; McNeil et al. 1991; Garland et al. 1992) is further evidence that mandatory testing of persons engaged in selected voluntary activities is unlikely to identify many HIV carriers. Persons who think they have a high probability of testing positive—or who have tested positive in a voluntary test—will avoid the activity in which testing is mandatory. So mandatory testing will yield a disproportionately large number of negative results, making the test cost *per positive result* very high (Petersen et al. 1990; cf. Henry and Campbell 1992).[14] The lower the prevalence of HIV in the tested population, moreover, the higher will be the ratio of false to true positives. If the rate of false positives equals the prevalence, the number of false and true positives will be equal. The false-

---

13. Another factor, however, in the reduction in the marriage rate was that the applicants were required to arrange and pay for the test themselves. Incidentally, the decision of many couples to be married in another state rather than take an AIDS test casts further doubt on the argument examined (and rejected) in Chapter 3 that refusal to be tested is such a strong signal of probable infected status that the availability of testing is likely to lead, without governmental prodding, to universal testing. Presumably in most of those cases one prospective spouse took the initiative in suggesting marriage in another state and the other went along.

14. On this basis it has been questioned whether the benefits of screening marriage applicants for syphilis, as is done in all but seven states, exceed the costs (Haskell 1984).

positive rate, though low when a person who tests positive is retested before being pronounced infected, is not negligible. It goes without saying that a false positive can disrupt personal relationships and create great psychological distress.

Persons who would not have tested voluntarily, but who by virtue of mandatory testing learn that they are negative for HIV, may on average increase the amount of risky sex in which they engage, because they will find it even easier than before to find willing partners for such sex. The few positives will be barred or expelled from the occupational group (or, in the case of insurance that is conditional on being HIV-negative, denied insurance) but not, of course, rendered sexually inactive. To the extent that they are able to conceal their positive status and are not altruistic—and we saw in Chapter 3 that egoists are less likely to test voluntarily than altruists, which implies that egoists are likely to be disproportionately represented among those who discover their infection status only by virtue of mandatory testing—they may engage in risky sex more often than before they were tested and therefore accelerate the spread of the disease. The consequences may be exacerbated if exclusion from a preferred occupation, by lowering the HIV carrier's income, makes him less altruistic.

Our analysis thus yields the startling, though very tentative, conclusion that mandatory testing—one of the most severe measures seriously proposed, and already widely implemented, for limiting the spread of AIDS in the United States—is, unless universal or nearly so (see the next subsection), more likely to increase than to reduce the incidence of the disease. The qualification "in the United States" is intended to exclude the Cuban case, where mandatory testing is followed by the quarantining of the persons who test positive—a more severe measure than any seriously contemplated in this country. The principal objection to quarantining HIV carriers is that it is the equivalent of a sentence to life in prison (albeit a shorter than average life), since there is no cure for AIDS and, as far as anyone knows, the disease invariably ends in death rather than in recovery.[15] Isolation is thus a more costly method of controlling AIDS than of controlling other serious diseases in which quarantining is commonly employed. By the same token, the benefits may be greater because AIDS is more lethal than most other contagious diseases. And

---

15. Since, obviously, not every person who is HIV-positive, or even who has AIDS, has died, we cannot be certain that infection with HIV is *always* fatal. We have not, however, heard of anyone who has recovered.

more limited forms of quarantining (discussed in Pappas 1988 and Cappon 1991)—for example, of HIV carriers who refuse to desist from risky sex with persons who are not themselves HIV-positive, or of prison inmates who are HIV-positive—are less problematic. Actually, as we shall see, with universal mandatory testing, quarantining is unnecessary to achieve effective control over the spread of the disease.

Our conclusion about the likely effect of local mandatory testing on the incidence of AIDS requires qualification in two respects that are not, however, critical. The first concerns the sanctions for knowing that one is an HIV carrier. If those sanctions are effective, then people who are forced through involuntary testing to learn that they are HIV-positive may be deterred from engaging in risky sex. Such sanctions are unlikely to be very effective, however, for reasons discussed in a subsequent section of this chapter.

The second qualification, already touched on, concerns the relative number of altruists and egoists affected by mandatory testing. That ratio is important because if an altruist discovers that he is carrying the AIDS virus, he will switch to safe sex to protect his sexual partners.[16] This was the main reason for our predicting a higher demand for voluntary testing by altruists than by egoists. It might seem to follow that mandatory testing would have no effect on altruists because they all would have tested voluntarily. Not so: even an altruist, if for example he has a strong aversion to the possibility of learning that he is certain to develop a fatal disease, will not test voluntarily if the probability that he is infected, although greater than zero, is small. Mandatory testing will force this class of altruists to test. Upon learning the test results, those who test positive will presumably switch to safe sex. Those who test negative, however, will be able to make additional risky trades —and there is nothing inconsistent with altruism in assuming a risk of infecting oneself. Moreover, if we are right in predicting that a greater proportion of altruists than of egoists will test voluntarily, and if in addition egoists are at least as common as altruists in the relevant subpopulations, mandatory testing will force more egoists than altruists to test. And subject to the first qualification noted above, we know that HIV testing of egoists, especially but not only when concealment of a positive test result from sexual partners is feasible, is likely to accelerate the spread of AIDS.

---

16. This of course depends on just how altruistic the person is. We assume throughout this book, unless otherwise indicated, that an altruist is sufficiently altruistic to forgo risky sex once he knows for certain that he is infected. An assumption of weaker altruism would strengthen our principal conclusions.

Our analysis of avoidable mandatory testing requires only slight modification for the case in which testing is unavoidable, as in the case of mandatory testing of prison inmates and of some hospital patients. Here the cost of testing per person testing positive will be lower because persons having a high probability of testing positive will not have the option of avoiding the test by leaving or not joining the group that is subject to mandatory testing. But the effect on the epidemic, assuming that knowledge of infection status increases the spread of the disease, will be the same—or possibly even worse, since a higher percentage of the prison and hospital population tested will test positive,[17] and since the prison population is likely to be deficient in altruists. A partial offset is that HIV-positive prisoners can be quarantined without arousing powerful civil-liberties concerns[18]—but only for the duration of their imprisonment. Surprisingly, although anal intercourse is apparently common in many prisons (Doll et al. 1991b, pp. 30–31), and some prisons have a high rate of HIV infection because so many inmates are drug abusers, the few studies of the transmission of HIV within prisons find very low rates of transmission (Brewer and Derrickson 1992; cf. National Commission 1991). This may be because sex and particularly needle-sharing are much less common inside than outside prisons, despite suspicions to the contrary.

Universal mandatory testing. We have been assuming that HIV carriers can find sexual partners among persons who either have tested negative or do not know their infection status. But when we are considering mandatory testing that is potentially universal, as it nearly is in Cuba, the assumption is questionable. Imagine such universal testing or, what is the equivalent from the standpoint of controlling the epidemic, a subsidy so generous that everyone is induced to test voluntarily. Then everyone would know his HIV status. Anyone interested in having risky sex who had tested negative would disclose his test result with whatever documentation was necessary to establish the truth of the disclosure, because anyone who could not produce such proof would immediately be suspect. The reason for the suspicion and resulting disclosure is that universal mandatory testing would greatly reduce the cost of establishing one's

---

17. For empirical confirmation, see Centers for Disease Control (1992a); Harding (1987); Vlahov (1991); Horsburgh et al. (1990); Henry and Campbell (1992); Morse et al. (1990); and Sacks et al. (1992).

18. Stated differently, a prisoner can be quarantined at lower incremental cost to himself than would be possible for other HIV carriers, because he is isolated from the general population anyway. For a useful general discussion of AIDS quarantining, see Ford and Quam (1987).

noninfected status. Under a regime of voluntary testing, that cost includes the cost of getting tested in the first place, which may be considerable when psychic costs are factored in; so people who say that because of the cost (broadly understood) they have not been tested and therefore cannot reveal their infection status are making a plausible statement. With universal mandatory testing, the cost of disclosure falls essentially to zero (just as in the example of the students' grades, in Chapter 3) and the statement cannot be made in a believable form; as a result, any nondiscloser will be assumed to be infected. Notice also that mandatory testing would be universal in a relevant sense if persons within a particular occupation in which testing was mandatory drew their sexual partners from other members of the same occupation exclusively. But that would be unlikely.

This analysis suggests an inverted U-shaped function relating the extent of HIV testing to the growth of the disease. When testing first becomes feasible, the private demand for testing may cause the growth of the disease to accelerate (as discussed in Chapter 3). That acceleration in turn increases the demand for testing, because that demand is higher the greater the prevalence of the disease. The demand for testing can be stimulated further by subsidies, or supplemented by mandatory testing. If generous subsidies, or mandatory testing, or improvements in test accuracy that reduced the full price of testing, moved the demand for testing close to 100 percent, the effect in forcing persons who test positive to reveal (if only by their silence) their infection status to potential sexual partners would begin to dominate the effect of testing in enabling persons who test negative to obtain additional risky trades. The incidence of the disease would then begin to fall, and eventually there would be positive assortative matching of sexual partners by infection status, and zero growth of the disease. But we are far from the 100 percent testing level. Should we be? Would that be a more efficient equilibrium than the present one?

Universal testing would be costly. The costs would include the expense of the test itself and of readministering the test periodically, since the test is no guaranty against future infection. The expense is not trivial; at a price of $20 per person, testing the entire U.S. population annually would cost $5 billion. The necessity of readministering the test must be emphasized. A negative test result is a highly perishable good; it certifies (test error to one side) merely the absence of HIV antibodies on the date of the test. The person tested may have become infected later the same day—or indeed up to six months earlier. Periodic retesting could be limited to high-risk groups, but such "discrimination" would be enormously resented. The costs of universal testing also include the disutility to persons who prefer not to know their disease status, and other psychic costs of testing. Undoubtedly these costs dwarf the price—otherwise there would be much more voluntary testing, given its modest pecuniary cost. (The Illinois experience is pertinent here, too.) So $5 billion a year would be a *very* low lower-bound estimate of the costs of universal mandatory testing.

One might suppose that the benefit-cost ratio would rise if the results of the tests were made available to anyone who requested them. A variant of contact tracing, which would enable one's potential sexual partners to verify one's disclaimer of HIV-positive status, this would be a civilized alternative to William Buckley's proposal that persons who are HIV-positive be branded on the buttock with that information to provide fair warning to potential sexual partners (Buckley 1986), or to the Cuban program of locking up HIV carriers, presumably until they die.

Lifting the veil of privacy from HIV test results is a proposal independent of mandatory testing. It would discourage voluntary testing by increasing its cost, but we know that that might not be a bad thing. Coupling universal mandatory testing with (in effect) public access to the results, however, would require a formidable bureaucracy, which would further increase the cost of such testing. And public access would not be necessary if we are right that a system of universal mandatory testing automatically identifies HIV carriers to their potential sexual partners.

We should consider intermediate states between (very) local mandatory testing and (truly) universal (at least within one country) mandatory testing. Suppose, for example, that all marriage applicants in the United States were required to take an HIV test, so that substitution toward marriage in states not requiring the test would no longer be an option.[19] The rate of true positives would rise and that of false positives would fall. However, the total cost (pecuniary and nonpecuniary) of testing would be great, and by increasing the cost of marriage would cause substitution toward other forms of sexual relationship, in which the risk of transmitting AIDS is greater. Against this it can be argued that such testing is necessary to protect the unborn, since AIDS is transmitted with high efficiency from a pregnant woman to her fetus. Society does not require genetic testing of marriage applicants, however, so it is questionable whether we should require a costly test to identify what is after

---

19. This is essentially the situation with regard to syphilis.

all one of the lesser threats to the unborn. The virtually nationwide testing of marriage applicants for syphilis, another heritable disease and probably a more serious threat to the unborn than AIDS because syphilis is so much more common, has been found not to be cost-justified (Haskell 1984).

"Taxing" HIV Carriers

In discussing local mandatory testing, we assumed that exclusion from an occupation or from buying an insurance policy would follow from testing positive. But we did not treat these consequences as a penalty, which they are, however, even if such radical measures as quarantining persons who test positive for HIV are set to one side. Suppose a person who tests positive cannot obtain life or medical insurance, or will lose his job and is unlikely to be able to find as good a one elsewhere in the economy, or (if he is a doctor or dentist, for example) will have his professional opportunities curtailed. These consequences are penalties; equivalently, they are taxes on voluntary testing; under either description they should lead to less testing (for empirical confirmation, see Phillips n.d.). In the case of local mandatory testing, the penalties do not affect the amount of testing directly but do so indirectly, by affecting the choice of occupation. The greater the penalty for testing positive, the greater will be the cost of entering an occupation in which an HIV test is required.

Local mandatory testing also reduces the incentive to engage in risky sex by increasing the expected costs of that activity through the imposition of a penalty. Universal mandatory testing that carried a similar penalty (loss of medical insurance, for example) would have the same effect. The penalty thus operates as a tax not only on testing but also on risky sexual trades—so we call it a *trade* tax. The *proportional* increase in expected cost brought about by the trade tax is unlikely to be great, because for most people the expected cost of a painful premature death is much greater than that of losing insurance. Yet the fact that allowing a person infected with the AIDS virus to externalize some of his medical and disability costs by forbidding employers and insurers to "discriminate" against such persons is unlikely to increase the spread of the epidemic does not make such a policy a good one (Clifford and Iuculano 1987; Epstein 1988). The spread of the disease is to a significant extent the by-product of a voluntary lottery of risky sex. Should the players in that lottery be subsidized by the cautious people in the society?[20] No doubt, to repeat an earlier caveat, one should distinguish between people who were infected before AIDS was discovered and those infected afterward; the former had no opportunity to learn the high cost of the lottery ticket. Their claim for social insurance is stronger, and internal subsidization (see note 20) is one method of providing it.

Another argument that has been made for the antidiscrimination principle is that the expected medical costs of HIV carriers may be no greater and the life expectancy no shorter than in the case of certain other high-risk persons whom insurance companies insure, including people who are accident-prone (Vogel 1989, pp. 991–992). This argument neglects the fact that insurance companies are constrained both by law and by the costs of information in trying to determine the risk posed by the various persons they insure. The existence of such constraints provides no economic basis for imposing additional ones.

If we stay within the framework of our economic analysis and ignore ethical considerations, including those bearing on the question whether or not to provide social insurance, the strongest argument for forbidding discrimination by insurance companies against HIV carriers or AIDS victims is that to permit such discrimination gives the companies an incentive to require applicants for insurance to test—and increased testing can increase the spread of the disease. In addition, forbidding discrimination shifts some of the costs of AIDS that are borne by the government, which picks up most of the medical tab for people who do not have medical insurance, and hence by the taxpayer, to workers, consumers, insurance policyholders, and other groups, a shift that may or may not reduce administrative costs.

Radical penalty proposals, such as for quarantining or tattooing persons who are infected with the AIDS virus, are likely to be dismissed out of hand as barbarous. This they may be, in treating people like cattle, or like inmates of Nazi concentration camps. But there is also an economic point to be made. Precisely because the penalty is so severe, its principal effect in a regime of voluntary testing or local mandatory testing would simply be to discourage testing, in the second case by discouraging entry into the occupation in which testing was required. This might be a good result from the standpoint of controlling the epidemic, but it is not one sought by the proponents of branding or isolation. Such

---

20. The antidiscrimination rule operates as a form of internal subsidy, in which regulation makes one group of customers or employees bear costs for the benefit of another (Posner 1971).

a measure would serve the proponents' stated goal only if conjoined with universal mandatory testing—but we have seen that under such a regime no further measures to control the epidemic would be necessary. Individuals who tested positive would find it virtually impossible to find partners for risky sex, because lack of proof of negative infection status would be taken as an admission of positive infection status. Thus they would be "branded" as AIDS carriers without any need to mutilate their bodies. Cuba could have achieved its goal of controlling AIDS with universal testing alone, without having to quarantine persons who tested positive.

Any suggestion that voluntary testing with penalties for positive test results might reduce the spread of AIDS must be qualified when one is considering a subpopulation in which altruists are likely to predominate. For example, an altruist who would otherwise test voluntarily in order to protect his sexual partner may decide not to do so if as a consequence of testing positive he would be unable to obtain medical insurance. This conclusion may seem inconsistent with our assumption that an altruist will refrain from risky sex if he knows he is infected; for the cost of losing one's medical insurance is incurred only if the test reveals that one is HIV-positive. However, the altruist who does not test does not *know* he is a carrier, and the altruistic benefit of testing, discounted by the probability that he is a carrier, may be less than the selfish cost of losing his insurance, similarly discounted, plus the selfish cost of giving up risky sex.

Or consider the extremely rare case of nonsexual transmission of AIDS from a medical worker to a patient. If there is no cheap equivalent of safe sex that will protect the patient, the penalty on medical workers who test positive may induce many of them not to test, even if they are altruists (it depends on their degree of altruism). In this situation, if testing positive is to be penalized the testing should be mandatory. But given the very small probability of transmission in this case, probably there should be no penalty.

Much of the analysis of mandatory testing in the previous section of this chapter could also be restated in terms of taxation, viewed of course as a regulatory rather than as a revenue-raising device. Mandatory testing operates as a tax on both altruists and egoists, but while it should induce some altruists to avoid unsafe sex (those who would not have tested voluntarily because of their aversion to the test, would not have used condoms because of their aversion to condoms, and who test positive under the regime of mandatory testing), it may induce many egoists to forgo safe sex. Subsidizing condoms is a fairly straightforward subsidy of safe sex, though not completely so, as we shall see in the next chapter. The corresponding tax on unsafe sex is not easy to devise, though we shall consider some possibilities shortly.

Criminal Punishment and Tort Liability

An important class of trade taxes involves the use of criminal or tort law to impose formal legal sanctions, whether fines, imprisonment, or orders to pay damages, on people who deliberately, recklessly, or carelessly expose others to a risk of infection, even if their risky behavior does not result in the transmission of the infection. This is to be contrasted with imposing criminal punishment or tort liability on persons who deliberately, recklessly, or carelessly infect others with the AIDS virus. The latter type of tax, a tax on the transmission of the disease itself, we call a *transmission* tax.

The three degrees of culpability—deliberate, reckless, careless—can be viewed, consistently with the economic analysis of intentional and nonintentional torts (Landes and Posner 1987, ch. 6), as different degrees of probability of an infective consequence of risky sex. Consider a simple economic model of negligence in which a person is negligent if and only if $C < PL$, where C is the cost of avoiding an accidental injury, P is the probability of the injury if avoidance is not undertaken, and L is the loss if the accident occurs. Obviously, the higher P and L are, other things being equal, the more likely the accident is to be adjudged negligent. L is very high in the AIDS setting, and P is higher the greater the likelihood that one is infected and one's partner is not.

Under conventional tort principles, which have been applied to other sexually transmitted diseases, m would be liable for battery if $P_m = 1$ (and m knew this but f did not) and $P_f < 1$.[21] Whether there is tort liability for merely negligent sexual transmission of a disease (that is, where m should but does not know that $P_m = 1$, or where P_m though smaller than 1 is substantial and, again, m should know this) remains unsettled (*Cornell Law Review* staff 1984; see also Schoenstein 1989), but probably there is liability (Gostin 1990). However, if the victim consented to risky sex knowing his partner's probability of being infected already, tort liability would be barred by the doctrine of assumption of risk. That may be the

---

21. See *Crowell v. Crowell*, 180 N.C. 516, 105 S.E. 206 (1920).

usual case where there is no fraud, so that liability for transmitting the AIDS virus may turn out to be very largely liability for deliberate concealment of risk—for battery rather than for negligence.

A transmission tax may seem a more discriminating form of taxation from the standpoint of minimizing the growth of the AIDS epidemic than a trade tax, since it avoids penalizing behavior that does no actual harm. Ever since Pigou, and notwithstanding Coase, the taxing of conduct that inflicts an external cost has been the economist's favorite remedy for negative externalities. Imposing sanctions on the knowing, reckless, or careless transmission of the AIDS virus can be viewed in this light. An obvious objection to relying heavily on what we are calling a transmission tax to control the disease, however, is that a person who is carrying the AIDS virus, and even more clearly one who has already converted to the active form of the disease, is already on death row. Threatening him with criminal or civil sanctions is unlikely to weigh heavily in his decisions. This is a form of the last-period problem discussed extensively in other areas of economics: If a person is about to leave the market anyway, exclusion from it is not an effective sanction.

The objection must not be overstated. Many people infected with the AIDS virus remain asymptomatic, in good or at least relatively good health, for a decade or more after becoming infected.[22] They should be no less deterrable by threat of imprisonment, fine, or tort damages than, say, a 70-year-old man whose life expectancy is 10 years. However, given the relatively low infectivity of the AIDS virus, a carrier is unlikely to infect another person immediately upon becoming infected himself. The other person, moreover, may not discover that he is infected for several years—often not until he converts to the active disease state. These lags, which are cumulative, together with normal delays in instituting and concluding legal proceedings, will not only reduce the interval between the imposition of punishment and the death by AIDS of the person punished; they will also create daunting problems of proof, such as the problem of proving that the infected person was infected by the defendant and not by someone else.

An attractive alternative is punishing not the act of transmission but the act of exposure. The punishment of exposure is a form of trade tax.

---

22. Recall that the median incubation period—the period between infection with HIV and conversion to full-blown AIDS—is about 10 years. However, serious although not life-threatening medical problems are apt to develop in the HIV carrier before this time, though this depends on precisely how AIDS is defined.

A number of states have made it a crime for a person who knows that he is infected with the AIDS virus to penetrate sexually another person without disclosing his infected status to that person.[23] Difficulties of proof (no greater, however, than in the case of rape, which is *unconsented-to* sexual intercourse) to one side, this strikes us as a sensible measure. Sweden has harsh sanctions (including quarantining—though this has been done to only seven persons) for exposing others to a risk of AIDS; the threat of these sanctions is said to deter voluntary testing. Sweden also has a very low rate of AIDS (see Henriksson and Ytterberg 1992, esp. p. 329), though this may also be related, as we shall see, to the lesser stigma attached to homosexual activities in Sweden than in most other countries, notably the United States, which has the highest rate of AIDS of any wealthy country. Within the framework of our analysis, the fact that exposure liability will discourage voluntary testing is not an objection.

Paradoxically, however, such liability both strengthens the case for local mandatory testing and weakens our analysis of voluntary testing. Exposure liability increases the cost to a person who knows he is an HIV carrier of engaging in risky sex. The more people who are tested, the larger will be the fraction of HIV carriers who know they are carriers, and hence, possibly, the fewer HIV carriers who will engage in risky sex (or risky needle-sharing). So the critical thing is the expected cost, to the HIV carrier who knows he is such, of exposure liability. Probably it is small. Unless records of test results are kept and made available to tort plaintiffs or to prosecutors, which because of concerns about privacy is unlikely, it would be difficult to prove that the carrier knew he was such because he had been tested and the result disclosed to him. Ordinarily it would not occur to anyone even to seek such proof until he, or someone, was suspected of having been infected by the carrier, and by then the carrier might be too far advanced in the disease to be effectively punishable either criminally or civilly. We doubt therefore whether exposure liability will have a large effect on the decision of a person who tests positive to desist from risky behavior, unless, as suggested in Chapter 3, knowledge of one's HIV-positive status might induce altruistic sexual behavior. All things considered, the prudent conclusion is that testing, whether voluntary or mandatory, is, unless universal or close to it, as likely to increase the spread of AIDS as to curtail it.

---

23. See, for example, Mich. Compiled Laws §333.5210 (1991). The parallel in tort law is knowingly, recklessly, or carelessly inflicting emotional distress by exposing one's sexual partner to HIV even if the partner does not become infected (Gostin 1990).

Additional Regulations and the Question of Stigma

Nothing in the preceding section should be taken to imply that effective sanctions for *refusing to test* under a regime of mandatory testing are infeasible. Most persons taking the test do not know whether they are HIV-positive—whether they are on death row—and therefore a sanction for refusing to take the test imposes an incremental cost. This is a form of trade tax. It shows that such taxes can alter behavior with respect to AIDS, although the particular tax in question (punishment for refusing to be tested) may alter behavior in an undesirable direction.

Other trade taxes might not have the perverse effects that a sanction for refusing to be tested might have. An example would be a tax on homosexual bathhouses. The punishment of trafficking in illegal drugs could be viewed in a similar light: by reducing the number of intravenous drug users, it would reduce the amount of needle-sharing and hence the spread of AIDS by drug users. Both examples involve complications, however, discussed in the next chapter.

Half the states of the United States retain laws against sodomy, usually understood to mean anal or oral intercourse between men. Were these laws actually enforced, the growth of the epidemic would be slowed. However, they are not enforced, and no one supposes they can be, consistent with civil liberties and public opinion (see generally Posner 1992, pp. 310, 344). Notice that from the standpoint of limiting the spread of AIDS, the laws are undiscriminating, in punishing oral intercourse as severely as anal intercourse, even though the former is much less likely to spread the disease, in punishing safe sex as well as risky sex, and in making no exception for long-term, monogamous homosexual cohabitations. Indeed, one can argue that far from criminalizing such cohabitations, states should authorize homosexual marriage in order to reduce the cost of (a form of) safe sex—and that the sodomy laws, if they have had any effect on AIDS at all, probably have increased the spread of the disease. We will return to this point.

Female prostitutes, because of their very large number of sex partners, have a high incidence of AIDS in countries in which many heterosexual males are HIV carriers. The United States is such a country by virtue of heavy intravenous drug use in some subpopulations; in addition, many U.S. prostitutes are intravenous drug users themselves. However, despite their high rate of infection, female prostitutes in the United States do not appear to be a significant source of infection for their sexual partners (as noted in the Introduction). If they were—as they are in the Third

World—this would be an argument for punishing prostitution more severely than is done at present, but not necessarily a powerful argument; many infected customers of prostitutes might be diverted to other women, whom they would infect. In contrast, male prostitutes, who like female prostitutes have a high rate of AIDS, may be important sources of transmission of HIV—not only to their customers (invariably male; there is virtually no demand by women for the services of prostitutes) but also to women, because many customers of male prostitutes are bisexuals (Morse et al. 1992). There is some evidence, however, that as "specialists" in sex, male prostitutes are more knowledgeable about the risk of AIDS than their customers and are relatively unlikely to engage in risky-sex activities with them (Pleak and Meyer-Bahlburg 1990, pp. 580, 582–583)—unless they are paid a risk premium (see Chapter 1).

Some counties in Nevada permit brothels, under license, and require frequent mandatory testing of the prostitutes employed in them. These 36 brothels are reported to have succeeded, through house rules requiring safe sex, in keeping their employees free of HIV (Campbell 1991; *Economist* staff 1991). Apparently the threat to fire any employee who tests positive, a threat backed up by frequent testing, which minimizes the cost to the employer of determining its employees' infection status, operates as a sufficiently high tax on risky sex to discourage them from practicing it. Not only are the prostitutes protected, but the brothels are prevented from becoming sources of infection. Insofar as men are diverted to these brothels from other sexual channels, their chances both for infecting (if they are HIV-positive) and for becoming infected (if they are HIV-negative) are reduced. Subsidizing these brothels might therefore be a method—a politically infeasible one, of course—of reducing the spread of AIDS.

The question whether to punish or test prostitutes is part of a larger issue: Are efforts to penalize forms of activity that generate large risks of AIDS, such as male homosexuality, intravenous drug use, and (in some circumstances) prostitution, a promising method of reducing the spread of the epidemic? In the case of prostitution, there would be high enforcement costs and also substitution to other risky—possibly riskier—forms of sex. The question is more difficult in the case of drug abuse, and we discuss this further in the next chapter. By reducing the amount of such abuse, punishment can be expected to reduce the amount of needle-sharing, viewed as a complement to such abuse—but at the same time it will increase the probability that such needle-sharing as does occur will be infective.

As for male homosexuality, if as seems likely homosexual orientation is for the most part innate and unalterable,[24] efforts to discourage homosexual activity, whether by stigmatizing it or by discriminating against homosexuals in employment or other activities, are unlikely to have much effect on the amount of the activity—and this quite apart from the enforcement problems that have made the sodomy laws a dead letter. Stigmatization and discrimination impose costs, but not costs so great as to deflect many people from attempting to satisfy their imperative sexual needs. On the contrary, as we implied in Chapter 2 in noting the hostility in the black and Hispanic communities toward homosexuals, stigmatization or discrimination could increase the spread of AIDS by increasing the incentives of homosexuals to conceal their homosexuality. Desire for concealment discourages homosexual men from joining gay organizations, which are important vehicles for dissemination of information concerning the risks of AIDS. Doll and colleagues (1991, p. 174) thus find a negative correlation between belonging to such an organization and engaging in unsafe sex. Desire for concealing one's homosexuality also impels many male homosexuals into (heterosexual) marriage (Ross 1983), which increases the danger that AIDS will spread through the heterosexual population, because these men continue to engage in homosexual activity. Desire for concealment might also induce homosexual men to dabble in heterosexual sex to establish their heterosexual credentials (see Doll et al. 1991b, p. 36) and might induce both heterosexual and homosexual men to avoid practicing safe (hetero)sex lest their practicing it be thought an acknowledgment that they consider themselves at risk of becoming infected with the AIDS virus, or of transmitting such infection, because of homosexual activity. For the same reason, it is true, a desire to conceal one's homosexual status may discourage one from testing, and this may actually reduce the spread of the disease. However, to encourage hostility toward homosexuals is an oblique and costly method of discouraging HIV testing, compared to simply stopping subsidizing it.

Entry Controls and International Trade in Risky Sex

Under existing law, aliens known to be HIV-positive are denied entry to the United States, while aliens who have been admitted and desire

---

24. Posner (1992, pp. 101–105, 295–299) reviews the evidence; see also Green (1992).

resident status (as opposed to aliens who visit the country for tourism or business) must undergo a medical examination that includes an HIV test, and if they test positive they are excluded (Wolchok 1989). Despite the many criticisms that have been leveled against these policies, they are more attractive from an economic standpoint than mandatory testing, though on balance they too are probably not cost-justified.[25]

With mandatory testing, no direct restriction is placed on the sexual activity of those who test positive, whereas HIV-positive persons barred from entering the United States are thereby rendered sexually inactive in this country. In effect, foreign countries are barred from exporting infected persons to the United States; the analogy is to the efforts of many nations (and some cities and states of the United States) to forbid the importation of toxic wastes and other economic "bads." As with many policies affecting international trade, whether this regulation of the international trade in sex is efficient may depend on whether the social welfare that is to be maximized is that of a particular country or that of the whole world. If the latter, one might wish to encourage HIV-infected persons to migrate to areas in which medical costs are low and the prevalence of HIV or AIDS high, so that the incremental effect of the HIV-positive immigrant will be minimized. Assuming, however, as is politically more realistic, that the relevant community whose welfare is to be maximized is limited to the United States, the cost to foreign countries, as well as to the excluded immigrants or visitors themselves (who might derive utility from entry into this country irrespective of medical costs or transmission probabilities), falls out of the picture, although there may be some costs to Americans who would have transacted with the infected foreigners (presumably nonsexually)[26] if entry had been permitted. Compared to mandatory testing, then, the benefits of excluding HIV-positive foreign visitors or immigrants—benefits that include the avoidance both of transmission risk and of medical costs for which the entrants might not have paid—are larger and the costs smaller.

It might seem that if HIV-positive homosexuals (say) are excluded from the United States, this will reduce the supply of potential sex part-

---

25. Like mandatory testing itself, they are a standard response to epidemics (Druhot 1986).

26. Americans, other than those already infected, who would have had sex with the HIV-positive entrants presumably are benefited by being prevented from encountering them.

ners to American homosexuals and may cause some of the latter to travel more abroad and, when doing so, to engage in greater sexual activity. As a result they may become infected, carry the virus back to the United States, and infect other Americans. But because potential entrants are demanders as well as suppliers of sex, it is unclear that keeping them out reduces the net availability of sexual partners to Americans.

As the prevalence of AIDS declines in this country, immigration and entry controls will become more; rather than, as one might think, less, economically attractive as a policy instrument. The more persons in a country who are infected, the smaller are the disease costs of allowing the entry of foreign visitors, since those who are HIV-positive will be only a small fraction of the total sources of infection to the country's uninfected population. If the disease were totally eliminated among the native population, however, the benefits from excluding all HIV-positive visitors might be very great: might be equal, in fact, to the costs of a restarted epidemic. The analogy is to England's strict policy of quarantining animals brought into the country. Because England is rabies-free the potential disease cost created by even one unquarantined animal is high, as it would not be in the United States, where rabies is already widespread among the animal population. The analogy suggests that the time to have imposed a ban on immigration by HIV-positive persons was at the outset of the AIDS epidemic.[27]

This analysis is helpful in evaluating Cuba's draconian program. When it was instituted, the prevalence of AIDS and HIV infection in Cuba was very low. The major costs of such a program—the disutility of the persons interned—are minimized when prevalence is low, while the benefits in protecting the uninfected are maximized. However, the program imposes disutility not only on the (few) persons interned, but also on the many persons who would prefer to assume the risks of risky sex rather than to be tested. So here is an argument for foreign countries that have a low prevalence of AIDS to test visitors from the United States, which has a high prevalence!

All this said, there is a very powerful, and perhaps conclusive, objection, unrelated to the stage of the epidemic, to the imposition of *comprehensive* entry controls by a country such as the United States that millions of people visit each year as tourists or business travelers. The objection is cost: not so much the cost of the test itself—the United States could

---

27. In countries where AIDS is rare, foreigners may be an important source of infection (see Isomura and Mizogami 1992).

require each visitor to pay the cost of having an HIV test, as Illinois did with applicants for marriage licenses—but the fact that, given the aversion of many people to HIV testing (even at zero pecuniary cost to them), requiring the test would cause a substantial diminution in the flow of foreign tourists and business travelers to the United States, to the detriment of its economy. This cost could be reduced by not requiring proof of HIV-negative status and instead relying on criminal penalties to deter the entry of people who know they are carrying the virus. But the benefits would be slight, since most entrants would not know their HIV status.

The number of immigrants is much smaller than the number of tourists and other temporary visitors, and both the risk of their infecting Americans and their expected cost to welfare programs such as Medicaid are greater because their average duration here is longer. The benefit-cost ratio of testing, and of exclusion of those who test positive, is therefore higher in the case of immigrants. This is not to say that it equals or exceeds 1. Immigration of HIV carriers may not increase the incidence of AIDS in this country significantly, because such immigration, by raising the prevalence of the disease initially, will induce greater substitution of safe for risky sex. This is one more example of how attention to the possibility of behavioral responses to the epidemic can reverse strong intuitions concerning the effect of public intervention.

Thus far in discussing immigration we have focused on the exclusion of people who are HIV-positive. But the point about behavioral response to immigration of HIV carriers implies that such a focus is too narrow. If all carriers can be identified and kept out, so that all immigrants are free from infection, the immediate effect will be to reduce the prevalence of HIV infection in this country and thus the riskiness of unsafe sex. The sexually active population will respond, however, by reducing its demand for safe sex, and that effect will be greater the higher the number of uninfected immigrants. The result will be a higher incidence of AIDS, or in epidemiological terms a longer delay in the epidemic's reaching saturation. Thus, at least from the narrow standpoint of disease control, admitting a large number of HIV-negative immigrants might be worse than admitting a few HIV carriers!

CHAPTER 6

Subsidies Designed to Change Behavior

In this chapter we analyze two types of subsidy aimed at retarding the spread of AIDS. The first is education in the dangers of AIDS and in ways of avoiding becoming infected with the AIDS virus. Because there is as yet no vaccine or cure for AIDS, thus leaving behavioral change as the only feasible means of prevention, AIDS education has been said to be "among the government's chief public health priorities" (Gostin 1989, p. 1624). We interpret public expenditures on education about AIDS as subsidization of the demand for information relating to the disease and show that, because the disease itself is the key determinant of the demand for such information, subsidization is unlikely to and probably does not in fact affect knowledge about the disease and hence behavioral responses to it.

The second type of subsidy that we discuss in this chapter is the subsidization of goods or services, such as condoms, clean needles, and HIV testing and counseling, that are believed to be complements of safe sex.[1] Subsidies for medical research are discussed in the next chapter. Subsidies for HIV testing and counseling need not detain us; if the analysis in Chapter 3 is sound, such subsidies are as likely to increase as to reduce the incidence of AIDS.

---

1. One good or service is a "complement" of another when a fall in the price of the one causes an increase in the demand for the other. A blackboard is a complement of chalk and a clean hypodermic needle is (with a qualification to be noted later) a complement of intravenous drug use.

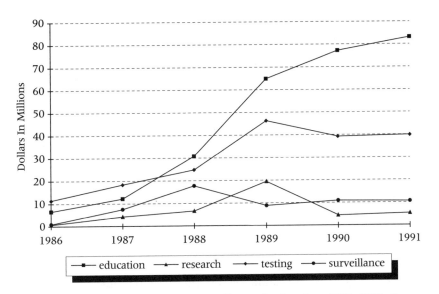

Figure 6-1 Annual total state AIDS expenditures, by function, 1986–1991. *Source:* AIDS Policy Center, Intergovernmental Health Policy Project, George Washington University.

Publicly Financed Education about AIDS and Its Prevention

We distinguish between programs aimed at educating medical professionals and those aimed at educating the lay public, and focus on the latter. They include sending pamphlets on AIDS to all households in a state (or the nation—as the U.S. Public Health Service did in 1988), targeting high-risk groups such as drug addicts and male homosexuals with information about AIDS and its prevention, and teaching AIDS awareness and prevention in schools and colleges (Bush and Boller 1991; Gostin 1989; Turner et al. 1989, ch. 4; Quam and Ford 1990). Advertising in the mass media has been employed, as well as direct-mail advertising and classroom instruction. Aggregate annual expenditures, federal and state, for these programs exceed $700 million (U.S. Congress 1991; Rowe and Ryan 1988, p. 427 [tab. 3]). Figure 6-1 shows the rapid growth of these expenditures on the state level, where they now dominate all other categories of state expenditures on AIDS other than medical treatment itself.[2]

---

2. The source of the data for this figure is volume 4 of the *Intergovernmental AIDS Reports,* published by the Intergovernmental Health Policy Project of George Washington Univer-

To simplify analysis, we take as given a goal of reducing the incidence of AIDS, so that the "efficiency" of public expenditures on education about AIDS is assessed relative to that goal rather than to an "economic" goal such as utility maximization. And we accept the possibility that education in disease risk could reduce the incidence of unhealthy or risky behavior.[3] Even with these assumptions it does not follow that public expenditures on AIDS education are economically justified; and if they are, a question would still remain concerning how the expenditures should be allocated across subpopulations, whether defined geographically (for example, states or cities) or otherwise, to maximize the impact of the expenditures. The "where" and the "how much" issues are related because an inefficient allocation across subpopulations makes it less likely that educational expenditures will have the desired effect on behavior.

Public education about AIDS is intended to subsidize the acquisition of accurate information. Some people (homosexual physicians, for example) are already well informed about the dangers of AIDS and the means of protecting against them (Klein et al. 1987). Further expenditures on educating them about AIDS would have no effect on their behavior. Other people are not well informed. Although by now most people in this country know the main methods by which the AIDS virus is transmitted, many do not know how great (or small) the risk posed by the various methods of transmission is or what they can do to reduce the risk to themselves. According to one study, as of 1987, 92 percent of the public knew that the AIDS virus could be transmitted by sexual intercourse with a person infected with the virus, but only 80 percent knew that condoms are effective in preventing infection (Institute of

---

sity in Washington, D.C. We have not been able to obtain the data necessary to create a comparable time series of federal expenditures.

3. Evidence that it can is extensive. See, for example, Atkinson and Skegg (1973); Papaevangelou et al. (1988); Dwyer, Viney, and Jones (1991); Ellickson et al. (1988); Haaga, Scott, and Hawes-Dawson (1992); Wenger et al. (1991); and Warner (1977, 1989). For skepticism about the efficacy of AIDS education, see Dannemeyer and Franc (1989), and of education in healthy styles of living generally, see Tolley et al. (1992); Kenkel (1991); and Zeckhauser and Shepard (1976). More optimistic views about the efficacy of AIDS education are expressed in Ostrow (1989) and in Hinman (1991). We return to the issue of efficacy later in the chapter. Special education in disease or accident risk must be distinguished from general education, which may reduce that risk by reducing the costs to individuals of assimilating information (Leigh 1990).

Medicine 1988). As late as 1989, 11 percent of the public thought that the virus could be transmitted by a toilet seat and 16 percent by a drinking glass (Gallup Poll 1989, p. 15), and as late as 1990, 16 percent believed that it could be transmitted by insects and 32 percent were unaware that a person could be an HIV carrier and yet look and feel healthy (Centers for Disease Control 1992b).

A model of the demand for information about AIDS and of the effect of a subsidy. Risky sex has two possible outcomes: infection and noninfection. The expected utility of risky sex lies between the utility of each outcome. A person who is informed about safe sex can raise his expected utility by eliminating the bad outcome (unsafe sex with an infected person), but at some cost, since safe sex is less pleasurable than unsafe and the information itself may be costly (in time and effort) to obtain. If AIDS is rare in the population from which a person draws his sexual partners, the greater utility, net of disease risk, of unsafe sex than of safe sex may exceed the value of information in enabling him to reduce disease risk; in fact that value may be very low. This is one reason why many persons who are well informed about the dangers of AIDS (for example, highly educated persons who have had a monogamous heterosexual relationship for many years) engage in unprotected sex. As the prevalence of AIDS in the population from which one's sexual partners are drawn rises, the demand for information about safe sex will increase to a point at which a subsidy may induce a shift from unsafe to safe sex. When the prevalence of AIDS reaches a *very* high level, however, the subsidy may become redundant (and therefore change no one's behavior) because the high prevalence generates in the relevant population a high *private* demand for the information.

More formally, a person considering whether to have sex with another person faces two uncertainties: P, his subjective probability that the other person is or is not infected (p, for positive, versus n for negative) with the AIDS virus; and Q, his subjective probability that an objectively unsafe sexual practice (u in our notation, versus s for safe), such as unshielded anal intercourse, is indeed unsafe. Let b (for bad) and g (for good) denote the two possible consequences of an objectively unsafe practice, so that with full information u would be regarded as b with probability Q of 1. And let $U(a,i,q)$ be the utility of engaging in activity a ($= u$ or s) with a partner of infection status i ($= p$ or n) and an objective quality of the activity q ($= b$ or g). Then the expected utility to an uninformed or imperfectly informed person—EU_N (that is, a person for whom $Q < 1$)—of engaging in unsafe sex is

(6.1) $EU_N(P) = (1 - P)[QU(u,n,b) + (1 - Q)U(u,n,g)]$

$+ P[QU(u,p,b) + (1 - Q)U(u,p,g)].$

The first term on the right-hand side of the equation is the probability that one's partner is negative $(1 - P)$ multiplied by one's subjective utility of engaging in the objectively unsafe (though actually harmful only if one's partner is HIV-positive)[4] activity, u. The second term is the subjective utility of engaging in the objectively unsafe activity under the alternative possibility that one's partner is HIV-positive.

A person who learns that a particular practice can transmit AIDS (that is, that u is b) is assumed to choose safe over unsafe sex. The expected utility of being informed (EU_I) is, therefore,

(6.2) $EU_I(P) = (1 - P)[QU(s,n,b) + (1 - Q)U(u,n,g)]$

$+ P[QU(s,p,b) + (1 - Q)U(u,p,g)].$

The difference between the two utility functions is the expected gain from being informed (equivalently, the value of the information):

(6.3) $EU_I(P) - EU_N(P) = PG_p + (1 - P)L_n.$

In this equation, $G_p = [(1 - Q)(U(s,p,b) - U(u,p,b))]$ denotes the gain in utility from switching to safe sex when one learns that unsafe sex is indeed dangerous (b) and one's partner turns out to be HIV-positive. $L_n = [Q(U(s,n,b) - U(u,n,b))]$ denotes the loss in utility from switching to safe sex when one learns that u is dangerous, but, because one's partner is negative, there is a loss (measured by one's aversion to safe sex) from switching in this instance.

If c is the cost of acquiring this information, an individual will desire to be informed if $EU_I(P) - EU_N(P) > c$, and hence if $PG_p + (1 - P)L_n > c$. This is illustrated in Figures 6-2 through 6-4, which represent expected utility levels of safe and unsafe sex as functions of the probability of

---

4. And even then, since the probability of infection from unprotected sex with an infected person is less than 1, not all such sex is *really* harmful. We ignore this irrelevant complication.

infection. The horizontal line represents safe sex (*s*). Figure 6-2 shows the expected utility of unsafe sex (*u*), if one is not informed, as a function of the probability of infection. That expected utility is a weighted average (dependent on *Q*) of the expected utilities of two states of the world—a higher if *u* is *g* and a lower if it is *b*.

Figure 6-3 illustrates the expected utility of sex, both safe and unsafe, on the assumption that information about the dangers of AIDS is costless. The kink results from the fact that, if *P* is very low, knowledge that unshielded sex is potentially dangerous will not cause the individual to choose safe sex, while as soon as *P* reaches the point at which the fully informed person switches to safe sex, further increases in *P* have no effect on his utility, because he is protected against infection by having switched.

Figure 6-4, a composite of the previous two figures, shows the net gain from being informed, at a cost of *c*, as a function of *P*. At P_0 the individual is indifferent between being informed or not; more precisely,

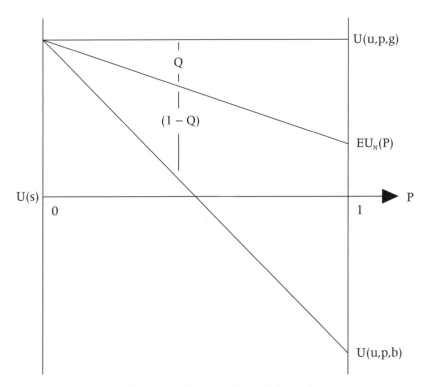

Figure 6-2 Expected utility of unsafe sex to the uninformed.

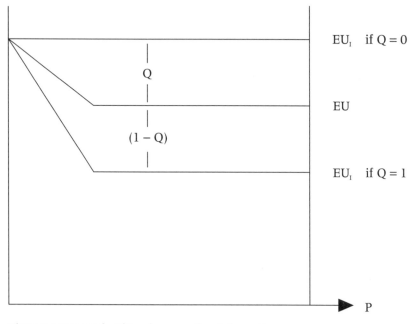

Figure 6-3 Expected utility of sex: costless information.

his expected utility of sex is the same whether or not he is informed. To the left of that point, where *P* is lower, the cost of information exceeds the benefit. To the right, where *P* is higher, the benefit exceeds the cost. Thus the demand for information is monotonically increasing in the probability of infection of one's sexual partner; that is, *every* increase in the probability of infection increases the demand for information.

Figure 6-5 brings us to the heart of our analysis. It illustrates the effects of a subsidy $s < c$ on the demand for information and, through the effect on information, on sexual behavior. The figure is the same as Figure 6-4 except that now the expected utility of being informed is uniformly greater because of the subsidy. As a result of the increase in expected utility, the point at which people are indifferent between being informed and uninformed shifts to the left (to P_s); that is, they become indifferent between these states at a lower probability of infection.

Figure 6-5 demonstrates that the marginal effect of an education subsidy on the demand for information is not monotonic (that is, not continuously increasing) in the probability of infection. Only the behavior of individuals in region $[P_s, P_0]$ is affected by the subsidy. Individuals with

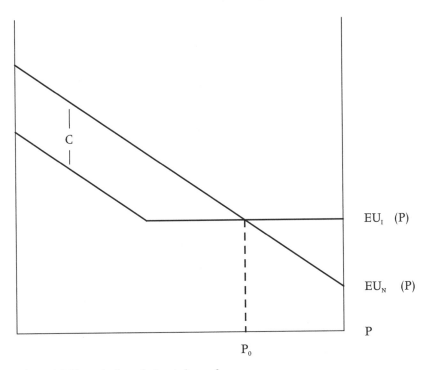

Figure 6-4 Net gain from being informed.

lower risk than P_s are not affected because even though the information is now cheaper, it does not have sufficient value for them to demand it. There is also no effect on individuals with higher risk than P_0, because they would demand the information even if it were not subsidized. So expenditures on AIDS education targeted either on sexually conservative heterosexual married couples, or on the homosexual community in San Francisco, may be wasted because these expenditures are unlikely to alter sexual behavior.[5] (For evidence, see Calsyn et al. 1992.)

The effect of a high risk of AIDS in inducing people to become better informed about that risk is one more example of the self-limiting character of a disease transmitted by voluntary behavior, once rational behav-

---

5. A similar point is made in Siegel, Weinstein, and Fineberg (1991). For a striking example of ignorance about AIDS in a low-prevalence area, see Keeter and Bradford (1988). For evidence that knowledge of AIDS varies between low- and high-prevalence cities in the direction predicted by our analysis, see St. Lawrence et al. (1989) and the first row of our Table 2-1 (in Chapter 2), which is drawn from the St. Lawrence study.

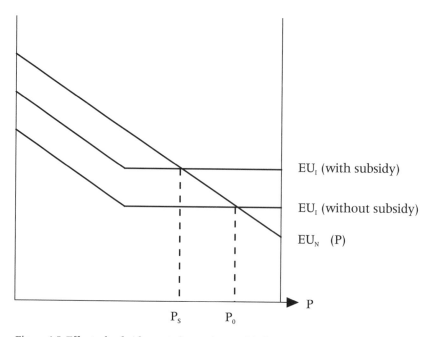

Figure 6-5 Effect of subsidy on information and behavior.

ioral response is allowed for. And maybe not so rational: the effect of high risk in limiting incidence by increasing the demand for information about risk and prevention is actually magnified if, as the empirical studies that we mentioned in Chapter 2 suggest, people who know an AIDS victim are—irrationally—less likely to engage in risky sex than people who do not know one. The greater the prevalence of the disease in an area, the more likely are people in the area to know at least one AIDS victim.

The optimal allocation across risk groups. Although our model casts doubt on the intuitive proposition that public expenditures for AIDS education should be concentrated in high-risk subpopulations, as well as on any suggestion that they should be concentrated in low-risk ones instead, it would be equally premature to conclude that such expenditures should be concentrated in subpopulations that are at intermediate risk. That would require assuming that all persons in high-risk populations were equally well informed. If there are any uninformed people in the high-risk group, the limited effects of education concentrated on that group in terms of the number of persons whose behavior is likely to be altered would still have to be traded off against the benefit, in reducing the spread of an epidemic, from changing the behavior of a small number, all of whom, however, are at high risk of getting (and then transmitting) the disease. But if the high-risk population is already nearly saturated with the disease, and if members of that population do not engage in risky trades with other populations, the infecting of the few remaining noninfected persons will not result in substantial further growth of the disease.

The best approach, therefore, might be, if feasible, to target educational expenditures on (1) the uninformed members of (2) intermediate-risk groups. So maybe the encouragement of AIDS education in schools is preferable to mailings to every household in the nation, advertisements in the mass media, or mailings or other educative efforts targeted on members of high-risk groups. Teenagers are more likely than either the population at large or the high-risk population to be in the intermediate-risk group *and,* independently of that fact, to be relatively uninformed.[6] Recall (from note 3 in this chapter, and also from Chapter 2) that general education appears to enhance awareness of disease risks. Many teenagers have not completed their general education. An educational campaign may also be more effective when directed toward a group (the young) that is not yet habituated to the practices that the campaign seeks to change. But this argument can easily be turned around: education is needed more if the barriers to behavioral change are greater, and also if the targets of the educational campaign have more to unlearn, having acquired much of their knowledge about an activity at a time when it was regarded as safe (Viscusi 1991).

When AIDS education cannot be finely targeted on the uninformed in an intermediate-risk (or high-risk but not saturated) region, the marginal product of a dollar spent on providing such education will be higher, the larger the fraction of uninformed persons in the region. But this is true only up to a point, for there are likely to be sharply diminishing returns to such expenditures. Through its effect in inducing a reduction in risky sex, an education subsidy reduces the size of the population at risk, so further expenditures have less effect on the infection rate. In the limiting case, if the subsidy drove the probability of infection to zero,

---

6. For empirical evidence of this, see Huszti, Clopton, and Mason (1989); Hingson, Strunin, and Berlin (1990); and Kraft, Bostic, and Tallent (1990). However, the first of these studies expresses skepticism about the effectiveness of AIDS education targeted on teenagers.

further expenditures on AIDS education would be worthless unless there were a danger of the epidemic restarting. And long before the probability of infection fell to zero, the subsidy would cease to have any effect for a different reason: it would drive the AIDS risk down so far that people would not switch to safe sex even if fully informed of the risk, because the cost of safe sex would exceed the slight benefit. Thus to be effective the education subsidy would have to increase over time because more and more money would have to be spent in order to alter behavior as risk fell.

The optimal second-best policy toward public education about AIDS (if expenditures cannot be targeted on the uninformed, which would be best) requires allocating educational expenditures across regions in such a way as to equalize the marginal reduction in HIV infection; otherwise total reduction could be increased by a reallocation. Obviously, other things being equal, more funds should be allocated to more populous areas. As for the cost of education, which will vary from region to region with such factors as the general education level of the population, extra dollars spent on less easily educable persons will probably be more productive because without the additional expenditure these persons would not become informed, while the highly educated may be educable about AIDS at less or even zero expenditure of public funds. Some persons, it is true, may be so difficult to educate that the added dollars are wasted. Evidence that the first effect dominates, however, is found in a survey of persons who received the Public Health Service's nationwide mailing of an AIDS brochure in 1988. College graduates were less than half as likely as non–college graduates to report that they learned a "great deal" or "quite a lot" from the brochure (Gallup Poll 1988).

Is public AIDS education cost-justified? Even if the problem of efficient allocation of expenditures, across different areas and populations, on educating the public about AIDS were solved, there would be reasons for skepticism about the likely efficacy of such expenditures. First, the general efficacy of government campaigns to dissuade people from unhealthy practices has yet to be clearly established (cf. note 3). Too many studies of the effects of AIDS education fail to correct for other sources of information besides the government, measure success by increased ability to answer questions about AIDS correctly rather than by altered behavior, or examine only near-term behavioral effects. Since, however, many of the same sexual practices increase both pregnancy risk and the risk of sexually transmitted diseases, the finding in a recent multivariate study that sex education in schools reduces teenagers' pregnancies by almost 6 percent is some evidence that AIDS education might succeed in reducing the incidence of HIV infection (Evans, Oates, and Schwab 1992).

Second, like other government endeavors, government information programs are apt to be deflected from the optimal path by political pressures. Under pressure from moral conservatives, who want to raise the perceived cost of nonmarital intercourse and reduce awareness of what they consider deviant sexual practices, publicly supported AIDS education programs tend to emphasize abstinence over condom use and the risks of vaginal intercourse over those of anal intercourse.[7] Not only does this emphasis reduce the efficacy of the programs in conveying information likely to be actually used to reduce the risk of transmitting the virus; but if the public realizes that government education programs are distorted by political pressures, the programs will lack credibility.

Third, to assume as we have thus far that AIDS education has a negative effect on the demand for unsafe sex and therefore on the growth of the epidemic may be false. We saw in Chapter 3 that the acquisition of information about disease risk can actually increase the demand for unsafe sex. Could that be the case here? A central aspect of AIDS-education programs is informing people about the probability of becoming infected if they engage in particular practices. The danger varies from region to region, subgroup to subgroup, practice to practice. Heterosexuals may overestimate the danger of transmission through vaginal intercourse. Homosexuals may underestimate the efficacy of condoms. In addition to the earlier examples of exaggerated beliefs in the infectivity of the virus, we note that more than 25 percent of the respondents in a large 1989 survey of persons 18 years of age and older thought there was a significant danger of getting AIDS from "shaking hands, touching, or kissing on the cheek someone who has AIDS" (Hardy 1990). The more that people exaggerate the infectivity of the AIDS virus, the more prone they will be (up to a point—an important qualification, as we shall see) to avoid even low-risk, but not safe, sexual activities. In that event, full, truthful information, by dispelling some of the perceived risks of risky sex, will *reduce* the demand for safe sex. A pamphlet published by the Centers for Disease Control states, for example, that "regardless

---

7. Moral conservatives in the Christian tradition have since the Middle Ages been reluctant even to allude, in public, to deviant sexual practices, lest people be made aware of possibilities for sexual enjoyment that they hadn't thought of on their own (Posner 1992, pp. 49–50).

of what you have heard, the AIDS virus is easily avoided" (Centers for Disease Control 1991a). Over time people have in fact become less fearful of low-risk activities, as well as more fearful of high-risk ones. For example, between 1987 and 1989 the percentage of people who believe that you can get AIDS from a toilet seat fell from 18 percent to 11 percent, while the percentage who believe that you can get it from vaginal intercourse rose from 88 to 95 percent (Gallup Poll 1989, p. 16). A study of the impact of the Public Health Service's 1988 nationwide mailing of an AIDS brochure found that it *reduced* people's feelings of being personally at risk from AIDS (Snyder 1991).

Now consider regional differences. The lower the prevalence of AIDS, the lower is the risk of infection from unsafe sex and hence the smaller the benefits of safe sex. Before the educational program, people in low-prevalence regions may exaggerate the danger of infection and hence the benefits of safe sex. A truthful educational program may cause them to reduce their estimate of those benefits and as a result induce them to practice safe sex *less* frequently than before. A fraudulent program, which exaggerated the risks of unsafe sex, would be a possibility, but it would be very costly, since it would undermine the credibility of all government informational activities. Other objections to scare tactics are that they may convince some people that they already *are* infected and might as well drop precautions, and that by obscuring the *relative* safety of different sexual practices they may shift some people from relatively safe to completely unsafe practices. People falsely persuaded that oral sex is as dangerous as anal sex may decide to continue with the latter. People persuaded by moral conservatives that only abstinence is safe may, thinking that abstinence and risky sex are the only alternatives, choose the latter.

At the same time that people in low-risk classes learn that the risk is lower than they believed and increase their consumption of risky sex, however, people in high-risk classes learn that the risk is higher than they believed and may reduce their consumption of risky sex. Why "may"? Because, as we mentioned in discussing scare tactics, a person who learns that he is in a high-risk group will increase his estimate of his own probability of being infected as well as that of potential sex partners, and we know that the demand for risky sex is an increasing function of one's own perceived probability of being infected. Recall Figure 1-1: an increase in one's own perceived probability of being infected will enlarge the upper right-hand shaded area in the figure, which is an area in which both partners prefer risky to safe sex. Recall too that under certain assumptions, if the perceived probability of being infected already exceeds 50 percent, further increases in that perceived probability may increase the demand for risky sex.

We are assuming a particular distribution of misestimations of the AIDS menace: high risks are underestimated, low risks exaggerated. (If both types of risk were exaggerated, an AIDS education program would be truly perverse.) This assumption is plausible; it is not inconsistent with the normal assumptions of economics about rational behavior; and it is supported by research on other diseases (Viscusi 1985, 1990) as well as on AIDS itself (Capilouto et al. 1992; Schneiderman and Kaplan 1992), and by the Gallup Poll data on beliefs regarding toilet seats and vaginal intercourse. When people learn of the existence of a new disease, but do not yet have good information about the probability of becoming infected by it, they will, as rational persons, ascribe some kind of average probability to it. If the true probability is extremely low, as is the risk of AIDS to many persons, the subjective probability ascribed on the basis of inadequate information will tend to be higher than the true probability, and additional information will cause these persons to lower their subjective probability of becoming infected. For persons at high risk, the true probability of infection will tend to lie above the ascribed probability, and additional information will cause them to raise the latter. This, by the way, is a reason, though not a conclusive one, for concentrating educational expenditures in high-risk populations. Few members of those populations will *overestimate* the risk of infection, while some will underestimate it.

The foregoing analysis casts doubt on a program of indiscriminate public education about AIDS, but not necessarily on a program limited to high-risk populations. However, another reason for skepticism about AIDS education is that there is a private demand for and supply[8] of information about the disease, and one expects that demand to increase with the prevalence of the disease. Especially in high-prevalence areas, therefore, public expenditures on the dissemination of AIDS information may increase the level of information only slightly as public resources are substituted for private resources in the supply of the information. The substitution will not be complete; we may assume that incomplete property rights in information, or other sources of market failure, prevent

---

8. The mass media are important sources of information about AIDS (Price and Hsu 1992, p. 31; Edgar, Hammond, and Freimuth 1989), as are physicians and other health workers, and word of mouth.

the private market in information from supplying the socially optimal amount of information about the dangers of AIDS. (This issue is examined in a different context in the next chapter.) But public subsidization of such information may have little net effect where private demand is brisk. Thus, although the anti-smoking "campaign" of the last three decades has been shown in careful studies to have reduced the consumption of cigarettes markedly (Schneider, Klein, and Murphy 1981; Warner 1977, 1989), very little of that campaign was publicly financed. The Surgeon General's declarations concerning the dangers of smoking received wide publicity without the aid of public expenditures, although the cost to the industry of forcing cigarette companies to advertise the dangers of smoking should be counted as a public expenditure.[9] The dangers of AIDS have received and continue to receive *enormous* media attention (Brown 1992)—far more, surely, than the dangers of cigarette smoking have ever received. To recur to a point made in Chapter 5, the benefits of public efforts at AIDS prevention may be largely exhausted in the surveillance and reporting activities of the Centers for Disease Control (and its parent agency, the Public Health Service), activities that are amplified, elaborated, and disseminated, at no public expense, by the media, the medical profession, family, and friends.[10]

So despite widespread complaints that not enough is being spent on public education about AIDS (see, for example, Griffin 1992), the hundreds of millions of dollars being spent every year not only may be excessive from the standpoint of economic efficiency but may have little or no incremental effect on the incidence of AIDS. We do not wish to overstate our point. To the extent that public expenditures merely replace private expenditures, the social costs of the public program are reduced, since the reduction in private expenditures is a social saving. And the case for public education about AIDS is not uniformly weak. We have already mentioned teenagers. In addition, some subpopulations that are at high risk from AIDS (blacks and Hispanics, for example—and many of them are teenagers too)[11] may be uninformed about that risk because they have high costs of information as a result of poor education and

---

9. It is another example of an internal subsidy. See note 20 in Chapter 4.

10. On the role of the Centers for Disease Control in the detection of AIDS and the early dissemination of information about AIDS to the medical community, see Panem (1988, pp. 7–13).

11. See the references in Chapter 2; see also Aruffo, Coverdale, and Vallbona (1991).

other factors. Nonwhites in the Gallup Poll cited earlier were more likely than whites to overestimate the riskiness of low-risk activities and underestimate the riskiness of high-risk activities (Gallup Poll 1989, p. 15). With regard to these subpopulations, all but one of the factors discussed in this chapter that favor public education in the risk of AIDS line up on one side: high prevalence that makes the benefits of switching to safe sex (and hence of education in safe sex) great and minimizes the possibility that the risk of AIDS is at present overestimated; uninformed target population; low general level of education of the target population; minimum public-private substitution effect. The last three points counteract, for these subpopulations, the self-limiting effect of AIDS in generating information about risky and safe sex.

As with most policy proposals regarding AIDS, however, only qualified endorsement is possible. Disregarding the saturation issue, the possibility that some persons are not educable at reasonable cost, and the fact that an increase in one's own probability of being infected will (other things being equal) increase one's demand for risky sex unless one is an altruist, we recall from Chapter 2 that even well-informed, fully rational poor persons may choose to gamble with their health or safety or may apply a heavy discount rate to the costs of AIDS; in either event, they may not respond to expenditures on AIDS education. At least this is so if the focus of these expenditures is on conveying information rather than on altering attitude and life style by trying to make risky sex "uncool." Although attempts to alter preferences might seem even less likely to be effective than efforts to repair deficits in information, there is some evidence that adolescents' attitudes toward drugs and cigarettes can be altered by providing them with suitable role models (Ellickson et al. 1988), and perhaps the same is true with respect to their attitudes toward sex without condoms. However, contrary evidence is the unexpected failure of basketball star Earvin "Magic" Johnson's well-publicized announcement of his HIV status, and his efforts (including the publication of a paperback book aimed at his fans, *What You Can Do to Avoid AIDS*) at increasing awareness of the disease, to stimulate condom sales (*Wall Street Journal* staff 1992).

Empirical implications. We can estimate whether the existing allocation of AIDS-education expenditures across states is efficient by regressing expenditures per state on three regional variables: population, level of general education (proxied by the percentage of high school graduates), and AIDS prevalence. For the pattern to be efficient, the coefficient of the first variable should be positive and of the second negative. The third either should be positive or, more likely, should describe an inverted U shape. We have estimated two regressions, one of federal expenditures by state on AIDS education, and one of state expenditures on AIDS education. Our independent variables are the cumulative total of AIDS cases per state (a measure of prevalence), population per state, and percentage of the state's population to have completed college. The results of these regressions, presented in Table 6-1, do not support the hypothesis that public expenditures on AIDS education are being allocated efficiently across states.

In both regressions, the coefficient of the education variable is both positive and significant, which is inconsistent with the hypothesis that expenditures on AIDS education are being allocated efficiently. In the state regression, the population variable has the correct sign, but is not significant at the conventional 5 percent level; it is, however, positive and strongly significant in the federal regression. The variable representing the stock of AIDS cases is positive in both regressions but significant only in the state one. Thus, federal allocation seems more strongly influenced by population, state allocation by prevalence. A possible interpretation of this finding is proposed in Chapter 8; for now the significant point is that efficiency considerations seem not to explain the allocation of public expenditures for education about AIDS. Notice the high percentage of variance (R^2) explained by the regression equation despite the small number of variables.

Table 6-1 Regressions of AIDS education expenditures (*t*-statistics in parentheses)[a]

Dependent variable	Independent variables			
	Cumulative cases	Educational attainment	Population	R^2
State expenditures	1,427 (4.49)	119,743 (2.03)	.09798 (0.96)	.74
Federal expenditures	238.6 (1.70)	123,043 (4.73)	.17558 (4.07)	.79

a. The *t*-statistic is the ratio of the coefficient of a variable to its standard error. A *t*-statistic greater than 1.96 indicates that there is a 5 percent or less probability that the sign of the coefficient (that is, whether it is positive or negative) is due merely to chance. Details of the regression analyses in this chapter are available from the authors on request.

Another test of efficient allocation of expenditures on public AIDS education, but one we have not conducted, is whether educational expenditures targeted on the uninformed, as distinct from indiscriminate expenditures, such as on media advertising, tend to be concentrated in high-prevalence areas. With such targeting, the benefit from switching to safe sex (which is greater in such areas) will tend to dominate the benefit from educating a population a high percentage of which may already be informed, at least if the problem of saturation is disregarded. AIDS education in public schools may, as suggested earlier, be an example of such a targeted expenditure and thus enable this test to be conducted.

More fundamental than the question of efficient allocation across regions or groups is whether public expenditures on AIDS education are affecting the level of knowledge about AIDS at all. The next three tables examine this question. In Table 6-2, AIDS awareness per state, as determined in a recent nationwide survey (Centers for Disease Control 1991b), is regressed on the same measure of educational attainment as in Table 6-1, on the per capita number of cumulative AIDS cases in the state, on state expenditures on AIDS education the previous year, and on federal expenditures on such education the previous year. The survey used a number of awareness variables. We used the one that seemed most significant from the standpoint of disease control: whether it is possible to be infected by a person who appears to be in good health. (The answer, of course, is yes.) An even better variable might be *changes* in AIDS awareness over time, rather than *levels* of awareness at a point in time; but the necessary time-series data are not available on a state-by-state basis.

The educational-attainment variable has the expected positive sign and is highly statistically significant, implying that the more educated

Table 6-2 Regression of AIDS awareness on public education expenditures and other variables, 1991 (*t*-statistics in parentheses)

Educational attainment	Cumulative cases per capita	State expenditures	Federal expenditures	R^2
.6841	79.25	.000000571	.000000207	.31
(3.77)	(0.45)	(1.82)	(−2.99)	

the population of a state is, the more it knows about AIDS.[12] The variable representing state educational expenditures has the right sign and is almost significant, but not quite, while the federal variable, although statistically significant, has the wrong sign—implying that raising federal expenditures on AIDS education *lowers* public knowledge of AIDS![13]

A weakness of the regression in Table 6-2 is that it uses *current* education expenditures, thus disregarding the fact that expenditures on education may yield a benefit in future years (as is implicit in models that treat education as creating human capital). We are unable to obtain federal AIDS education expenditures per state for any years before 1990, but we do have data on state expenditures per state from 1986 (Figure 6-1), and in Table 6-3 we substitute cumulative 1986–1990 state data, depreciated at an annual rate of 20 percent, for the corresponding state data in Table 6-2. We also add another dependent variable—a measure of ignorance rather than knowledge: the fraction of the state's population that believes that the AIDS virus can be transmitted through insect bites.

With this adjustment, a larger amount (56 percent versus 31 percent) of the variance in the awareness equation across observations is explained, and the positive coefficient of the state-expenditures variable approaches a little closer to, but still does not reach, statistical significance at the conventional 5 percent level. However, in the "unawareness" equation, although the state-expenditures variable has the

---

12. For other evidence of the strong positive correlation between general education and knowledge about AIDS, see Kanouse et al. (1991, pp. 40–41). An alternative interpretation, however, is that since education is positively correlated with income (as discussed in Chapter 2), the education variable is a proxy for income. This conjecture is supported by the finding in Kenkel (1991) that education has a positive effect on health even after correction for differences in knowledge about health. See also Ehrlich and Chuma (1990, pp. 774–775). On this interpretation, high-income persons demand more information about AIDS not because they can absorb it at lower cost but because health is more valuable to them. Some evidence that high-income persons have changed their behavior more in response to the AIDS menace than low-income persons was presented in Chapter 2. See also Bozinoff and MacIntosh (1992).

13. The coefficients of the expenditure variables in this and the next table are so minute (indeed, so close to zero that in the next table we show the coefficient of the expenditure variables as zero) because the expenditure of one more dollar on an education campaign will not have a large effect on a statewide statistic, such as the fraction of the population that is aware that a healthy-looking person may be infected by HIV. Table 6-4, which replaces total with per capita expenditures, enables us to derive meaningful coefficients for the expenditure variables.

Table 6-3 Regression of AIDS awareness on depreciated public education expenditures and other variables, 1991[a]

Dependent variable	Independent variables				
	Educational attainment	Prevalence	State expenditures	Federal expenditures	R^2
Aware	.9729 (6.21)	−5.058 (−4.15)	0 (1.87)	−0 −(1.96)	.56
Unaware	−.3582 (−3.36)	−.5276 (−0.64)	−0 (−0.23)	0 (1.36)	.28

a. The variable labeled "Prevalence" denotes cumulative cases per capita. The *t*-statistics are, as before, in parenthesis.

correct sign (negative), it is not even close to being statistically significant. The coefficient of the federal-expenditures variable remains wrong in both equations, but is less significant than it was in the previous table. The most surprising result in Table 6-3 is that the prevalence of AIDS is significantly *negatively* related to (that is, reduces) AIDS awareness, rather than positively as our analysis predicts; it is also negatively related to AIDS unawareness, as our analysis predicts, but here the coefficient is not statistically significant. The educational-attainment variable has the correct sign and is highly significant in both equations.

The regressions in Table 6-4 differ from those in Table 6-3 by substituting per capita expenditures for total expenditures in the two expenditures variables. The results are much as before. The amount of variance explained continues to be high, and the educational-attainment variable

Table 6-4 Regression of AIDS awareness on depreciated per capita public education expenditures and other variables, 1991

Dependent variable	Independent variables				
	Educational attainment	Prevalence	State expenditures	Federal expenditures	R^2
Aware	.9650 (5.52)	−4.659 (−2.08)	.08 (.05)	−1.047 −(0.89)	.53
Unaware	−.2751 (−2.45)	3.081 (2.15)	−.1399 (−0.14)	−1.912 (−2.53)	.32

continues to have the correct sign and to be highly significant. Prevalence has the wrong sign and is statistically significant in both equations, while the federal-expenditures variable has, at last, the correct sign, and is statistically significant, in the unawareness equation—but not in the awareness one.

Although we are not surprised that our regressions do not support the hypothesis that public expenditures on AIDS education increase knowledge about AIDS, we are surprised that increases in the prevalence of AIDS do not increase knowledge. A possible explanation that is consistent with our theoretical analysis, however, is that the coverage of AIDS by the media is so extensive that the effect of high prevalence of the disease in increasing the demand for information about it is outweighed by the effect of information deficits that are not rectified by the mass media in increasing the prevalence of the disease. There may, in other words, be a two-way causal relation between awareness and prevalence.

Another report of the national survey mentioned earlier also finds higher AIDS misperception scores in regions of high AIDS prevalence than in regions of low prevalence (McCaig, Hardy, and Winn 1991), which, although contrary to our prediction that the demand for information is monotonically increasing in P, is consistent with the results of our regression analysis. The report notes, however, a serious interpretive difficulty: an exogenous lack of information about disease risk and preventives could, as we suggested in discussing the parallel finding in our regressions, cause a higher incidence of the disease (ibid., p. 1594).

Thus far we have assumed that the only possible effect of AIDS education is to alter behavior involving risky sex. Another possible effect, however, is to alter public opinion toward redistributive policy measures regarding AIDS. This possibility is explored in the next chapter.

Subsidizing Complementary Goods: Condoms, Needles, Marriage

A different kind of subsidy program for combating AIDS is to reduce the cost of safe sex or other protective measures by subsidizing complementary goods, such as condoms and clean needles, or monogamous sex.

Condoms. Although the purchase price of condoms is low, the full price, when condom search costs are included, is not, especially when there are restrictions on where condoms may be sold (for example, not in vending machines or on school premises). Making condoms available at zero price from vending machines or other sites conveniently located on school premises, bars, and other "hangouts" of the highly sexually active might reduce the cost of safe sex significantly. But this is far from certain. First, there would be a danger of arbitrage, because people would have an incentive to play middleman by emptying the dispensary of its supply and reselling the condoms at a positive price. The effect would be to siphon off the subsidy into the pockets of the middlemen, thereby defeating the object of the subsidy, which is to lower the price of condoms. This danger could be controlled by limiting the number of condoms per person to some reasonable estimate of how many are needed for personal use. But this would not be possible with vending machines, and many people, especially teenagers, are embarrassed about obtaining condoms in a face-to-face transaction.

Another measure would be to subsidize the manufacture and distribution of condoms specially designed to withstand the greater stress on the condom of anal compared to vaginal intercourse. But surely the private market will evoke an adequate supply of such condoms without government subsidy if there is a private demand for them. Such condoms are already marketed in other countries.

A condom subsidy may seem especially attractive from an economic standpoint in the case of subpopulations that have high costs of absorbing information because of incompleteness of or deficiencies in general education, low IQ, language problems, or illiteracy. However, more information than one might think is required in order to use a condom as an effective AIDS prophylactic (Martin 1990)—not to mention information about the benefits of such use—although the total amount of necessary information may be somewhat less than that provided by an AIDS education program.

Some moral conservatives object to the free distribution of condoms to teenagers and other vulnerable groups on the ground that by lowering the cost of sex it promotes immorality. This objection, whatever its ethical force, would have no bearing on our analysis if two conditions were satisfied: condoms were foolproof preventives of HIV infection and people who used condoms used them every time they had sex. Because neither condition is satisfied in reality, the objection of these moral conservatives does bear on our analysis. Anything that lowers the cost of sex will increase the amount of it, and an increase in the amount of sexual activity will increase the incidence of AIDS, provided that at least some of the activity is unsafe. Suppose that as a result of free distribution of condoms the percentage of sexual trades in which a condom is used increases from 30 to 40 percent in some subpopulation, but the number of trades (60 percent of which remain unsafe) also increases because the expected costs of sex are now lower. Suppose further that 10 percent of the "safe" trades are unsafe in fact, because condoms, as actually used (or not used), are imperfect preventives of sexually transmitted disease. Feeling safer, for example, teenagers might begin to have sex at an earlier age and not always use a condom, or might sometimes use it incorrectly. The resulting increase in risky sexual trades would not completely offset the increased use of condoms; otherwise, the number of risky trades would have been greater before the condom program. But it would reduce the program's effectiveness and could, depending on the failure rate of condoms (which, we recall, may be high for anal intercourse in high-risk populations), actually increase the spread of the disease. Approaching the question from the other direction, we point out that if condoms were outlawed, the cost of risky sex would skyrocket. There would be some substitution either toward abstinence, as the conservatives hope, which is safer than "safe" sex, or, more plausibly, toward oral sex, mutual masturbation, and other risky sexual practices that may however be safer than full intercourse with condoms. Thus, highly risky sex would be riskier than before the condom ban, but there would be less of it.

It is thus an empirical question whether subsidizing condoms reduces or increases the incidence of AIDS. The Swedish experience with AIDS suggests (no stronger word is possible) that it reduces the incidence. Although the average age of initiation of sexual intercourse is lower in Sweden than in the United States, the rate of AIDS in Sweden is only one-tenth of what it is in the United States (see Table I-1 in the Introduction), in part, it seems, because sex education (much of which is education about condoms) is emphasized in Swedish homes, schools, and media, and condoms are widely available, including to teenagers (Posner 1992, p. 165). (In contrast, the major television networks in the United States will not broadcast condom advertisements; see *Wall Street Journal* staff 1992.) The wide availability of condoms, by reducing the fertility risk of sex, may of course be a factor in the early age of sexual initiation. But the net effect of that availability on both fertility risk (Posner 1992, pp. 166, 271) and disease risk appears to be negative. However, the principal obstacle to wider use of condoms in the United States may not be ignorance or price, but the variety of nonpecuniary costs mentioned in Chapter 1. These costs may well exceed a subsidy limited to reducing the price or increasing the availability (reducing search costs) of condoms. We conclude that condom subsidies are unlikely to be a major factor in the control of AIDS, at least in wealthy nations like the United States.

Needles. A program of distributing clean hypodermic needles (or distributing bleach for disinfecting used needles) free of charge to intravenous drug users may seem analytically identical to a program of giving away condoms,[14] but this is not so. Unlike condoms, clean needles are not a major source of disutility. Needle-sharing does confer utility on some intravenous drug users (O'Brien 1989, p. 77; Sibthorpe et al. 1991, p. 706), and is associated with psychiatric disturbance (Metzger et al. 1991). But much needle-sharing is the consequence simply of the cost, kept artificially high by regulatory measures, to intravenous drug users of obtaining new needles (ibid., p. 639; Magura et al. 1989). In addition, the price elasticity of demand for addictive drugs is high (Becker, Grossman, and Murphy 1991); a present reduction in the price of an addictive good, if expected to be permanent, confers future utility because addiction implies heavy future consumption of the drug.

For both reasons—there is less aversion to clean needles than to condoms, and the price elasticity of demand for addictive drugs is high—the effect of a clean-needle subsidy in increasing the amount of intravenous drug use is likely to be greater than the effect of a condom subsidy in increasing the amount of sex. Consistent with this prediction, there is evidence that "changing sexual risk behaviour in drug injectors is more difficult than changing syringe-sharing" (Donoghoe 1992, p. 411; Sibthorpe et al. 1991, p. 706; see also Käll and Olin 1990, Lewis and Watters 1991). This prediction may seem ominous because, other things being equal, the more intravenous drug use there is, the more transmission of the AIDS virus there will be. Other things are not equal, however. If there is no significant disutility to using clean needles, intravenous drug users will switch to them if the full price, including search and expected-punishment costs, is reduced to zero.

Three qualifications are necessary. First, as noted in Chapter 2, drug use is a risk factor for AIDS quite apart from transmission via needles; it fogs the mind, and thereby increases the probability of forgetting to take precautions in sex. So if a clean-needle subsidy led to an upsurge in intravenous drug use, the incidence of AIDS might rise as a result of more risky sex (not needle-sharing) by intravenous drug users. But this

---

14. For useful descriptions of clean-needle programs, see Donoghoe (1992); O'Brien (1989); and W. Anderson (1991). On needle-sharing generally, see Battjes and Pickens (1988).

depends on where the upsurge comes from. If it is from people who previously had substituted other mind-altering drugs, such as alcohol, for intravenous drug use because of the risks posed by needle-sharing, there may be no (more likely, little) increase in the overall incidence of drug abuse. And recall that alcohol abuse is likely to impair the immune system and thus increase susceptibility to HIV infection.

Second, as with condoms, any increase in intravenous drug use due to the fact that disease risk had been reduced would produce an increased number of infections in cases in which the user forgot to use a new needle or forgot to decontaminate the old one, or did so incorrectly. Third, it may be difficult to reduce the full price of clean needles to zero because intravenous drug users would be reluctant to identify themselves to the distributor. This problem could be solved in principle by distributing needles from vending machines at no charge,[15] by placing the machines at convenient locations throughout neighborhoods frequented by addicts, and by stipulating that the use of such a machine to obtain needles could not be used directly or indirectly as evidence of the user's having violated the drug laws. The solution is imperfect, however, because, just as with a condom subsidy, there would be an incentive to empty the machines and resell the needles at a positive price. This problem may be insoluble with vending machines but can be overcome through the device of the needle exchange (O'Brien 1989), the patrons of which exchange a dirty needle for a clean one. Most of the pilot programs aimed at discouraging needle-sharing are needle-exchange programs. But it is difficult for a drug user to achieve anonymity when he must deal face to face with the dispenser, and as long as the drug trade is illegal—and even if it were legal but stigmatized—drug users will continue to attach a high value to anonymity.

Much of the desired effect of a clean-needle subsidy might be achieved by repealing the laws, which exist in about a quarter of the states—notably including New York, which accounts for 17 percent of all new AIDS cases in the United States (Centers for Disease Control 1991a, p. 5 [tab. 1])—forbidding the sale of hypodermic syringes or needles without a doctor's prescription (Pascal 1988). Even in the remaining states, pharmacies, influenced by the "war on drugs," often refuse to sell syringes or needles without proof of medical need, or in other than bulk quantities (Compton et al. 1992), although there is some evidence that

---

15. Germany has made needles available from vending machines at low though not zero price (Des Jarlais and Case 1992, pp. 688–690).

needle-sharing is indeed less common in at least some of these nonprescription jurisdictions (Calsyn et al. 1991). Not much can be done about the restrictive laws and practices as long as the nation is committed to an all-out "war on drugs." And remember that anything that increases drug addiction can indirectly increase AIDS, though we have suggested that the effect is likely to be small.

Decontamination of old needles is a feasible alternative to the free availability of new ones; and given that household liquid bleach, available in any grocery store or supermarket at low cost with no questions asked, is an effective method of decontaminating needles, it is difficult to believe that a subsidy of clean needles would have much effect on the spread of AIDS among intravenous drug users, at least now that knowledge of decontamination is widespread in the intravenous-drug-using community. Cognitive impairments, high discount rates, and risk preference may already be larger causes of the high rate of HIV infection among intravenous drug users than the costs of obtaining clean needles.

Marriage. Not all methods of subsidizing safe sex or safe intravenous drug use, it might be argued, need involve as acute moral, political, and operational problems as free condom distribution to teenagers or free needle distribution to intravenous drug users. It might seem obvious, for example, that subsidizing marriage through generous tax exemptions for married people would reduce the spread of AIDS by reducing the amount of promiscuous sex (implying multiple sex partners of mostly unknown infection status). So might permitting *homosexual* marriage—though here the objections of moral conservatives would be deafening—or at least creating the quasi-marital status available to homosexuals under Danish and Swedish law (Posner 1992, pp. 313–314). The problem is that unless something of this sort is done for homosexuals, subsidizing heterosexual marriage may be counterproductive from the standpoint of controlling AIDS. For if heterosexual marriage is subsidized and thereby made more attractive, but society makes no effort to reduce the stigma or other costs of homosexuality, the marriage subsidy will induce male homosexuals to marry women at an even greater rate than they do, and bisexual activity is an important source of transmission of the AIDS virus to women. The fraction of male homosexuals who marry women is higher, the more repressive the society is toward homosexuality (Ross 1983), because marriage makes it easier to conceal homosexual orientation. This gives further support to our earlier point that efforts to restore traditional sexual morality are unlikely to be effective in reducing the spread of AIDS. It is not surprising that forbidding discrimination on the basis of sexual orientation and permitting homosexuals to enter into marriage-like arrangements are integral elements of Sweden's apparently successful program for controlling AIDS (Henriksson and Ytterberg 1992, p. 332).

The effect of homosexual marriage in limiting the spread of AIDS might, it is true, be small if the bulk of the persons who entered into such marriages were those who already had a monogamous homosexual relationship. But it would not be zero, even if *all* the persons who entered into these marriages had a monogamous relationship already. Divorce rates are lower than rates of dissolution of cohabitations (Posner 1992, p. 190), which implies that married persons probably have, on average, fewer sexual partners over the course of their lifetime than cohabitors do.

CHAPTER 7

Subsidies for Medical Research

In this chapter we examine the optimal and the actual pattern of public expenditures for biomedical research relating to AIDS.[1] The research is of four types: research on the biology of the virus, on tests to determine whether a person is infected, on possible vaccines and cures, and on meliorative treatments—treatments that prolong the life or reduce the suffering of the AIDS victim without curing him or rendering him noninfective. Contrary to the usual view, which treats the types of research interchangeably from the standpoint of whether government should fund it, we argue that the case for public expenditures is weaker for the second two types of research than for the first two. Because the optimal pattern and the actual pattern of expenditures appear to diverge, we are led in the second section of this chapter to begin an exploration of the forces that actually shape public policy toward AIDS.

The Optimal Public Expenditure for AIDS Research

We distinguish between two possible economic rationales for subsidizing medical research on AIDS: external costs in the market for risky sexual activity (or other activity that creates a risk of AIDS), and external benefits in the market for medical research and for information more generally. If because AIDS generates external costs the disease is more prevalent than is optimal,[2] there is an argument, though by no means a

---

1. On the economics of medical research generally, see the helpful discussions in Weisbrod (1989, pt. 1) and Tolley et al. (1992).

2. Recall that because AIDS is to a significant (and increasing) degree a by-product of utility-maximizing behavior, the optimum prevalence of the disease is greater than zero.

conclusive one, for government intervention. One form that such intervention might take is the subsidization of efforts to develop a vaccine or cure for the disease.

We suggested in Chapter 4 that the external costs of AIDS are exaggerated. But they are positive, and even if they were zero, the subsidization of medical research on AIDS might confer external benefits and be justified on that ground. When property rights are incomplete, as they are in the case of basic scientific research,[3] which cannot be patented, and as they may be even with respect to some patentable vaccines and cures, the private market may produce an inefficiently small amount of a good unless subsidized.

The different types of AIDS biomedical research. Evaluation of the external-benefits argument for subsidizing AIDS research requires consideration of the private demand for the four types of research that we have distinguished (basic research, HIV tests, vaccines or cures, meliorative treatments). If, because of incomplete property rights, the private demand for each type of research is inadequate, there is an economic case for a public subsidy based on the concept of external benefits. (We conducted a similar inquiry in Chapter 6.) It is doubtful that this condition is satisfied for all four types of research. First, a distinction must be made between basic research, on the one hand, and the development of therapeutic products, whether diagnostic, preventive, curative, or meliorative, on the other hand. Newly invented vaccines and other drugs, including chemical or biological agents used to test for the presence of antibodies, can, unlike basic research, be patented, or in some cases adequately protected under trade-secret law from competitive appropriation. The result is a considerable measure of property-rights protection that induces pharmaceutical companies and other manufacturers to invest substantial resources in medical research. Industry contributes some 45 percent of the total U.S. investment in research in the health sciences (Institute of Medicine 1990, pp. 49–50).

It is true that few AIDS drugs have been patented, but that is because of the heavy federal investment in their development (Griffin 1991, pp. 387–397), and we are interested here in the situation that would exist without such investment. Moreover, the best-known AIDS drug, AZT, *has* been patented, though the scope of its patent protection is being disputed in litigation—precisely because of the government's contribu-

---

3. And other information: recall that one economic rationale for public education about AIDS (Chapter 6) is that of external benefits.

tions to the development of the drug. We cannot be certain that the system of intellectual-property rights, which includes the patent and trade-secret laws, would optimize the development of AIDS drugs. The biggest problem—apart from the limitations in those laws, such as the 17-year limit of patent protection, and the costs and delays of obtaining such protection—is that a vaccine or cure that eliminates a disease confers benefits, which the manufacturer of the vaccine or cure cannot capture, on future generations.[4] Even if the vaccine reduces but does not eliminate the disease, it will benefit nonvaccinated persons, present and future, by reducing their risk of infection; and again this is a benefit that the manufacturer cannot capture.[5] The vaccine market is in fact small (Institute of Medicine 1985, p. 55 [tab. 4.5]), which is one reason why liability suits arising from the rare instances of vaccine injury have driven some manufacturers out of the market (ibid., p. 63).

Yet the existence of intellectual-property laws does at least raise a question whether public expenditures need be devoted to AIDS research beyond the stage of basic research, the stage at which the virus is identified and its biological properties—its infectivity, mutability, and so on—determined. Moreover, perhaps because profit-making opportunities in basic research are limited, this is an area in which private philanthrophy has traditionally been a major source of investment. In 1986, total philanthropic giving in the United States amounted to $90 billion, of which more than $12 billion was for health and hospitals (Ginzberg and Dutka 1989, p. 82). How much of this went for research—let alone AIDS research—is unknown. But it has been estimated that private philanthropy accounts for 4 to 5 percent of all health research in this country and is concentrated in basic research, of which therefore it represents a larger, but unknown, fraction (Institute for Medicine 1990, p. 59). Public expenditures for such research augment, but also replace, philanthropic giving.

Even if the external-benefits rationale for subsidizing AIDS research were totally discredited, a case for subsidization would remain, based on external costs. We give two examples. First, persons who practice safe sex and are thus at little or no risk from AIDS nevertheless would benefit

---

4. For this to be true of a cure, however, it must render the cured person noninfective. One can imagine a cure for AIDS that would leave the infected person a completely asymptomatic but undiminishedly infective HIV carrier.

5. However, a possible negative externality of vaccination, though one inapplicable to AIDS, is mentioned in the Conclusion.

from a cure because safe sex is costly. The inventor could not capture this benefit in the price for the cure unless it was so efficacious and cheap that everyone now using safe sex promptly dropped it (because no one would fear the disease any more) and as a result the incidence of the disease, and thus the demand for the cure, rose, as indeed happened with syphilis. Second, the market price of a patented vaccine would deter some people from being vaccinated, and incomplete vaccination is a formula for spreading a communicable disease, as we noted earlier. The unregulated market price might be very high, moreover, because a patent is a legally protected monopoly.

The cause and the mechanics of transmission of AIDS are now largely though not completely understood, and cheap and accurate tests for the presence of the virus have been developed and made widely available. So one might expect the amount of federal funding for AIDS research to be declining. But it is not, as we shall see.[6] Another reason for such an expectation is that, with every year that passes, the fraction of AIDS victims who became infected before enough was known about the disease to enable avoidance by behavioral changes—the victims whose plight makes the strongest case for publicly financed AIDS research as a form of social insurance—declines. The fact that federal funding is not declining is thus a clue that public-choice analysis (positive) may be as important as welfare economics (normative) to an understanding of governmental intervention in the epidemic. A further clue is that much federal spending on AIDS research is devoted to the development of vaccines, cures, and treatments rather than to basic research in the structure and behavior of the AIDS virus. In 1987 vaccine development was receiving almost half as much federal research funding as biological research, and treatment development almost twice as much (Siegel, Graham, and Stoto 1990). In fiscal year 1991, by our calculations, 63 percent of the Public Health Service's $771 million budget for medical research on AIDS was going for the development of vaccines and other therapeutic agents, broadly defined, rather than for basic research, even though there is a much larger private market for the former type of research than for the latter.[7]

---

6. It has leveled off, however, in real (that is, inflation-adjusted) terms. See Table 7-1 and Figure 7-3 later in this chapter. Moreover, AIDS research includes a considerable amount of basic research in infectivity, genetics, virology, cytology, immunology, and so forth that has potential applications to other diseases.

7. These calculations are based on a January 22, 1992, printout of the Public Health Service's budget. We added the figure for basic science research–biomedical research to the figure for neuroscience and neuropsychiatric research to obtain our estimate of expen-

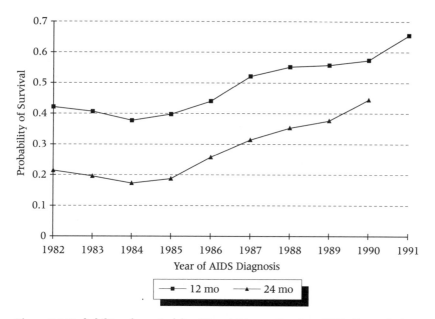

Figure 7-1 Probability of survival for 12 and 24 months after AIDS diagnosis, by year of diagnosis, 1982–1991. *Source:* Computed from CDC Public Information Data Set, 7/1/92.

The federal government pays many of the nation's medical bills under the Medicaid and Medicare programs (though because of their age few Medicare recipients have or are likely to get AIDS),[8] and therefore has a financial interest in reducing those bills through the development of a cheap and effective vaccine or cure. It has a smaller, and possibly no or even a negative, stake in the development of treatments, such as the drug AZT, that merely prolong the lives of persons infected with the AIDS virus. Such treatments, because they do not prevent the opportunistic diseases that mark the active phase of the disease, may actually increase total medical costs by extending the period during which infected persons demand and receive medical treatment.

The data do not permit a confident estimation of whether the costs of treating an AIDS patient over his lifetime are increasing in real terms. Figure 7-1, summarizing CDC data, shows that the average lifetime of

---

ditures on basic research, and added the figures for basic science research–therapeutic agents and basic science research–vaccines to the figure for product evaluation, research, and monitoring to obtain our estimate of expenditures on vaccines and therapeutic agents.

8. Medicare is estimated to pay only 1 percent of the total cost of treating persons with AIDS (Baily et al. 1990).

such patients is increasing. It is likely that this increase has raised the lifetime costs of treating them, but it is not certain. AZT may reduce the length of hospital stays of pre-AIDS victims—HIV-positives whose weakened immune systems make them susceptible to disease but not yet to the (more serious) diseases that denote the onset of AIDS itself. And by postponing the onset of AIDS,[9] AZT reduces in present-value terms the costs of treating AIDS patients (Paltiel and Kaplan 1991). At the same time, however, by prolonging the period during which HIV victims are infectious, AZT may, by reducing the exit rate (see equation 1.5), increase the spread of the disease (Anderson, Gupta, and May 1991). This effect may be amplified by the encouragement to testing which AZT provides because of belief that it can delay conversion from the asymptomatic state to the active disease state. But the analysis is not yet complete. By prolonging the HIV carrier's life, AZT makes him more responsive to criminal and tort laws designed to deter risky activities by infected persons, and possibly more altruistic.

We have made our own estimate of the effect of AZT and other AIDS therapy on the medical costs of AIDS (many of which, to repeat, are borne by the same government that is subsidizing the development of the therapies). Our findings, summarized in Figure 7-2,[10] suggest that AZT has caused a real (that is, inflation-adjusted) increase in the lifetime medical costs of the disease. We attempted to exclude not only cost increases due to inflation but also increases due to changes in medical costs, such as basic hospital charges per day of hospitalization, that are unrelated to treatment for AIDS. AZT was introduced in 1987—and that is the year in which AIDS medical costs began to rise.

Research on HIV tests presents an interesting issue of optimal subsidization. On the one hand, there is a private market for such tests, and the protection of patent law is available to the inventor. On the other hand, a particularly effective way of combating the epidemic would be to develop a test so cheap, quick, and accurate (a cheap, foolproof partner-administered test) that it would increase the demand for HIV testing to the point where almost every sexually active person would test voluntarily; for at that point the further spread of the disease would be halted. The external benefits of such a test might warrant subsidization.

---

9. This effect of AZT therapy is currently being questioned, however, as discussed in the Introduction.

10. The assumptions underlying this graph are complex and contestable. Details are available from the authors upon request.

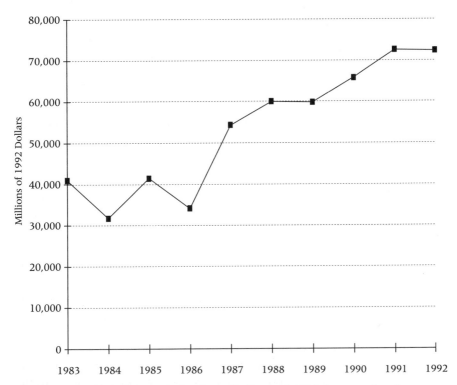

Figure 7-2 Estimated individual lifetime medical cost of AIDS, by year of patient diagnosis, 1983–1992. (Figures are in millions of 1992 dollars.) *Source:* The sources of these estimates and the details of their derivation are available from the authors.

Unlike a cheap, foolproof partner-administered test, but like AZT and similar drugs, vaccines and cures for AIDS may have a perverse effect on the spread of the disease by reducing the average cost of the disease to persons at risk of catching it. A complete but not costless cure for AIDS would reduce the expected costs of the disease to potential victims and by so doing increase the amount of risky sex. Another sexually transmitted disease—syphilis—illustrates this effect. As we saw in Chapter 2, not only is its prevalence much greater than that of AIDS, but the discovery of a cure was followed, albeit with a lag, by an increase in that prevalence.[11] Since total costs are the product of cost per case and total number of cases, a program that reduces the cost per case (to the cost

---

11. Much in the spirit of our analysis, Weisbrod (1983, p. 8) remarks that "discovery of the effectiveness of antibiotics in treating certain venereal diseases may lead to an in-

of the cure, if the cure is completely effective) may increase total welfare even though it also increases the prevalence of the disease. However, the benefits of such a program will tend to be fewer than those of a program aimed at developing a cure for a disease that is not spread by voluntary contact or alterable by changes in style of life. Stated differently, the benefits of curing a sexually transmitted disease are not so much the avoidance of suffering and death as the facilitation of preferred sexual practices, since most such diseases, including AIDS, can, even if incurable, largely be avoided by a change in sexual practices. This just restates our earlier point that, if ignorance and involuntary exposure are set to one side, the costs of safe sex cap the expected costs of AIDS, since no rational person would incur the latter if the former were lower. In a partial but nonetheless illuminating sense, much public subsidization of research on AIDS could be regarded as a subsidization of risky sex. This helps explain the opposition of moral conservatives to such subsidies.

The general point is not limited to AIDS or other sexually transmitted diseases. It can also be used against the current heavy public spending on research to cure cancer or heart disease. The development of a cure would reduce the incentive that people now have to reduce the risk of such diseases by behavioral changes, such as quitting smoking, exercising more, or following a healthier diet. Such changes are costly to people who enjoy smoking and do not enjoy exercise or a healthy diet, but the costs are not as great as those of the disease itself. These lesser costs, to the extent that incurring them is effective in preventing the diseases, could be regarded as placing an upper bound on the benefits of the research. The qualification is vital, however. Safe sex reduces the risk of AIDS to a trivial level; diet and exercise have nowhere near the same impact on the risk of heart disease or cancer.

A formal analysis of the optimal level of public spending on AIDS medical research. To get a better fix on the issue of public spending on AIDS research, we analyze the demand of a representative individual for such spending, beginning with research on a cure. Let E denote the level of spending, $F(E)$ the probability of finding a cure as a function of that spending,[12] P the potential probability of the individual's becoming in-

---

crease, not a decrease, in venereal diseases as sexual activity increases in response to the reduced danger."

12. The analysis is different if the objective of the research is to find a vaccine. That case is discussed below.

fected in the future,[13] and *C* (defined more precisely below) the cost of the infection if no cure is found; therefore *PC* is the expected cost of failing to find a cure. There are four possibilities, depending on whether a cure would be found without any public subsidy of research and whether the representative individual will in fact become infected. However, on the simplifying assumption that the cure is costless once discovered (the cost of discovery is of course positive), three of the four possibilities involve no cost to the individual: cure found anyway (that is, without a public subsidy), individual infected; cure found anyway, but individual not infected; cure not found anyway, but individual not infected. Hence the only benefit from the subsidy is in possibly avoiding *C*, defined as the loss of utility in the case in which the individual is infected *and* no cure is developed outside the subsidized research program.

We make two further assumptions—that a cure is a public good in the sense that its consumption by one person does not reduce its consumption by another (this is implicit in its zero cost), and that representative individual *i* pays a tax share of t_i, so that $St_i = 1$. With these assumptions, the net expected benefit (*V*) of the research to *i* is given by

(7.1) $V_i(E) = F(E)(0) + (1 - F(E))(-PC) - t_iE.$

The critical middle term on the right-hand side denotes the expected benefit of the cure $(-PC)$ discounted by the probability $(1 - F(E))$ that no cure will be found as a result of the public program. If the quest for a cure is hopeless—that is, if $F(E) = 0$ for all levels of *E*—there is no benefit from the research, just as there is no benefit if the person would never have caught the disease; so his wealth is diminished by the full amount of the tax plus the full expected cost of the disease (*PC*). At the other extreme, if a cure is certain to be found as a result of the public program—that is, if $F(E) = 1$ for some level of *E*—the middle term disappears; the entire expected disease cost is averted.

By differentiating both sides of the equation and setting the result equal to zero, we can derive the optimal expenditure by individual *i:*

---

13. This is not quite the same *P* as in earlier chapters, as there the individual was assumed to be sexually active. For purposes of the present analysis, the relevant population includes persons who are not sexually active.

(7.2) $PC(dF/dE) = t_i.$

The left-hand side is the marginal benefit of the research and the right-hand side is the marginal cost. We see that the demand for research will be higher the greater i's probability of getting the disease, the more costly the disease, the greater the marginal effect of expenditures in producing a cure (that is, the higher dF/dE is), and the smaller the tax on i (that is, the larger the population). Although we speak of the cost of the disease, we remind the reader that the more pertinent cost is that of avoiding the disease through some form of safe sex.

The analysis of the demand for research on a vaccine, as distinct from research on a cure, is similar though not identical, if what is under discussion is a vaccine like the polio vaccine, which is administered to the entire population because it is ineffective if administered after a person becomes infected, as opposed to a vaccine like the rabies vaccine, which is administered only to persons who become infected because it is effective in the incubation stage of the disease.[14] Everybody has an actual or expected benefit from cure research, but in the case of the first type of vaccine, the polio type, persons who are already infected have no demand. Since they, and even more plainly persons who already have converted to the active disease state, have a greater demand for a cure than persons merely at risk of someday becoming infected, we can expect a research bias toward cures over polio-type vaccines,[15] other things being equal. The qualification is vital: Depending on the state of medical and scientific knowledge, expenditures on developing a cure may be so much less productive than those on developing a vaccine that little public support could be generated for a research program biased in favor of the former.

Consider now a rabies-type vaccine against AIDS, which would be administered after a person discovered that he was infected with HIV. The efficacy of the vaccine might of course depend on how far the virus had spread in the person's body. If the vaccine was effective only if ad-

---

14. The former is called a preventive vaccine, the latter a therapeutic vaccine. Scientists are trying, so far without much success, to develop both types of vaccine for HIV (Goldsmith 1991). They are especially pessimistic about the possibility of developing a therapeutic vaccine (Berzovsky 1991, p. 452). Another possibility is a perinatal vaccine, that is, a vaccine designed to prevent the transmission of the virus from mother to fetus (or infant, through breast feeding).

15. For empirical support, see Wachter (1992).

ministered early in the course of the infection, persons at risk of HIV would have a strong incentive to be tested, because they could avert AIDS by being vaccinated soon after becoming infected. So vaccine research, like research on cheaper, more accurate HIV tests, may eventually have profound behavioral, as well as direct medical, consequences.

$F(E)$, the productivity of public research expenditures in developing an AIDS vaccine or cure, depends on two things. First is the productivity of research expenditures in general in leading to an AIDS vaccine or cure. Second is the productivity of *private* research expenditures on the disease, since the greater that productivity, the likelier it is that a cure or vaccine will be found without heavy, or perhaps any, public expenditures. These variables make clear that simple comparisons between public research expenditures for different diseases cannot reveal overspending or underspending for particular ones. Public research expenditures per AIDS death are much higher than the corresponding ratios for cancer, heart disease, diabetes, stroke, and senility.[16] But because AIDS is a relatively new disease about which less is known than in the case of the older and longer-studied diseases, research expenditures on it may be more productive. Moreover, AIDS is an infectious disease, unlike cancer, heart disease, or diabetes, and therefore faster-growing (which means, however, potentially faster-falling because of behavioral changes); and because the disease is transmitted mainly by stigmatized practices, private spending for research on it appears to be much lower than in the case of these other diseases.[17] Like AIDS, polio was a relatively rare communicable disease, but a careful study found a rate of return of 11 to 12 percent on the research investment, public and private, in discovering an effective polio vaccine (Weisbrod 1983, pp. 75–76). The proper focus of economic concern with the heavy public expenditure on AIDS research is thus not the high ratio of expenditures to AIDS deaths, but the fact that much though not all of the expenditure is on research and development that an unregulated market would generate, since it is not

---

16. For example, in fiscal year 1989 the federal government spent $1.3 billion on AIDS research, $1.4 billion on cancer research, $1 billion on research on heart disease, and less than $.3 million on diabetes research (Winkenwerder, Kessler, and Stolec 1989, p. 1602 [tab. 4]).

17. We have no precise figures on private spending on AIDS medical research. As of 1987 foundation grants for such research had not yet reached $600,000 (Wells 1987). Recently it has been estimated that in the last 10 years, all private grants to AIDS (not just research grants) have exceeded $200 million (Sebastian 1992).

basic research,[18] and that to a significant extent the disease is the consequence of freely chosen risky activities—and more so every year.

The voluntaristic character of much (though by no means all) HIV infection undermines the argument that more money should be spent on AIDS research because the average age of AIDS victims is much lower than that of victims of the other major diseases. The argument has some merit, however, for reasons closely related to the discussion in Chapter 4 of the cost-savings effect of AIDS. The largest effect of medical research on a disease of the aged may be to induce death from another disease, as where progress in treating heart disease "saves" the patient for cancer. That effect is less, the younger the patient. But that is not the whole story. The fact that, because of the low average age of victims of AIDS, the average disutility of dying from AIDS is greater than that of dying from the other diseases gives people a bigger incentive to make the changes in sexual behavior or drug use necessary to avoid becoming infected by the AIDS virus than they have to make the changes in diet and exercise necessary to minimize the risk (or consequences) of heart disease, cancer, or diabetes. To put this differently, the peculiar horror of AIDS in destroying young lives evokes greater private efforts at avoidance, arguing a smaller role for government. A related point is that because behavioral changes are less effective in preventing the other diseases we have mentioned than they are in preventing AIDS, the optimal expenditure on research into *medical* preventives may be greater in the case of the other diseases.

Even on an age-adjusted basis, public expenditures on AIDS medical research may be disproportionate. For example, in 1988, when federal expenditures on AIDS research and cancer research were approximately equal (see note 16), the number of deaths from cancer of persons under the age of 45 was only a few hundred short of the number of deaths from AIDS in the same age group, whereas the number of cancer deaths of older persons—whose lives were not worthless—was more than 60 times the number of AIDS deaths of older persons.[19]

---

18. Although to the extent that AIDS generates external costs, the market may take too long, from an overall social standpoint, to produce a vaccine or cure.

19. In that year, the last for which we have the number of cancer deaths broken down by age, there were 15,034 deaths from cancer of persons under 45 compared to 15,778 AIDS deaths in that age group, and 284,711 total cancer deaths versus 19,882 total AIDS deaths. In the 45- to 54-year-old bracket alone, the number of cancer deaths exceeded all AIDS deaths, and exceeded all AIDS deaths of persons 45 or older by a factor of almost 6.

We should also consider, however, what would happen to any savings from curtailing public expenditures on AIDS research. Even if a shift of, say, $500 million from AIDS research to cancer research would increase social welfare, it is far from certain that such a shift would be feasible politically. As we point out in the next chapter, federal expenditures for medical research fell markedly in the 1980s—except for research on AIDS. This may have reflected a shift, in principle reversible, from other medical research to AIDS research. Another possibility, however, is that fear about AIDS caused a diversion of resources from other government programs altogether, or from the private sector in the form of higher taxes or a larger federal deficit. In that event, curtailing federal expenditures for AIDS research might well result in a shift of resources toward economically less defensible government programs or, via a reduction in taxes or in the deficit, toward increased private spending which might or might not be as productive as research into AIDS—research that in addition has spillover effects for the understanding and control of other diseases and for the growth of biological knowledge generally. Indeed, an unknown fraction of AIDS research grants are actually not specific to AIDS (see note 6), and should be reclassified as basic biomedical research.

Actual Expenditures and the Median Voter

In examining the demand for AIDS research from the standpoint of a representative rather than any actual individual, our formal analysis assumed that everyone has the same demand for expenditures on AIDS research. The analysis also revealed, however, that infected and uninfected persons have different demands for the allocation of research expenditures between vaccines and cures. If this point is ignored, demand would be uniform if everyone had the same probability of getting the disease, but that is not true either. Suppose that only certain groups in the population are at risk. Others will anticipate no benefit from research expenditures, so they will, unless altruistic, prefer that those expenditures be zero. To put this differently, avoidance and vaccination are substitutes in prevention, and to persons for whom the cost of avoidance is close to zero, because they don't want to engage in risky activities,

---

Cancer figures are from Public Health Service (1988), AIDS figures from the CDC's AIDS data set.

the benefits of research aimed at developing an effective vaccine are also close to zero.

In the simple model of political behavior in which policies are assumed to reflect not some generalized "public interest" but the preference of the median voter, public subsidies for AIDS research will be zero if fewer than half the voters are at risk, because the risk of infection faced by the median voter will be zero. Fewer than half the voters *are* at risk of AIDS. So why is the federal government spending $2 billion a year on AIDS research (biomedical and other), monitoring, HIV testing and counseling, and education?[20] Two possibilities, both undermined though not demolished by the analysis in the preceding section, are (1) that these expenditures are optimal from either a utility-maximizing or a disease-reducing standpoint (and thus could be said to serve the public interest) and (2) that voters are altruistic. Another explanation, one more consistent with the data, is that advocates for male homosexuals have succeeded in persuading the public at large that AIDS is a danger to everyone, not just to discrete high-risk groups such as male homosexuals, hemophiliacs, and intravenous drug users. Since AIDS originated in this country in the homosexual community and has been spread to heterosexuals in part by bisexuals, one might have thought it politically risky for homosexual advocates to emphasize the dangers that "their" disease poses to the broader public. It may be risky,[21] but there is a compensating gain. The more the public at large is persuaded that it is at risk from AIDS, the more willing it will be to support public expenditures to combat the epidemic. The major beneficiaries will be persons at high risk. Thus there will be a net wealth transfer to the homosexual community. A related point is that the more AIDS is regarded as "our" disease rather than just "their" disease, the more altruistic people will be toward the victims of AIDS. Paradoxically, the more hostile the public is toward homosexuals, the more likely are homosexuals to benefit from emphasizing the public danger posed by "their" disease. For if convinced that AIDS was a threat only to homosexuals (or other, equally stigmatized groups, such as intravenous drug users), a public that was hostile toward them might be un-

---

20. This is the AIDS budget of, and these are the principal AIDS activities of, the Public Health Service. See Table 7-1. Most other federal expenditures on AIDS are to defray the cost of treatment.

21. For example, people who believe that AIDS can be spread through casual contact are more likely to favor highly restrictive public policies (including branding) than are people who do not believe this (Price and Hsu 1992, pp. 31, 34). Such a belief harms homosexuals by making them seem more dangerous than they are.

willing to support the expenditure of public funds on programs aimed at preventing or curing the disease.

Notice the ambivalent role that public expenditures on AIDS education play in efforts to obtain greater public expenditures for AIDS research and education. The more the educational programs rely on scare tactics, the more they reinforce the public demand for subsidies to combat AIDS. The more the programs counteract exaggerated fears of AIDS, however, the more they undercut that public demand (except insofar as such programs may increase the prevalence of the disease). Because the administrators of the programs have a personal and professional interest in maintaining and expanding the programs, we can expect the content of the programs to tilt in the direction of scare tactics—especially since such a tilt conforms to the desire of moral conservatives to emphasize abstinence over safe sex, as only abstinence is completely safe. This is not to say that the scare tactics necessarily are wrong. In the early stages of the epidemic they may *conceivably* have been an appropriate means of educating voters, thereby overcoming the standard free-rider problem of political information—though we doubt this, for the reasons given in Chapter 6.

The essential point (from equation 7.2) is that the median voter's optimal expenditure (via taxation) on research is greater, the more prevalent he believes the disease to be. The effect of expenditures devoted to advertising the dangers of AIDS on his demand for a public research subsidy therefore depends on the effect of those expenditures in increasing his estimate of the risk posed to him by the disease. Unless the median voter's *perceived* potential risk of infection exceeds the *true* potential risk, which equals the fraction of the electorate that will someday be infected, the expenditures are wasted from a political standpoint. A median-voter model of AIDS policy implies, therefore, that the electorate overestimates the prevalence of the disease. Public opinion polls summarized in Blendon, Donelan, and Knox (1992, pp. 981–982) support this prediction. For example, 20 percent of Americans say they are "very concerned" about contracting AIDS, 34 percent of persons 18 to 39 years old feel "at risk," and twice as many consider themselves at high or medium risk as the number believed by experts to be in these risk groups (ibid., p. 982; see also Price and Hsu 1992). At the same time, and what is also consistent with the analysis, Americans are becoming more compassionate or altruistic toward victims of AIDS. Between 1987 and 1991, the percentage believing that AIDS victims should be treated with compassion rose from 78 to 91 and the percentage believing that they should be isolated from the rest of society fell from 21 to 10 (Gallup and Newport 1991). A political explanation is further supported by Tables 6-2 and 6-3, which suggest that public expenditures on AIDS education are not well designed to increase the public's actual knowledge of AIDS. Perhaps the real objective of these education programs is different.

We expect overestimation of the risk of AIDS to be greater than in the case of less deadly diseases, such as gonorrhea. The benefits to the infected or at-risk groups from medical research, and hence their incentive to support efforts to increase the public's estimate of the risk of infection, are greater the more deadly the disease, provided other factors are held constant such as the number of persons infected or at risk, the productivity of research expenditures, and the supply of private research.

The economic-efficiency and median-voter models yield different predictions concerning the time path of public expenditures on medical research on AIDS. The former predicts a high level of expenditures (after a brief start-up period) because the marginal product of a dollar of expenditures in generating useful knowledge about a disease is high when very little is yet known about the disease, eventually declining as diminishing returns to research set in and emphasis shifts to the development of specific treatments and cures—at which point the private market can take over—and as the expected benefits of further research decline because fewer people remain at risk, many having either died or switched to safe sex. In the median-voter model, initial expenditures may be too low because few people feel themselves at risk (this was the initial reaction to the AIDS epidemic), but the level of expenditures may continue to increase for too long if more and more people come to feel threatened by the disease and they exaggerate the threat.

Annual federal expenditures, both in total and by the Public Health Service, which accounts for most of the government's expenditures on AIDS medical research and AIDS educational programs, are listed in Table 7-1 and are graphed in real (inflation-adjusted) terms in Figure 7-3. Table 7-1 suggests that homosexual-rights advocates may be correct in arguing that the federal government was too slow to react to the epidemic (notice the low level of expenditures through 1985),[22] and this supports the median-voter model. However, the leveling off in the growth of research expenditures in real terms (shown in Figure 7-3) is consistent with the economic-efficiency model. The data as a whole are

---

22. Further evidence is that the President's budget requests contained no item for AIDS funding until the 1984 fiscal year (U.S. Congress 1985).

Table 7-1   Annual federal expenditures on AIDS (in millions of 1992 dollars)[a]

Year	Total expenditures	Public Health Service expenditures
1982	8	6
1983	44	29
1984	104	61
1985	208	109
1986	507	234
1987	926	502
1988	1,591	962
1989	2,275	1,301
1990	2,978	1,590
1991	3,648	1,888
1992	4,345	1,967
1993	4,916	2,068

a. The source for this table is a data sheet dated February 16, 1992, furnished by the Public Health Service. The 1992 figures are the amounts appropriated, not the amounts expended; the 1993 figures are the President's budget requests. In 1988, when federal expenditures on AIDS were $1.6 billion, state expenditures were estimated to be $.5 billion (Rowe and Ryan 1988, p. 425).

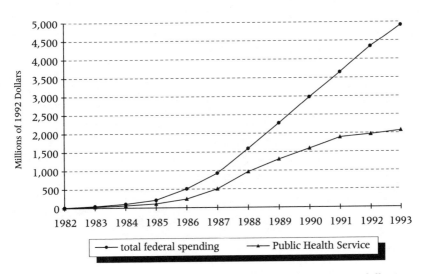

Figure 7-3 Annual federal expenditures on AIDS (in millions of 1992 dollars). *Source:* See Table 7-1.

consistent with neither model. Notice the divergent paths of research expenditures and of other federal expenditures on AIDS. With the increase in the number of persons who have AIDS, the focus of the most articulate lobby for governmental assistance in combating the epidemic, that of male homosexuals, has shifted from efforts to obtain research subsidies to efforts to obtain subsidies for the medical expenses of persons requiring thereapeutic assistance. Since most other classes of AIDS victims do not constitute politically effective interest groups, we predict that the pattern of federal expenditures on AIDS will follow the changing relation of male homosexuals to the epidemic.

Further evidence that public spending on AIDS is not being driven by the preferences of the median voter is that surveys show that a plurality of adults (45 percent in one survey) consider AIDS research a higher priority for public spending than prevention (29 percent) or treatment (25 percent) (Kanouse et al. 1991, p. 60 [fig. 5]). The actual spending pattern is the reverse. The issue of explaining the pattern of public expenditures on AIDS is explored further in the next chapter, where we present an interest-group analysis of public intervention in the epidemic.

The analysis in this section suggests that the strongest case for public subsidies is presented by the Centers for Disease Control itself in its role as an early-warning system for new epidemics. Since the social costs (as through quarantining) of effectively combating an epidemic are lowest in the earliest stage of an epidemic, and the private demand for effective measures is weakest then, there is a powerful case for having a public machinery devoted to identifying new epidemics and recommending public and private measures for limiting their spread.

CHAPTER 8

The Redistributive Factor in Public Policy toward AIDS

In the last four chapters we have examined the range of public policies, both regulatory and fiscal, toward AIDS. Most do not seem easily defendable by reference to the presence of external effects, by other criteria related to economic efficiency, or even by the goal of minimizing the prevalence of AIDS; nor do they seem justified by the fiscal or proprietary interest of government as a provider of Medicaid and other benefits that the epidemic may or may not have made more expensive. Some policies, including many of the educational programs and much funding for medical research on vaccines, cures, and treatments for AIDS rather than on the fundamental biology of the disease and the development of cheap, accurate partner-administered HIV tests, seem wasteful from an economic standpoint, in the sense that the expenditures would be more valuable in other uses. And the social-insurance rationale for subsidizing treatments, cures, and vaccines is diminishing with the increasing fraction of infected persons who deliberately assumed the risk of infection.[1] Other policies, notably the extensive public support and encouragement of HIV testing using the tests available at present, may be perverse, because they may accelerate rather than retard the spread of the disease. More efficient policies, such as subsidizing the distribution of hypodermic needles and (less clearly) of condoms, have, though strongly advocated, not been widely adopted. Naive models of democracy, such as the median-voter model examined in the preceding chapter, are no more successful than welfare economics in explaining the pattern of AIDS policies.

---

1. We are not aware of any efforts to justify or explain the entire pattern of existing AIDS policies on social-insurance or other ethical grounds.

So what *is* going on? Economists used to believe that most governmental interventions in the economy were motivated by a genuine desire to ameliorate market failures or achieve other broadly supported "public interest" goals, and that if the interventions failed in fact to serve the public interest, this was a result of ignorance or incompetence on the part of individual legislators or administrators, or of poor institutional design. The hypothesis of ignorance cannot be completely rejected in the case of AIDS policies. After all, if the analysis in this book is correct, public health professionals, who have been highly influential in the formation of public policies toward AIDS, have made analytical mistakes by paying insufficient attention to economic factors in the growth and control of diseases. But ignorance need not be exogenous; it can be influenced by incentives. Mistakes in analyzing AIDS do not necessarily result from any lack of intellectual skill on the part of public health professionals, but instead may result from biases induced by training, by personal interest, or by pressures exerted by politically influential groups. Nowadays when economists observe ineffectual or perverse public policies, they look for a possible redistributive motive rather than for motiveless ignorance. They look particularly for redistribution from diffuse groups, such as consumers or taxpayers, to concentrated groups, rather than redistribution that is arguably justifiable on efficiency grounds, such as anticartel policy, or on other public-interest grounds, for example as a form of social insurance. That will be our focus too. The plausibility of such an approach is supported by the extensive literature on the redistribution of income from consumers (patients) to producers (physicians) and other providers of health care (see note 6). Although we have found only two studies that extend the analysis to *public* health, the branch of biomedical science that emphasizes protection against communicable diseases, they support the hypothesis that public-health policies have likewise been a "device used by organized interest groups to redistribute wealth to themselves" (G. Anderson 1990, p. 576; see also Tollison and Wagner 1991).

The reason a compact group can organize for effective political action at lower cost and greater per capita benefit than a larger, more diffuse group is the same reason why a cartel having only a few members is more likely to succeed in redistributing wealth from a diffuse group of consumers to itself than a cartel having many members is likely to succeed in redistributing the wealth of a small, concentrated group of consumers (Olson 1965; Stigler 1975; Peltzman 1976; G. Becker 1983). The larger the group, and the lower the stake to each member, the more likely are efforts to organize the group to be defeated by free-rider problems.

The government's response to the AIDS epidemic may not be very efficient, may not even be calculated to defeat or at least diminish the disease, and may not reduce the federal deficit, but it may be redistributing wealth from taxpayers and the sexually active population at large to high-risk populations, such as male homosexuals, and, above all, to medical and public health professionals, especially those engaged in research, and also to pharmaceutical companies. Griffin (1991, pp. 387–399) presents evidence of heavy federal subsidies to pharmaceutical companies for research, development, and sale of AIDS drugs, and some evidence of high profits,[2] while Ohsfeldt and Gohmann (1992) present evidence that interest group pressures have affected state regulation of insurance coverage for victims of AIDS. That evidence is consistent with our regression analysis in Chapter 6 of expenditures on AIDS education. The allocation of federal and state expenditures across states for this purpose did not appear to be consistent with a public-interest or efficiency model of public policy. In particular, other things being equal, states with highly educated populations had more rather than, as one might expect in an efficiency model, less per capita public financing, both state and federal, of AIDS education than states with less highly educated populations; and state expenditures were only weakly related to population.

Male homosexuals constitute a substantial although not enormous group within the general population[3] and have a strong stake in reducing the cost of satisfying their sexual needs. They are particularly endangered by AIDS; and while there is little systematic information about their characteristics, it appears that homosexuals are disproportionately concentrated in a few major cities, such as New York, San Francisco, and Los Angeles, where they have considerable political clout; that they are above average in education and income; and that they are well represented in the communications media. Furthermore, the long incubation period of AIDS means that infected people have a greater expected bene-

---

2. And we saw in Chapter 4 that government is the principal purchaser of vaccines and further supports the demand for them by requiring vaccination of schoolchildren. An interesting economic issue that we do not explore in this book is whether, contrary to widespread belief, government is subsidizing the pharmaceutical industry by maintaining the demand for vaccination at an inefficiently high level.

3. Most estimates of the percentage of the male population that has a predominantly homosexual orientation are between 2 and 5 percent (Posner 1992, p. 295; Johnson et al. 1992, p. 411; Smith 1991; Rogers and Turner 1991). The most reliable is 2 percent, including bisexuals (Smith 1991). Estimates for more tolerant societies are not significantly higher (see, for example, Biggar and Melbye 1992), suggesting that the low estimates are not the result of concealment.

fit from medical research than people who contract a disease that runs its course faster than the feasible pace of medical progress.

For all these reasons, homosexual men have the earmarks of a politically effective interest group[4]—though they are also strongly disapproved of by many heterosexuals (Posner 1992, p. 64; Price and Hsu 1992, p. 34), so strongly that until about twenty years ago they were unorganized, politically powerless, and indeed nearly invisible to the population at large. That remains the condition of intravenous drug users today. It is highly probable that, like other poor people, a disproportionate number of intravenous drug users do not vote, thus further reducing their political influence.[5] All this makes it highly unlikely that AIDS policies are shaped to their preferences—if they were, the government would probably distribute hypodermic needles free of charge or at least lift the restrictions on the sale of needles by private suppliers.

Finally, medical and public health professionals, along with drug companies, have a considerable stake in redistributive policies. This is particularly true of the medical and public health research community. During the 1980s, when Republican administrations were trying with some success to curtail nondefense, nonentitlement federal spending, the growing appropriations for AIDS research protected the Public Health Service's overall budget from being cut (Booth 1988). For in addition to research on AIDS proper, a good deal of research in general fields of biomedical research such as virology, immunology, and epidemiology was classified as AIDS-related to protect its federal funding. Medical professionals have an impressive track record in obtaining government largesse, protection from competition, and above all deference to their professional judgment.[6] Once an issue is defined as lying within the scope

---

4. Indeed, it has been conjectured that they have become an effective interest group in part because the AIDS epidemic has increased the expected benefit to them of government assistance (Posner 1992, p. 215). The epidemic has further aided the formation of a politically effective homosexual interest group by fostering organization within the homosexual community to raise money for AIDS victims and to provide mutual support, by exposing prominent Americans (such as Liberace, Roy Cohn, and Rock Hudson) as homosexuals, and by arousing the sympathy of heterosexuals by the spectacle of suffering, and examples of caring and commitment, among homosexuals.

5. The number of intravenous drug users in this country is unknown but is estimated to be somewhere between 500,000 and 2 million (Spencer 1989). The higher figure seems too high.

6. The anticompetitive character of much public regulation of health care is the subject of a large literature illustrated by Frech (1988), Kessel (1980), Lippincott and Begun (1982), and Weingast (1980), and summarized in Gravelle (1985) and Jacobs (1987). For

of some profession's expert knowledge, it is natural for the public at large and even politicians to defer to the professionals' judgment on the issue (Abbott 1988). Medical and public health professionals have succeeded in convincing the public and the political establishment that AIDS is primarily a medical and public health problem and that its solution therefore should be left largely to them (Fox, Day, and Klein 1989). To a large extent it *is* such a problem. But it is also an economic problem, as we have tried to show. The economic perspective is alien to the biomedical community, however—perhaps because economists are likely to assign a larger role to behavioral change, and a smaller one to public health measures and medical research, in the control of disease than the biomedical community, partly at least as a matter of self-interest, is likely to do.

The public subsidization of HIV testing is an interesting though equivocal illustration of a policy that promotes the welfare of the high-risk population and of health professionals at the expense of the rest of the population. The availability of HIV tests benefits persons in high-risk groups, as well as the professionals who develop, refine, and administer the tests and interpret, communicate, and counsel concerning their results. The test, as we have emphasized, enables high-risk persons to obtain risky sex (provided they test negative) that they could not obtain otherwise. It confers other private benefits as well. But it also imposes a cost on high-risk groups. It may enable some infected persons to abandon safe for risky sex and thus place the high-risk population at even higher risk of infection. In addition, a cheap and accurate HIV test, as the essential precondition of mandatory testing, fuels calls for such testing. That is why at first the leaders of the homosexual community opposed HIV testing; they feared it would set the stage for mandatory testing and quarantining of carriers identified as such by the test, as had occurred in other epidemics.

This point to one side, persons who do not belong to high-risk populations have little incentive to be tested, so they do not benefit proportionately from the contribution that they make, through the taxes they pay, to defraying the costs of HIV testing. Rather than certainly benefiting

---

a general self-interest model of health policy, see Feldstein (1988). It should be unnecessary to add that we do not believe that health professionals are motivated solely by pecuniary self-interest. Such a belief would be contrary to the entire spirit of our analysis, which emphasizes nonpecuniary costs and benefits and analyzes altruistic as well as selfish motivation.

from cheap HIV tests, persons in the low-risk population may be hurt, because the availability of the tests can increase the spread of the disease, potentially to persons who at present are at little risk from it. True, if the full price of the tests, including any disutility associated with delay in obtaining test results, squeamishness about having blood drawn, false positives, and false reports of test outcomes, fell to much lower levels than at present, voluntary testing might become so widespread that it would bring about a dramatic reduction in the spread of the disease. But we do not appear to be close to having a test that would have these characteristics and consequences.

Another policy that benefits high-risk populations (and the medical profession) but may harm low-risk ones is subsidizing the development and improvement of drugs such as AZT that prolong the life of a person infected with the AIDS virus but neither cure him nor render him incapable of transmitting the disease, though it may as we noted make him more amenable to the deterrent effects of criminal and tort law. Despite the last point, the subsidy is likely to increase the spread of the disease, and although this is a harm to high-risk as well as to low-risk populations (since, of course, not everyone in a high-risk population is infected), it is offset in the case of the former by the benefits in increased longevity to infected persons, who are disproportionately represented in high-risk populations.

The subsidization of research aimed at developing a vaccine against AIDS also benefits primarily persons in high-risk populations, and the same is true of subsidizing research aimed at finding a cure. We saw in the preceding chapter that such subsidies can increase the incidence of the disease.

Education in the danger of AIDS, when aimed, as much of it is, at persons who are at low risk of becoming infected, confers little benefit on those persons. Since most persons are at low risk, this may explain the finding in Tables 6-2 and 6-3 that raising federal expenditures on AIDS education does not increase public knowledge about AIDS. However, insofar as it makes the low-risk public more fearful of the disease than they otherwise would be, it may incline them to support public intervention more than they otherwise would; we presented some evidence of this in Chapter 7. Perhaps, therefore, such education is best explained as aimed at people in their capacity as voters, to the benefit of the high-risk populations that are seeking other forms of intervention, such as subsidization of research and treatment. Those populations also benefit from regulations, which are increasingly common, forbidding insurance companies to charge high premiums to, or to refuse to insure, members of those populations. We noted in an earlier chapter that such regulations transfer wealth from low-risk to high-risk persons.

Another point consistent with our emphasis on redistribution in favor of politically effective groups is that forms of intervention that would be particularly costly to male homosexuals have been successfully resisted. Mandatory testing of all persons in high-risk populations, followed by notification of positive test results to employers, spouses, insurance companies, and other persons or firms having substantial personal or business relations with the tested individual, or even by the quarantining of individuals who tested positive—all conventional responses to epidemics of an infectious disease—would have a substantial effect in reducing the spread of the disease. The cost would be high—too high, we think. But more to the point in an interest-group analysis, it would be borne largely by the high-risk population itself. Cuba, whose government is not constrained by democratic political pressures, has, as we pointed out in Chapter 5, a program of universal mandatory testing and internment of persons who test positive. We do not recommend such a program, not only because it goes against the American grain but also because the disease can be controlled at lower cost by voluntary action on the part of persons at risk from it. Our point is only that this is not the kind of policy, regardless of its merits, that is likely to be adopted by a government subject to the interest-group pressures associated with democratic politics.

Although we believe that AIDS policies as a whole redistribute wealth to male homosexuals as well as to medical professionals, the per capita and possibly the total redistribution to the latter is in all likelihood much greater. For reasons explained in Chapter 6, it is unlikely that the hundreds of millions of dollars spent annually on AIDS education confer much benefit on homosexuals, most of whom are already knowledgeable about the disease. And the billions spent on research confer mainly a future, uncertain benefit on them, given the lack of progress to date in developing either a vaccine or a cure, but a present, certain benefit on the researchers and research institutions that receive these billions in the form of salaries and grants. In this respect AIDS policies resemble such familiar examples of redistributive policies as public housing, welfare, and, perhaps the best examples, remedial education (such as the Head Start program) and job training. In the last two cases, the government confers substantial financial benefits directly and immediately on the providers of services, but only uncertain future benefits on the ostensible beneficiaries of the programs. The per capita discrepancy in benefits is particularly great in the case of AIDS policies, since millions of persons are at risk of AIDS (or already have it or are infected by HIV), but only a few thousand are engaged in the research, education, and support activities that are financed by government AIDS programs.

The point at which interest groups of male homosexuals and medical professionals encounter not a diffuse and uninformed public with relatively little at stake in the battle against AIDS but another interest group is in the matter of distributing condoms to high-school students and, a related point, the content of sex education—whether it should emphasize the role of condoms in the prevention of disease and pregnancy. By lowering the cost of sex, condoms (and therefore information about condoms) increase its incidence. Moral conservatives, whose political power has been demonstrated in the abortion controversy, are opposed to premarital sex, as most sex engaged in by Americans of high school age is. The chosen weapon of moral conservatives against disease risk as well as against the risk of unwanted pregnancies is abstinence from all nonmarital sexual relations. This weapon is blunted if the government takes steps to make a substitute for abstinence, such as condoms, cheaper.

Since people have a smaller stake in correcting the behavior of other people than in reducing the cost of their own preferred behavior, we expect that in the long run AIDS policy will tilt away from the moral conservatives and in the direction of the advocates of homosexual rights, especially if, as we also believe, the policies favored by moral conservatives have little chance of being effective in controlling the epidemic. This last point is important as a reminder that redistributive considerations are not the only influences on public policy. Especially in an area of policy where expert opinion is important, as is true of public health, policy cannot fail to be influenced by considerations of social costs and benefits as well as by purely private gains and losses.

The analysis in this chapter has been, at best, suggestive. We have not presented a full, testable, and verified theory of public policies toward AIDS. But we are persuaded that the interest-group approach has more promise as a positive theory of those policies than either a normative economic approach or the median-voter model of political choice discussed in Chapter 7.

CHAPTER 9

AIDS and Fertility

In this chapter we examine the interaction between AIDS (and other sexually transmitted diseases) and fertility, or more precisely between behavior designed to avoid the risk of infection and behavior designed to avoid pregnancy. These risks—which we call disease risk and fertility risk—are related both analytically, because an unwanted pregnancy, like infection with HIV, is the result of a sexual trade that is desired ex ante and regretted ex post, and, through the modalities of protection, practically. We define "unwanted pregnancy," present a model of its relation to infection, and use the model to explore three questions: What is the likely effect of AIDS on the demand for different types of protection against unwanted pregnancies, including abstinence, condoms, the contraceptive pill, and abortion? What is the likely effect of AIDS on the birth rate? What will be the effect on the spread of AIDS if the Supreme Court continues to cut back on the constitutional right of abortion created by *Roe v. Wade?*[1] Although our focus is on AIDS, the analysis can be generalized to any sexually transmitted disease. It also has utility in explaining the increase both in sexual activity and in sexually transmitted disease following the development of the contraceptive pill—thus illustrating the potential for extending the analytical approach of this book beyond AIDS and other communicable diseases.

An Economic Model of Protection against Fertility Risk and Disease Risk

We consider cases in which individuals desire to avoid two consequences of vaginal intercourse: HIV infection and pregnancy. For simplicity we

---

1. 410 U.S. 113 (1973).

assume that the only methods of avoiding infection are either abstinence (or, what for our purposes is the equivalent, a nontransmittive sexual practice such as mutual masturbation) or the use of a condom, both of which methods are employed, ex ante, to prevent transmission of virus or sperm. Abstinence can also be analyzed along the axis of level or type of sexual activity rather than that of methods of preventing unwanted consequences of sex; we emphasize this distinction later. Throughout most of the analysis we assume that the only ex ante methods of contraception are condoms, abstinence, and the contraceptive pill but that there is also an ex post method—abortion. (The AIDS analogue to abortion would be a cure for HIV.) The analysis would not be affected by assuming other methods of contraception, such as coitus interruptus (withdrawal before ejaculation), douching, intrauterine devices, the rhythm method, voluntary sterilization, and diaphragms. Coitus interruptus resembles condoms in preventing both infection and pregnancy, though, again like condoms, imperfectly. The other methods are like the pill in having no effect on disease[2] but, with the exception of sterilization, are unlike it in being less effective in preventing conception.

The pill is a more effective contraceptive than the condom, the risk of accidental pregnancy being only 20–25 percent as great (Bernstein 1990; Trussell et al. 1990). The trade-off between the superior infection protection of the condom and the superior fertility protection of the pill makes an increase in the expected cost of either infection or fertility alter the relative demands for the two methods, with consequences for abortion and the birth rate. We assume that the decision with respect to prevention of both infection and pregnancy is the woman's even if the method is employed by the man, as in the case of condoms. This assumption is realistic in cultures in which women are relatively independent of men; both the probability of infection and the cost of an

---

2. Or little effect. The spermicide that the douche or diaphragm holds reduces the risk of transmission of the AIDS virus, and the rhythm method may (or may not) reduce the frequency of intercourse. And there is some evidence that the pill significantly reduces infectivity by thickening the cervical mucus—and other evidence that it increases infectivity (*Blue Sheet* staff 1991; Ehrhardt and Wasserheit 1991). The latter evidence is mainly statistical, consisting of correlations between use of the pill and incidence of AIDS. The difficulty is that widespread use of the pill may be correlated with a high level of sexual activity—not to mention a low level of condom usage. For other criticisms, see Meirik and Farley (1990). We shall assume that the pill has no effect on infectivity, but the reader should bear in mind that our conclusions are sensitive to this possibly erroneous assumption.

unwanted pregnancy are greater for women than for men, which would lead women to demand more protection. The assumption may be unrealistic, however, in the black subculture in the United States, where the terms of trade are highly unfavorable to women (as discussed in Chapter 2).

We assume realistically that for most women an abortion is a more costly method of eliminating an unwanted pregnancy than contraception is; otherwise the demand for contraception would be weak. Unless abortion were costly, moreover, the concept of "unwanted pregnancy" would be paradoxical; by refusing to have an abortion, a woman would be signifying that she wanted to be pregnant and have a child. In fact, depending on moral attitudes and other factors, including price and the slight medical risk, an abortion may be more costly than carrying the fetus to term, in just the sense that the cure for a particular disease might be more costly than the disease—which would not mean that the disease was wanted. The expense of abortion thus enables a clear analytical distinction to be made between "unplanned" and "unwanted" pregnancy. Events that are unplanned can confer utility, but the fact that an event occurs does not show that it confers utility; the cost of preventing it may simply have exceeded the event's disutility.

The woman will choose among ex ante methods of protection that are cheaper than the ex post method (abortion) by comparing the benefits (B) of each ex ante method with its costs, as in the following formula for the expected utility of method j:

$$(9.1) \quad EU_j = B_j - q_{jd}C_d - q_{jf}C_f - C_o.$$

The costs are expected disease costs (C_d) and expected fertility costs (C_f),[3] discounted by the respective probabilities (q_{jd} and q_{jf}) of the method's failing to prevent disease and failing to prevent fertility, and other costs (C_o), including pecuniary and information costs and any health risks associated with the method of prevention chosen. Fertility costs increase with the disutility of abortion, since if abortion were costless (counting as "cost" any disutility from the procedure, as well as pecuniary costs, time costs, and the slight health risk), fertility costs would vanish.

---

3. These can of course be negative, if the couple desires a child. If they are positive, then any pregnancy that results from the couple's sexual activity is unwanted in an economic sense, as explained before, even if the risk of pregnancy is consciously assumed because of the perceived costs of contraception and abortion.

The possibility of eliminating fertility costs ex post, through abortion, introduces a temporal dimension into the woman's decision process. This is shown in Figure 9-1, where the (implicit) horizontal axis is time and the woman's choices are graphed as a function of time from before engaging in vaginal intercourse to the birth of a child.

Figure 9-2 illustrates our earlier point about the distinction among wanted, unwanted, and aborted pregnancies. The horizontal axis is the cost of fertility—that is, the disutility of having a child in view of the costs of pregnancy and of bringing up the child, the latter cost resulting

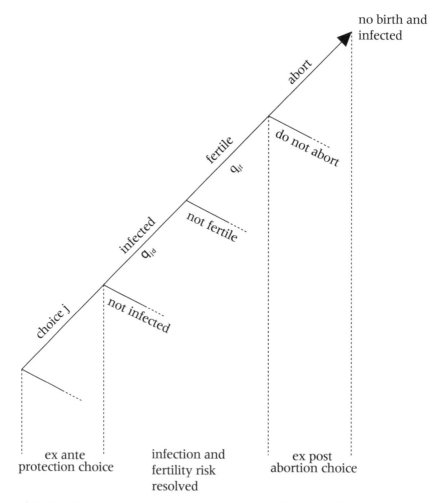

Figure 9-1 Woman's decision process in response to disease and fertility risk.

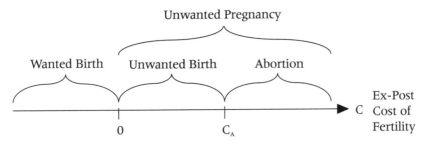

Figure 9-2 Types of pregnancy as function of fertility cost.

from such things as having to give up a job, or quit school, to take care of the child.[4] Three regions are demarcated: (1) where the cost of fertility is negative—to the left of 0—the birth is wanted; (2) where it is positive, but less than the cost of abortion, the birth is unwanted; (3) where it is greater than the cost of abortion, there is no birth. Notice that both (2) and (3) involve an unwanted pregnancy—the net cost of fertility is greater than zero. But an unwanted *pregnancy* will lead to an unwanted *birth* only if the cost of an abortion exceeds that of a birth.

Although our interest is in methods of prevention, it is helpful to begin with the default alternative ($j = 0$), where no ex ante method of prevention is used. The expected utility of this alternative is given by

(9.2) $EU_0 = B_0 - q_{0d}C_d - q_{0f}C_f.$

The benefits are sexual pleasure unimpeded by preventive methods plus the avoidance of the monetary and health costs of prevention. The costs are disease risk and fertility risk, as before. If the risk of disease is zero, the second term on the right-hand side of the equation drops out and the only costs are expected fertility costs. These turn into benefits if the couple desires children, but we put that case to one side.

At the other extreme from the no-prevention alternative is the abstinence alternative ($j = A$),

4. For empirical evidence that such costs influence the choice of contraceptive method in the direction predicted by the rational model, see Tanfer, Cubbins, and Brewster (1992). More generally, Kantner and Zelnik (1973) find in an empirical study of young unmarried women that "evaluation of one's own fecundity appears to relate strongly and rationally to the use of contraception." This parallels our finding in Chapter 2 that people's sexual decisions are rationally related to AIDS risk.

(9.3) $EU_A = B_A.$

Here the expected disease and fertility costs are zero, but if the pleasure of vaginal intercourse is highly valued, the individual's utility may be very low relative to the default alternative. That is, B_A may be smaller than B_0.

To analyze the effect of AIDS on fertility requires us to distinguish not only among methods of prevention, principally the pill, condoms, and abstinence, but also among the three fertility consequences of vaginal intercourse: wanted, unwanted, and aborted pregnancy. If the cost of fertility is negative, the pregnancy is wanted, whether or not it was planned; if the cost is positive, but smaller than the cost of abortion, the pregnancy is unwanted but will not be aborted; if the cost of fertility is larger than the cost of abortion, the pregnancy will be aborted (see Figure 9-2). In principle, all three outcomes are observable; and although wanted and unwanted, and in particular wanted but unplanned and unwanted, are difficult to distinguish empirically, unwanted can be proxied by the number of births out of wedlock, since a higher fraction of those births than of births to married women are likely to be unwanted. We are interested in the effect on each type of pregnancy of an increase in the risk of sexually transmitted disease, the kind of increase that the AIDS epidemic has brought about.

That epidemic has increased the demand for the types of prevention, specifically condoms and abstinence, that are effective against disease risk as well as fertility risk.[5] Condoms also reduce the risk of pregnancy, so it might appear obvious that the increased disease risk created by AIDS would lead, through greater use of condoms, to a reduction in the number of unwanted pregnancies and thus to a reduction in both the rate of abortions,[6] since abortions are a subset of unwanted pregnancies (see Figure 9-2), and in the rate of births out of wedlock, a higher fraction

---

5. The increase between 1982 and 1988 in the percentage of contraceptive users who used condoms is documented in Mosher (1990, p. 200 [tab. 3]).

6. An offsetting factor, but one probably too small to show up in the statistics of abortion, is that a woman who is HIV-positive has about a 30 percent chance of transmitting the virus to her fetus. Hence there is a high demand for abortion, conditional of course on contraceptive failing, by HIV-positive women (Sunderland et al. 1992), and possibly by women who merely suspect that they are HIV-positive and are reluctant to be tested. On the other hand, we are told that some women who know they are HIV-positive regard this as a reason for wanting to become pregnant, because they want to have a child before they die and the child will have a better than 50 percent chance of being HIV-negative.

of which, we said, are unwanted. And because marriage reduces the risk of AIDS, and married women tend to have more children than unmarried ones (Essock-Vitale and McGuire 1988), we might even conjecture that the ratio of legitimate to illegitimate births would rise faster than the number of illegitimate births declined (Posner 1992, p. 115).

Yet while the abortion rate has indeed declined since 1982 (U.S. Bureau of the Census 1991, p. 71 [tab. 102]), the marriage and legitimate-birth rates have both continued to fall (ibid., pp. 43 [tab. 50], 67 [tab. 92]). This suggests that the analysis in the preceding paragraph is deficient, which it is in implicitly comparing the condom only with the no-prevention alternative (equation 9.2), thereby disregarding preventive methods other than the condom. The effect of increased disease risk on pregnancy and abortion depends on substitutability among all possible preventive methods (plus the no-prevention alternative) along both their disease-preventing and fertility-preventing dimensions. If, for example, the only choice were not between the condom and no prevention but between the condom and the pill, AIDS would cause a substitution from the pill toward the condom, and the rates of unwanted and aborted pregnancies would both rise because the condom is a less effective fertility preventive than the pill.

If a third choice is allowed—abstinence—some users of the pill may substitute toward abstinence rather than toward condoms when disease risk increases; and with the level of sexual activity thus reduced, the number of pregnancies—wanted, unwanted, and aborted—will fall, along with the prevalence of all sexually transmitted diseases. As our reference to level of sexual activity suggests, abstinence is better viewed as an "activity level" response to disease risk than as a "care" response. This distinction is employed in the economic analysis of accidents and accident law[7] to distinguish between avoiding an accident by reducing the level of the activity that produces accidents as a by-product (for example, running fewer trains on a particular route) and conducting the same level of activity more carefully (for example, sounding the train's horn at crossings).

Not only can the level of an activity vary; so can the type of activity. Transportation accidents might be reduced by substituting canals for railroads. Here too there is an analogy to abstinence. From the standpoint of reducing fertility risk, the relevant abstinence is abstinence from vaginal intercourse, not from sexual activity altogether. An increase in disease

---

7. See Landes and Posner (1987) and Shavell (1987).

risk might thus induce an increase not in virginity but in oral sex, which carries zero fertility risk, and a switch from the pill to oral sex would reduce the rate of abortions and unwanted pregnancies.

There are further complications. Some couples use both the condom (for disease prevention) and the pill (for contraception) (Orr et al. 1992). Moreover, condoms are not a substitute for only the pill. They are also a substitute for other contraceptive methods, such as coitus interruptus, which are no more, and often less, reliable than condoms. We shall come back to this point; for now it is sufficient to have shown that the relation between AIDS and fertility is complex, and to have sketched an analytical framework that can be used to explore that relation empirically, using available data.

Tentative as it is, the foregoing analysis helps make sense of the Japanese government's reluctance, induced by AIDS, to relax its ban on the sale of the contraceptive pill in Japan. Originally motivated by concern with the health risks of the pill, the ban has gathered additional support as a method of retarding the spread of AIDS (Reid 1992). (And recall from Table I-1 in the Introduction the very low level of AIDS in Japan.) There need not be a high cost in unwanted pregnancies. The ban increases demand not only for condoms, but also for forms of "abstinence" (from vaginal intercourse, that is), like oral sex, that are even more effective from a contraceptive standpoint than condoms. Moreover, abortion has always been a less controversial procedure in Japan than in the United States, and the lower the cost of abortion, the lower the benefit of ex ante fertility preventives, such as the pill.

The analysis could be used to study the effect on preventive methods and fertility outcomes of an increase not in disease risk but in fertility risk. For example, we might expect that an exogenous increase in the demand for contraceptive sexual activity might result in substitution away from condoms and toward the pill or sterilization and a consequent increase in sexually transmitted disease with or without an increase in unwanted pregnancies. This appears to have happened when the "sexual revolution" of the 1960s (see Bell and Chaskes 1970; Biggar, Brinton, and Rosenthal 1989), continuing throughout the 1970s (see Centers for Disease Control 1991d, and especially Hofferth, Kahn, and Baldwin 1987)—a surge in the demand for nonmarital sexual activity aimed at pleasure rather than procreation—induced widespread substitution of the pill, first distributed in this country in 1960, for the condom. The pill both is a more effective contraceptive and avoids the condom's disutilities from a sexual-pleasure standpoint. A possible by-product of this substitution was the increased rate of syphilis and other sexually transmitted diseases (Felman 1989); consistent with this conjecture, women who have been surgically sterilized are less likely to use condoms than other women (Centers for Disease Control 1992c).

The causality is more complex than this simple sketch suggests. The increased demand for contraceptive sex was not entirely exogenous. Among its causes were both the invention of the pill[8] and the discovery of a cure for syphilis, developments that reduced two principal costs of sexual pleasure—fertility and disease. And as nonprocreative sex became more common, attitudes toward it became more tolerant—further increasing the demand for such sex, and hence for the pill, and hence for disease-risking sex. Moreover, much of the increase in the rate of syphilis as a result of the "sexual revolution" was among male homosexuals (Rolfs and Cates 1989), which had nothing to do with the pill.

The Effect on AIDS of Restricting Abortion

Consider now the effect of an increase in the cost of abortion, brought about by greater governmental restrictions on abortion,[9] on the AIDS epidemic. Of course, for women who would not consider an abortion even if there were no restrictions, the effect of restrictions on expected fertility costs ex post, and hence on the choice of a method of ex ante prevention, is nil. However, for women who are in the market for abortion—and there are many of them[10]—an increase in cost will affect their choice of ex ante method by increasing expected fertility costs. Since expected disease costs are unaffected, a method of prevention that has a low rate of failure as a fertility preventive but a high rate of failure as a disease preventive will become relatively more attractive, so there will be substitution toward it—substitution, for example, from condoms to the pill.[11]

---

8. For evidence that the pill, by reducing the fertility cost of sex, increases the frequency of vaginal intercourse, see Westoff, Bumpass, and Ryder (1969); Westoff (1974); and Brunborg (1984).

9. Although the Supreme Court reaffirmed the constitutional right of abortion in *Planned Parenthood v. Casey*, 112 S. Ct. 2791 (1992), it has authorized the states, in *Casey* itself and in *Webster v. Reproductive Health Services, Inc.*, 492 U.S. 490 (1989), to impose more restrictions than under the original regime of *Roe v. Wade*, decided in 1973.

10. There are more than 1.5 million legal abortions in the United States every year (Henshaw 1990; U.S. Bureau of the Census 1991, p. 71 [tab. 102]). On the demand for abortion, see Gohmann and Ohsfeldt (1992) and references there.

11. Or even to anal intercourse, which in Mediterranean and South American countries is a traditional form of contraceptive heterosexual intercourse. It is a prime example of a method of prevention that has low fertility risk and high disease risk.

Were that the only consequence of higher abortion costs, it would be plain that restricting abortion would have as an unintended by-product an increase in the incidence of AIDS, though the increase might be small. Another possible consequence of higher costs of abortion, however, is a substitution not from condoms to the pill but from sex to abstinence, which reduces to zero both fertility costs (the costs that increasing the cost of abortion raised) and disease costs. The centerpiece of the conservative program for reducing sexual risks, both of disease and of unwanted pregnancy, consists of efforts to induce the substitution of abstinence for nonmarital sex (Bennett 1988, pp. 2–4). The likely success of the program can thus be seen to depend on the elasticity of demand for abstinence with respect to measures, such as restricting the supply of condoms or of abortions, that increase the price of substitutes for abstinence. If the elasticity is low, and it is therefore unrealistic to believe that making abortion significantly more costly will result in a significant decline in nonmarital heterosexual intercourse, the effect of making abortion more costly may indeed be to increase the incidence of AIDS. It is therefore relevant to note that experience with earlier epidemics of sexually transmitted diseases suggests that preaching abstinence is unlikely to be a successful measure for controlling AIDS (Brandt 1988, pp. 368–369)—and that between 1982 and 1988, while American teenage girls used condoms in a significantly higher fraction of sexual encounters (Mosher 1990, p. 203), the rate of abstinence continued to fall (computed from Mosher 1990, p. 200 [tab. 2]). This is evidence that the elasticity of demand with respect to disease risk is much higher for condoms than for abstinence.

We emphasize once more the ambiguous character of the concept of "abstinence," and indeed of intercourse. Conservatives use "abstinence" to mean refraining from any sexual activity that involves orgasm, with the possible exception of solitary masturbation by teenage males. From the standpoint of the analysis of fertility, however, all abstinence means is refraining from *vaginal* intercourse. Mutual masturbation, petting to climax, and oral sex—all culminating in orgasm—are abstinent from a fertility standpoint, but not from the moral standpoint of sexual conservatives. Even if restricting contraception and abortion reduced (as it undoubtedly would) the amount of vaginal intercourse,[12] it would not

---

12. For empirical evidence that the frequency of a couple's vaginal intercourse is positively correlated with the effectiveness of the contraceptive method used by the couple, see Trussell and Westoff (1980).

significantly reduce the amount of sexual activity of which conservatives disapprove, and it might not even reduce the amount of AIDS.

Two further complications should be noted. First, substitution of the pill for condoms is not the only possible substitution effect from raising the price of abortion. A couple previously relying on abortion as a back-up to imperfect contraception may have been using a contraceptive method less safe than the condom, such as the rhythm method or coitus interruptus. An increase in the price of abortion may induce the couple to switch not to the pill but to condoms, resulting in a reduced disease risk as well as fertility risk. For this and other reasons, we are not able to predict the effect of restricting abortion on the incidence of AIDS.

Second, a complete analysis of the costs and benefits of restricting abortion cannot be limited to its effect on AIDS, but must also consider the effects on the number of pregnancies and births. There will be no effect on wanted pregnancies, the case where the demand for fertility protection is zero. And clearly there will be a negative effect on the number of abortions. The effect on unwanted pregnancies, however, is ambiguous. By increasing fertility costs, restrictions on abortion increase the incentive to take effective ex ante fertility precautions (our point about substitution from the condom to the pill) but increase the probability that if those precautions fail (and none of them is foolproof except abstinence) the pregnancy will result in a birth. Opponents of abortion generally focus on the second possibility. Cast in economic terms, their argument is that abortion has an external effect—on the fetus—that the mother and the abortionist do not fully internalize in the decision to abort. Evaluation of the argument runs into the problem, which we glanced at in Chapter 5, of defining the community whose welfare is to be taken into account in choosing welfare-maximizing policies. We shall not try to resolve that issue.

Conclusion

This book has challenged the conventional epidemiological and policy analyses of AIDS by examining the epidemic from an economic perspective, in which rational ex ante decisions designed to maximize utility in the face of uncertainty result ex post in increases or decreases in disease transmission. We therefore began our analysis by presenting a model of rational behavior toward the risk of AIDS. In this model, individuals who are contemplating sexual relations or other interactions that can transmit the AIDS virus compare the probability-adjusted costs and benefits of alternative practices, notably safe sex (for example, sex with condoms) and risky (unprotected) sex. Because safe sex imposes costs, chiefly in loss of sexual enjoyment, and because the expected cost of risky sex depends on the probability of infection, which is low for many people, rational behavior in the face of the risk of AIDS does not imply the elimination of all risky sex.

Simple and indeed obvious as this conclusion is, it has significant implications for policy that have been largely ignored in both the policy debates and the scholarly literature. It implies that once the virus is introduced into the population, and at least pending the development of a low-cost vaccine or cure, the optimal level of AIDS is greater than zero, and this creates an immediate problem for efforts to infer the need for public intervention from the fact that AIDS is a fatal infectious disease. The rational model also implies quite different, and less alarming, estimates of the future growth of the disease than most epidemiological models do because an increasing risk of infection leads rational persons to substitute away from risky sex, making the growth of the disease self-limiting.

We evaluated hypotheses generated by the rational model with data collected by ourselves and others concerning knowledge of AIDS, spread of the disease, behavioral changes in response to that spread, the growth in demand for HIV testing, and various demographic correlates of the disease, and found that the data support the model. The data do not prove, nor do we believe, that people are completely rational in sexual or other AIDS-risky behavior. They support the more modest hypothesis that this behavior has a sufficiently large rational component to exhibit patterns, regularities, and tendencies better explained by economic theory than by competing approaches. Puzzling discrepancies, for example the more than threefold difference between black and white women in the incidence of the disease, turn out to have an economic explanation.

Underscoring the difference between utility in the economist's sense and the public-health goal of minimizing the prevalence of disease, we showed how rational responses in the private market for unsafe sex, and in other risky activities, to the risk of AIDS—responses such as an increased demand for voluntary HIV testing—may have no effect on, or may even increase rather than, as generally assumed, decrease, the spread of the disease. A simple model of the demand for HIV testing implies that such testing enables people to obtain risky sexual trades by producing proof of negative infection status, and thus increases the amount of risky sex. This implication may—or may not—hold up when the analysis is complicated by taking into account such possibilities as altruistic behavior in the sexual marketplace and concealment of test results from the sexual partners of the person tested. The safest conclusion is that testing can increase the spread of the disease but is not certain to do so. A better understanding of the private demand for HIV testing is necessary in order to resolve the question, which is therefore an economic rather than a medical or epidemiological one.

Since the existence of an ex post cost in death and disability from AIDS is consistent with rational ex ante utility-maximizing behavior, just as the existence of fatal automobile accidents is consistent with driving being a form of utility-maximizing behavior, we were led to question the magnitude of the social as distinct from private costs of the disease. We found negative externalities, but fewer than are assumed to exist by the supporters of aggressive public intervention through regulation and subsidies. In particular, since the disease can be avoided with near certainty by the avoidance of particular risky activities, the cost of that avoidance caps the costs, both the voluntarily assumed costs and the external costs, of the disease. This conclusion led us to cast a critical eye on the various forms that the actual and proposed interventions have taken. Some of the programs, we found, may be downright perverse, such as the subsidization of voluntary testing, which (as just noted) may increase rather than decrease the spread of the disease, at least until almost everyone has been tested. Mandatory testing, unless universal, is likely to have the same effect as subsidized voluntary testing. Therefore, it is probably a mistake to impose mandatory testing on particular occupations such as health care or the military—while universal mandatory testing would in all likelihood involve costs in excess of the benefits.

A variety of punitive measures have been proposed—and some implemented—to combat AIDS. We classified punitive measures as trade taxes (taxes on risky activities) or transmission taxes (taxes on transmitting the virus). Many of these measures appear to be excessively draconian, ineffectual, or even counterproductive from a disease-reducing standpoint. We do endorse the criminalization of knowingly failing to disclose to one's sexual partner that one is infected with the AIDS virus. Although such a penalty reduces the demand for testing, that is not necessarily a bad consequence if we are correct that testing is as likely to increase as to decrease the incidence of the disease. The penalty may also reduce the incentive that testing gives persons who test positive for the AIDS virus, if they are not altruistic, to engage in risky sex. As throughout the book, many of our conclusions are counterintuitive. For example, we argue that testing immigrants for HIV and admitting only those who test negative may increase the spread of the disease more than admitting a few HIV carriers would do.

Subsidies for educating the public about AIDS are another example (like subsidies for HIV testing and counseling) of an almost universally supported anti-AIDS policy that is as likely to have no effect on or even to increase the spread of the disease as to decrease it. One effect of the subsidies is to increase the supply of information about AIDS to people who either have the information already or are unlikely to act on it because their risk of infection is very low. Another effect is to induce risky behavior because accurate information operates to dispel exaggerated fears held by persons in low-risk groups. A third possibility, which our regression analysis supports, is that these subsidies have no effect on the level of knowledge about AIDS and hence on behavior involving risky sex. Even if an education subsidy can be justified, moreover, its current allocation across the different risk groups appears to be inefficient—so one of our constructive proposals is for a different method of allocating educational expenditures across different regions and risk groups, assuming that such expenditures continue to be made.

The distribution of condoms free of charge is a more attractive proposal, but even it has many problems and could increase rather than decrease the growth of the disease. One of the most attractive of all actual or proposed subsidy programs is the subsidization of clean hypodermic needles for intravenous drug users. However, it is highly controversial because it would reduce the cost of drug abuse and thereby increase its incidence, which might in turn increase the amount of risky sexual behavior. And maybe it is unnecessary, since used needles can, as more and more intravenous drug users understand, easily be decontaminated with household liquid bleach.

Some public subsidization of basic (as distinct from applied) medical research on AIDS can be defended, although this depends in part on the potential level of private charitable support of AIDS research. The current level of public subsidization may be too great, however, especially since much current federal spending on AIDS research involves areas of research—research into possible vaccines, cures, and ameliorative treatments—that could be left largely though not entirely to the private sector because most of the fruits of such research, as distinct from those of basic research, are commercially appropriable. Moreover, the development of vaccines, cures, and meliorative treatments might not reduce, and might even increase, the prevalence of AIDS, while meliorative treatments may increase the epidemic's total costs, including costs of death and disability.

All this may sound "conservative," in the sense of hostile to government intervention. Yet a liberal philosopher who is also a homosexual-rights advocate has preceded us in arguing for de-emphasizing the external costs of the disease (Mohr 1988, ch. 8). And we have argued that the program of moral conservatives, which stresses abstinence from all orgasmic sexual activity outside of marriage, and from all use of illegal drugs, would probably be ineffective in reducing the spread of AIDS and could even be counterproductive, if for example it encouraged bisexual or homosexual men to marry women, a frequent occurrence in societies that are hostile to homosexuality. Moreover, conservatives' proposals for encouraging abstinence, for example by making condoms less available, seem more likely to induce substitutions within the class of orgasmic activities of which conservatives disapprove than true abstinence from nonmarital sex. The success of the Swedish approach to AIDS offers some (though weak) empirical evidence that Puritanism is not necessary to the effective control of sexually transmitted diseases.

In addition, some conservative criticisms of public aid for AIDS research and treatment have a hollow ring. Although federal funding of such research may be excessive, we argued that this is not provable simply by a comparison of the ratio of AIDS research expenditures per AIDS death to, say, cancer research expenditures per cancer death. Nor can AIDS be regarded as entirely a consequence of voluntarily undertaken risky activities, even when the mode of transmission is consensual sex or needle-sharing. If the 10-year estimate of the median incubation period of the disease is correct, even today about half the new cases of AIDS probably are the result of infection that occurred before people could have known that their sexual practices were creating a risk of fatal illness. The disease was first diagnosed in 1981, and it was not until 1983 that knowledge of the methods of transmission and prevention was widely diffused, and not until 1985, with the death of Rock Hudson, that media attention to the disease soared (Brown 1992, p. 728 [fig. 16.2]).

The essential normative point is that, from an economic perspective at least, the public sector may be too deeply involved in the campaign against AIDS. The proposals for further public intervention, whether they come from the liberal or the conservative end of the political spectrum, would if adopted amplify this excessive, and perhaps even perverse, governmental involvement.

That the forms and levels of public intervention in the AIDS epidemic appear not to be optimal from the standpoint either of economic efficiency or of disease minimization may illustrate a general characteristic of governmental activities even when those activities are undertaken in the public interest. From a public-interest standpoint, government intervenes when a social problem is too difficult for the free market to solve; and we expect a high failure rate in dealing with difficult problems. Nevertheless, we were led to explore the possibility of a redistributive explanation for the nonoptimal pattern of AIDS policy. We conjectured that pressure from small but organized groups consisting of male homosexuals, health professionals, government bureaucrats, moral conservatives, and pharmaceutical companies has deflected AIDS programs from the efficient path. Education expenditures have been used to increase the public's fear of AIDS and hence willingness to support subsidies for medical research and development. And subsidies (for example, for HIV testing) have been slanted in favor of members of high-risk populations other than intravenous drug users, who do not constitute an effective interest group, in part because of disapproval of their activities on moral grounds and in part because they are disproportionately non-voters. The overall AIDS program can perhaps best be understood as an involuntary compromise—more accurately, the result of a collision of contending forces—among male homosexuals and public health professionals, on the one hand, and moral conservatives on the other. We pointed out that, currently at least, the public health community is deriving greater benefits from government AIDS programs than the homosexual community.

We concluded with a look at the interaction between AIDS and fertility risks. We showed, for example, that restrictions on abortion may increase the spread of the disease—another counterintuitive result of economic analysis and another reason to doubt that moral conservatism is the answer to AIDS. Here and elsewhere our conclusions are unlikely to be popular, because many of them are contrary both to positions advocated by the AIDS lobby (consisting primarily of homosexual-rights advocates and health professionals) and to positions advocated by conservatives. For example, we agree with the latter that AIDS, with the important exception of persons who became infected before the discovery of the disease, is largely a by-product of voluntary "life style" choices; but we do not believe that this characterization dictates the optimal form of public intervention. We have serious reservations about mandatory testing, quarantining, and other regulatory proposals of conservatives, but equally serious reservations about the scale of the subsidy programs favored by liberals.

The main objective of our study has in any event been scientific rather than polemical. We have tried to show that economics can illuminate a variety of issues concerning the AIDS epidemic by treating systematically the behavioral choices that are shaping the epidemic and that determine the effects of measures taken against it. Economics can improve the predictions and prescriptions of the medical and public health professionals, including epidemiologists, who have devoted their knowledge and experience to combating the epidemic, and can sharpen the evaluation of public policy responses to AIDS. Economic epidemiology is not just a matter of relabeling familiar insights with economic jargon. It challenges the conventional wisdom, advances testable hypotheses, proposes counterintuitive insights.

The significance of this study is not limited to AIDS. It extends to communicable diseases generally (in fact we illustrated our analysis from time to time with examples of other sexually transmitted diseases), and thus to epidemiology and other branches of public health, a field that economists have largely ignored. Many such diseases are avoidable by behavioral change—such as boiling water, avoiding certain foods, or avoiding infected persons—at lower cost than by medical intervention. Vaccination—a fundamental tool of public health—presents a variety of subtle and neglected economic issues, including the cost of vaccination in lowering natural immunity[1] and the rapid diminution of its benefits when the prevalence of the disease drops to extremely low levels.[2]

The fact that behavior toward fertility risk can be analyzed within the same basic framework that we have used to analyze behavior toward the risk of AIDS leads us to hope that the approach taken in this book can be applied to a number of interesting and important problems unrelated to AIDS, other sexually transmitted diseases, or even communicable diseases generally, in the areas of health, education, public regulation and subsidization, and the family. Illustrative problems are changes in sexual mores, at which we glanced briefly in Chapter 9, and changes in the demand for and frequency of abortion. Contraception and disease prevention are closely related analytically. And aborted pregnancies can be analogized to HIV infection; both are forms of accident, resulting from the fact that the risky behavior that produces them is valued over the safe alternative. Just as an increase in the cost of sexually transmitted disease reduces the prevalence of that disease by inducing safer sex, so an increase in the cost of abortions, whether the increase is brought about by legal restrictions or by other means, induces a greater use of contraception and thus a reduction in the number of unwanted pregnancies, though the fraction of such pregnancies that are aborted will fall. A reduction in the cost of contraception will have a similar effect. Planned Parenthood and the Moral Majority agree in wanting to minimize the number of abortions, though by different routes—Planned Parenthood wants to encourage contraception, and the Moral Majority wants to restrict abortion. Economics helps us see that these approaches are consistent. It also helps us see, however, that if the welfare of the

---

1. In this case, contrary to the usual view, vaccination imposes a *negative* externality.

2. Recall the steady-state model of Chapters 1 and 2. If because of vaccination the percentage of healthy but susceptible persons (S in the model) falls to a very low level, the disease may disappear without further intervention. That happened with smallpox. Note that if vaccination is not compulsory, S may rise after falling, as the reduced risk of infection induces more people to choose not to be vaccinated.

fetus is disregarded (a big if), a zero rate of abortion would be inefficient even if a prohibition of abortion could be enforced at zero cost. But an adequate analysis of these issues is a task for another day.

This book is not the definitive study of AIDS. We have largely although not entirely ignored the evidence of systematic nonrational elements in human decision-making (Tversky and Kahneman 1981; Bell, Raiffa, and Tversky 1988).[3] We have neglected the Third World, in parts of which the incidence of HIV is much higher than it is in the United States. And we have slighted the ethical issues raised by the AIDS epidemic and responses to it. In particular, although we recognize the social-insurance argument for public subsidization of AIDS research and treatment, we did not attempt to evaluate it fully. Ours is an *economic* analysis, and we do not suggest that economics is the only fruitful perspective from which to view the social issues raised by the epidemic, merely that it is a neglected one. We have proposed a variety of economic models for analyzing the different aspects of the AIDS crisis, and have presented many new data. Our hope is that this book will be recognized as a convincing demonstration that the economic perspective is relevant to AIDS, as a useful contribution to the scientific and policy literatures on the epidemic, as a source of fresh and interesting data, insights, hypotheses, and research proposals, and as a persuasive illustration of the power of economics to explain social phenomena occurring outside explicit markets.

---

3. For an excellent brief summary of this literature, see Arrow (1988).

References

Abbott, Andrew. 1988. *The System of Professions: An Essay on the Division of Expert Labor*. Chicago: University of Chicago Press.

Aboulker, Jean-Pierre, and Ann Marie Swart. 1993. "Preliminary Analysis of the Concorde Trial." *Lancet* 341: 889–890.

ACFC Investigators. 1992. "AIDS and Sexual Behaviour in France." *Nature* 360: 407–409.

Adler, Jerry. 1991. "Safer Sex." *Newsweek*, Dec. 9: 52.

Altman, Ronald, et al. 1992. "Premarital HIV-1 Testing in New Jersey." *Journal of Acquired Immune Deficiency Syndromes* 5: 7–11.

American Health Consultants. 1992a. "CDC's Expanded AIDS Case Definition Sparks Controversy." *AIDS Alert* 7: 65–72.

——— 1992b. "Blood Supply 'Getting Safer All the Time.' " *AIDS Alert* 7: following p. 72.

Anderson, Gary M. 1990. "Parasites, Profits, and Politicians: Public Health and Public Choice." *Cato Journal* 9: 557–578.

Anderson, Roy M., and Robert M. May. 1991. *Infectious Diseases of Humans: Dynamics and Control*. Oxford: Oxford University Press.

Anderson, R. M., S. Gupta, and R. M. May. 1991. "Potential of Community-Wide Chemotherapy or Immunotherapy to Control the Spread of HIV-1." *Nature* 350: 356–359.

Anderson, Warwick. 1991. "The New York Needle Trial: The Politics of Public Health in the Age of AIDS." *American Journal of Public Health* 81: 1506–1517.

Aral, Sevgi O., and King H. Holmes. 1990. "Epidemiology of Sexual Behavior and Sexually Transmitted Diseases." In King H. Holmes et al., eds., *Sexually Transmitted Diseases* (2nd ed.): 19–36. New York: McGraw-Hill Information Services.

Aral, Sevgi O., et al. 1991. "Demographic and Societal Factors Influencing Risk Behaviors." In Wasserheit et al. (1991): 161, 168.

Archer, Victor E. 1989. "Psychological Defenses and Control of AIDS." *American Journal of Public Health* 79: 876–878.

Arrow, Kenneth J. 1988. "Behavior under Uncertainty and Its Implications for Policy." In Bell, Raiffa, and Tversky (1988): 497, 500–505.

Aruffo, John F., John H. Coverdale, and Carlos Vallbona. 1991. "AIDS Knowledge in Low-Income and Minority Populations." *Public Health Reports* 106: 115–119.

Åsard, Per-Erik. 1992. "Anal Sex." *Nature* 359: 182.

Atkinson, A. B., and J. L. Skegg. 1973. "Anti-Smoking Publicity and the Demand for Tobacco in the U.K." *Manchester School of Economic and Social Studies* 41: 265–282.

Bacchetti, Peter, and Nicholas P. Jewell. 1991. "Nonparametric Estimation of the Incubation Period of AIDS Based on a Prevalent Cohort with Unknown Infection Times." *Biometrics* 47: 947–960.

Bailey, Norman. 1975. *The Mathematical Theory of Infectious Diseases and Its Applications.* 2nd ed. New York: Hafner Press.

Baily, Mary Ann, et al. 1990. "Economic Consequences for Medicaid of Human Immunodeficiency Virus Infection." *Health Care Financing Review,* 1990 Annual Supplement: 97, 99.

Barr, Charles E., et al. 1992. "Recovery of Infectious HIV-1 from Whole Saliva: Blood Proves More Likely Virus Transmitter." *Journal of the American Dental Association* 123 (Feb.): 37–45.

Battjes, Robert J., and Roy W. Pickens, eds. 1988. *Needle Sharing among Intravenous Drug Abusers: National and International Perspectives* (NIDA Research Monograph 80). Washington, D.C.: Government Printing Office.

Bayer, Ronald, and Cheryl Healton. 1989. "Controlling AIDS in Cuba: The Logic of Quarantine." *New England Journal of Medicine* 320: 1022–1024.

Bayer, Ronald, and Kathleen E. Toomey. 1992. "HIV Prevention and the Two Faces of Partner Notification." *American Journal of Public Health* 82: 1158–1164.

Bazell, Robert. 1992. "Happy Campers: Cuba's Sanitarium for AIDS Patients." *New Republic,* March 9: 12–14.

Becker, Gary S. 1975. *Human Capital: A Theoretical and Empirical Analysis, with Special Reference to Education.* 2nd ed. New York: Columbia University Press.

———— 1976. *The Economic Approach to Human Behavior.* Chicago: University of Chicago Press.

———— 1983. "A Theory of Competition among Pressure Groups for Political Influence." *Quarterly Journal of Economics* 93: 371–400.

———— 1991. *A Treatise on the Family.* Enlarged ed. Cambridge, Mass.: Harvard University Press.

Becker, Gary S., Michael Grossman, and Kevin M. Murphy. 1991. "Rational Addiction and the Effect of Price on Consumption." *American Economic Review* 81 (May, Papers and Proceedings): 237–241.

Becker, Gary S., and M. Rebecca Kilburn. 1992. "The Value of Living, Misery, and Suicide." Unpublished paper, Department of Economics, University of Chicago.

Becker, Marshall H., and Jill G. Joseph. 1988. "AIDS and Behavioral Change to Reduce Risk: A Review." *American Journal of Public Health* 78: 394–410.

Becker, Neils. 1989. *Analysis of Infectious Disease Data.* New York: Chapman and Hall.

Bell, David E. 1988. "Disappointment in Decision Making under Uncertainty." In Bell, Raiffa, and Tversky (1988): 358–383.

Bell, David E., and Howard Raiffa. 1988. "Marginal Value and Intrinsic Risk Aversion." In Bell, Raiffa, and Tversky (1988): 384–397.

Bell, David E., Howard Raiffa, and Amos Tversky, eds. 1988. *Decision Making: Descriptive, Normative, and Prescriptive Interactions.* Cambridge: Cambridge University Press.

Bell, Robert R., and Jay B. Chaskes. 1970. "Premarital Sexual Experience among Coeds, 1958 and 1968." *Journal of Marriage and the Family* 32: 81–84.

Belongia, Edward A. 1988. "Border Hopping as a Consequence of Premarital HIV Screening: The Kenosha Diamond." *JAMA (Journal of the American Medical Association)* 260: 1883–1884.

Bennett, Charles L., Marilyn Cvitanic, and Anthony Pascal. 1991. "The Costs of AIDS in Los Angeles." *Journal of Acquired Immune Deficiency Syndromes* 4: 197, 201.

Bennett, William J. 1988. "AIDS: Education and Public Policy." *Saint Louis University Public Law Review* 7: 1–11.

Berger, Mark C., and J. Paul Leigh. 1989. "Schooling, Self-Selection, and Health." *Journal of Human Resources* 24: 433–455.

Bernstein, Gerald S. 1990. "Barriers: Contraceptive and Noncontraceptive Effects." In Voeller et al. (1990): 345, 348 (tab. 22-3).

Berzofsky, Jay A. 1991. "Approaches and Issues in the Development of Vaccines against HIV." *Journal of Acquired Immune Deficiency Syndromes* 4: 451–459.

Biggar, Robert J., Louise A. Brinton, and Miriam D. Rosenthal. 1989. "Trends in the Number of Sexual Partners among American Women." *Journal of Acquired Immune Deficiency Syndromes* 2: 497–502.

Biggar, Robert J., and Mads Melbye. 1992. "Responses to Anonymous Questionnaires concerning Sexual Behaviour: A Method to Examine Potential Biases." *American Journal of Public Health* 82: 1506, 1509.

Blendon, Robert J., Karen Donelan, and Richard A. Knox. 1992. "Public Opinion and AIDS: Lessons for the Second Decade." *JAMA (Journal of the American Medical Association)* 267: 981–986.

Bloom, David E., and Geoffrey Carliner. 1988. "The Economic Impact of AIDS in the United States." *Science* 239: 604–610.

Bloom, David E., and Sherry Glied. 1991. "Benefits and Costs of HIV Testing." *Science* 252: 1798–1804.

Blue Sheet editorial staff. 1991. "HIV in Women: Oral Estroprogestinic Contraceptive Use Was Associated with 50% Risk Reduction." *Blue Sheet* 34: 3–4.

Blythe, Stephen P., and Carlos Castillo-Chavez. 1989. "Like-with-Like Preference and Sexual Mixing Models." *Mathematical Biosciences* 96: 221–238.

Bongaarts, John. "A Model of the Spread of HIV Infection and the Demographic Impact of AIDS." 1989. *Statistics in Medicine* 8: 103–120.

Booth, William. 1988. "No Longer Ignored, AIDS Funds Just Keep Growing." *Science* 242: 858–859.

Boulton, Mary. 1991. "Review of the Literature on Bisexuality and HIV Transmission." In Tielman, Carballo, and Hendriks (1991): 187, 203.

Boulton, M., G. Hart, and R. Fitzpatrick. 1992. "The Sexual Behaviour of Bisexual Men in Relation to HIV Transmission." *AIDS Care* 4: 165, 173.

Bozinoff, Lorne, and Peter MacIntosh. 1992. "79% Say No Change in Behavior Necessary Because of AIDS." *The Gallup Report* (Canada), Feb. 3: 1–4.

Brandt, Allan M. 1985. *No Magic Bullet: A Social History of Venereal Disease in the United States since 1880.* New York: Oxford University Press.

———— 1988. "AIDS in Historical Perspective: Four Lessons from the History of Sexually Transmitted Diseases." *American Journal of Public Health* 78: 367–371.

———— 1990. "Sexually Transmitted Disease: Shadow on the Land, Revisited." *Annals of Internal Medicine* 112: 481–483.

Brettle, Ray P., and Clifford L. S. Leen. 1991. "The Natural History of HIV and AIDS in Women." *AIDS* 5: 1283–1292.

Brewer, T. Ford, and Janice Derrickson. 1992. "AIDS in Prison: A Review of Epidemiology and Preventive Policy." *AIDS* 6: 623, 626.

Brito, Dagobert L., Eytan Sheshinski, and Michael D. Intriligator. 1991. "Externalities and Compulsory Vaccinations." *Journal of Public Economics* 45: 69–90.

Brody, Jane E. 1987. "Personal Health." *New York Times,* March 4: C8.

Brookmeyer, Ron. 1991. "Reconstruction and Future Trend of the AIDS Epidemic in the United States." *Science* 253: 37–42.

Brookmeyer, Ron, and Mitchell H. Gail. 1988. "A Method for Obtaining Short Term Projections and Lower Bounds on the Size of the AIDS Epidemic." *Journal of the American Statistical Association* 83: 301–308.

Brookmeyer, Ron, and Jiangang Liao. 1990. "The Analysis of Delays in Disease Reporting: Methods and Results for the Acquired Immunodeficiency Syndrome." *American Journal of Epidemiology* 132: 355–365.

Brown, George R., and Joseph Pace. 1989. "Reduced Sexual Activity in HIV-Infected Homosexual Men." *JAMA (Journal of the American Medical Association)* 261: 2503.

Brown, Larry K., R. J. DiClimente, and N. S. Beausoleil. 1992. "Comparison of Human Immunodeficiency Virus Related Knowledge, Attitudes, Intentions, and Behaviors among Sexually Active and Abstinent Young Adolescents." *Journal of Adolescent Health* 13: 140–145.

Brown, Phyllida. "AIDS in the Media." 1992. In Global AIDS Policy Coalition (1992): 720–732.

Brunborg, Helge. 1984. *An Economic Model of Fertility, Sex and Contraception:* 173 (tab. 3.17), 254. Oslo: Central Bureau of Statistics of Norway.

Buckley, William F. 1986. "Crucial Steps in Combatting the AIDS Epidemic: Identify All the Carriers." *New York Times,* March 18: A27.

Buehler, James W., Ruth L. Berkelman, and Jeanette K. Stehr-Green. 1992. "The Completeness of AIDS Surveillance." *Journal of Acquired Immune Deficiency Syndromes* 5: 257–264.

Burgess, Ann W., and Timothy Baker. 1992. "AIDS and Victims of Sexual Assault." *Hospital and Community Psychiatry* 43: 447–448.

Bush, Alan J., and Gregory W. Boller. 1991. "Rethinking the Role of Television Advertising during Health Crises: A Rhetorical Analysis of the Federal AIDS Campaigns." *Journal of Advertising* 20: 28–37.

Butcher, Ann H., D. Thompson Manning, and Edgar C. O'Neal. 1991. "HIV-Related Sexual Behaviors of College Students." *Journal of the American College Health Association* 40: 115–118.

Calsyn, Donald A., et al. 1991. "Needle-Use Practices among Intravenous Drug Users in an Area Where Needle Purchase Is Legal." *AIDS* 5: 187–193.

——— 1992. "Ineffectiveness of AIDS Education and HIV Antibody Testing in Reducing High-Risk Behaviors among Injection Drug Users." *American Journal of Public Health* 82: 573–575.

Campbell, Carole A. 1991. "Prostitution, AIDS, and Preventive Health Behavior." *Social Science and Medicine* 32: 1367, 1371.

Capilouto, Eli J., et al. 1992. "What Is the Dentist's Occupational Risk of Becoming Infected with Hepatitis B or the Human Immunodeficiency Virus?" *American Journal of Public Health* 82: 587–589.

Cappon, Paul. 1991. "HIV: The Debate over Isolation as a Measure of Personal Control." *Canadian Journal of Public Health* 82: 404–408.

Carballo, Manuel, Oussama Tawil, and King Holmes. 1991. "Sexual Behaviors: Temporal and Cross-Cultural Trends." In Wasserheit et al. (1991): 122, 133.

Castillo-Chavez, C., ed. 1988. *Mathematical and Statistical Approaches to AIDS Epidemiology.* New York: Springer-Verlag.

Catania, Joseph A., Susan M. Kegeles, and Thomas J. Coates. 1990. "Psychosocial Predictors of People Who Fail to Return for Their HIV Test Results." *AIDS* 4: 261–262.

Catania, Joseph A., et al. 1990. "Methodological Problems in AIDS Behavioral Research: Influences on Measurement Error and Participation Bias in Studies of Sexual Behavior." *Psychological Bulletin* 108: 339, 341.

Catania, Joseph A., et al. 1992. "Condom Use in Multi-Ethnic Neighborhoods of San Francisco: The Population-Based AMEN (AIDS in Multi-Ethnic Neighborhoods) Study." *American Journal of Public Health* 82: 284–287.

Cates, Willard, Jr., and Katherine M. Stone. 1992. "Family Planning, Sexually Transmitted Diseases and Contraceptive Choice: A Literature Update—Part I." *Family Planning Perspectives* 24: 75–84.

Centers for Disease Control. 1988. "Partner Notification for Preventing Human Immunodeficiency Virus (HIV) Infection—Colorado, Idaho, South Carolina, Virginia." *Morbidity and Mortality Weekly Report* 37: 393–402.

——— 1989a. *National HIV Seroprevalence Surveys: Summary of Results: Data from*

Seroprevalence Surveys through 1989 (HIV/CID/9–90/006). Rockville: National AIDS Information Clearinghouse.

—— 1989b. "Trends in Gonorrhea in Homosexually Active Men—King County, Washington, 1989." *JAMA (Journal of the American Medical Association)* 262: 2985–2986.

—— 1990a. *Sexually Transmitted Disease Surveillance 1990.* Atlanta: Centers for Disease Control.

—— 1990b. "Estimates of HIV Prevalence and Projected AIDS Cases: Summary of a Workshop, October 31–November 1, 1989." *Morbidity and Mortality Weekly Report* 39: 110, 117 (tab. 2).

—— 1991a. *What Does AIDS Mean to You?* Sept. D056: 2. Atlanta: Centers for Disease Control.

—— 1991b. "Publicly Funded HIV Counseling and Testing—United States, 1990." *Morbidity and Mortality Weekly Report* 40: 666–675.

—— 1991c. "HIV/AIDS Knowledge and Awareness of Testing and Treatment—Behavioral Risk Factor Surveillance System, 1990." *Morbidity and Mortality Weekly Report* 40: 794, 795 (tab. 1).

—— 1991d. "Current Trends in Premarital Sexual Experience among Adolescent Women—United States, 1970–1988." *Archives of Dermatology* 127: 311–312.

—— 1992a. "HIV Prevention in U.S. Correctional System, 1991." *Morbidity and Mortality Weekly Report* 41: 389–397.

—— 1992b. "HIV/AIDS Knowledge and Awareness of Testing and Treatment—Behavioral Risk Factor Surveillance." *JAMA (Journal of the American Medical Association)* 267: 27–28.

—— 1992c. "Surgical Sterilization among Women and Use of Condoms—Baltimore, 1989–1990." *JAMA (Journal of the American Medical Association)* 268: 1833–1834.

—— 1993. *HIV/AIDS Surveillance,* Feb. (Year-End Edition). Atlanta: Centers for Disease Control and Prevention.

Chandarana, Praful C., et al. 1990. "The AIDS Dilemma: Worry and Concern over AIDS." *Canadian Journal of Public Health* 81: 222–225.

Chang, Sophia W., Mitchell H. Katz, and Sandra R. Hernandez. 1992. "The New AIDS Case Definition: Implications for San Francisco." *JAMA (Journal of the American Medical Association)* 267: 973–975.

Chase, Marilyn. 1992a. "Multiple Mutating HIV Strains Stymie Researchers Seeking a Vaccine for AIDS." *Wall Street Journal,* May 26: B1.

—— 1992b. "Researcher Sees U.S. Cost of Treating AIDS Virus Rising Sharply by 1995." *Wall Street Journal,* July 23: B6.

Chu, Susan Y., et al. 1992. "AIDS in Bisexual Men in the United States: Epidemiology and Transmission to Women." *American Journal of Public Health* 82: 220–224.

Cleary, Paul D. 1991. "Behavior Changes after Notification of HIV Infection." *American Journal of Public Health* 81: 1586–1590.

Clifford, Karen A., and Russel P. Iuculano. 1988. "AIDS and Insurance: The Rationale for AIDS-Related Testing." *Harvard Law Review* 100: 1806–1825.

Clotfelter, Charles T. 1985. *Federal Tax Policy and Charitable Giving:* 75. Chicago: University of Chicago Press.

Coase, R. H. 1960. "The Problem of Social Cost." *Journal of Law and Economics* 3: 1–44.

Coates, Thomas J. 1990. "Strategies for Modifying Sexual Behavior for Primary and Secondary Prevention of HIV Disease." *Journal of Consulting and Clinical Psychology* 58: 57, 58.

Coates, Thomas J., et al. 1988. "AIDS Antibody Testing: Will It Stop the AIDS Epidemic? Will It Help People Infected with HIV?" *American Psychologist* 43: 859, 860.

Cochran, Susan D., and Vickie M. Mays. 1990. "Sex, Lies, and HIV." *New England Journal of Medicine* 322: 774–775.

Cohen, Judith, Priscilla Alexander, and Constance Wofsky. 1988. "Prostitutes and AIDS: Public Policy Issues." *AIDS and Public Policy Journal* 3 (Winter): 16, 18.

Colgate, Stirling A., et al. 1989. "Risk Behavior-Based Model of the Cubic Growth of Acquired Immunodeficiency Syndrome in the United States." *Proceedings of the National Academy of Science* 86: 4793–4797.

Collier, Ann C., et al. 1990. "A Pilot Study of Low-Dose Zidovudine in Human Immunodeficiency Virus Infection." *New England Journal of Medicine* 323: 1015–1021.

Colón, Héctor Manuel, et al. 1992. "Changes in HIV Risk Behaviors among Intravenous Drug Users in San Juan, Puerto Rico." *British Journal of Addiction* 87: 585–590.

Compton, William M. III, et al. 1992. "Legal Needle Buying in St. Louis." *American Journal of Public Health* 82: 595–596.

Comptroller General of the United States. 1980. *Discussion of Selected Issues Affecting Federal Immunization Activities:* 11–12. Washington, D.C.: U.S. General Accounting Office.

Consumer Reports staff. 1989. "Can You Rely on Condoms?" *Consumer Reports,* March: 135–141.

Corby, Nancy H., et al. 1991. "AIDS Knowledge, Perception of Risk, and Behaviors among Female Sex Partners of Injection Drug Users." *AIDS Education and Prevention* 3: 353, 363.

Cornell Law Review staff. 1984. "Note, Liability in Tort for the Sexual Transmission of Disease: Genital Herpes and the Law." *Cornell Law Review* 70: 101–140.

Coutinho, R. A., et al. 1987. "Influence of Special Surveillance Programmes and AIDS on Declining Incidence of Syphilis in Amsterdam." *Genitourinary Medicine* 63: 210–213.

Creagh-Kirk, Terri. 1988. "Survival Experience among Patients with AIDS Receiving Zidovudine." *JAMA (Journal of the American Medical Association)* 260: 3009–3015.

Crystal, Stephen, et al. 1990. "AIDS Contact Notification: Initial Program Results in New Jersey." *AIDS Education and Prevention* 2: 284–295.

Csonka, G. W., and J. K. Oates, eds. 1990a. *Sexually Transmitted Diseases: A Textbook of Genitourinary Medicine.* London: Balliere Tindall.

Csonka, G. W., and J. K. Oates. 1990b. "Syphilis." In Csonka and Oates (1990a): 227, 232.

Curran, William, Larry Gostin, and Mary Clark. 1988. *AIDS: Legal and Regulatory Policy.* Frederick, Md.: University Publishing Group.

Dalton, Harlon L., et al., eds. 1987. *AIDS and the Law: A Guide for the Public.* New Haven: Yale University Press.

Daniels, Norman. 1992. "HIV-Infected Professionals, Patient Rights, and the 'Switching Dilemma.'" *JAMA (Journal of the American Medical Association)* 267: 1368–1371.

Danila, Richard N., et al. 1991. "A Look-Back Investigation of Patients of an HIV-Infected Physician." *New England Journal of Medicine* 325: 1406–1411.

Dannemeyer, William E., and Michael G. Franc. 1989. "The Failure of AIDS-Prevention Education." *Public Interest,* Summer: 47–60.

Darke, Shane, et al. 1992. "Drug Use and HIV Risk-Taking Behaviour among Clients in Methadone Maintenance Treatment." *Drug and Alcohol Dependence* 29: 263, 266.

Davies, Stephen. 1979. *The Diffusion of Process Innovations:* ch. 2. Cambridge: Cambridge University Press.

DeBuono, Barbara A., et al. 1990. "Sexual Behavior of College Women in 1975, 1986, and 1989." *New England Journal of Medicine* 322: 821, 824.

De Cock, Kevin M., et al. 1988. "Experience with Human Immunodeficiency Virus Infection in Patients with Hepatitis B Virus and Hepatitis Delta Virus Infections in Los Angeles, 1977–1985." *American Journal of Epidemiology* 127: 1250, 1258.

De Schryver, A., and A. Meheus. 1990. "Epidemiology of Sexually Transmitted Diseases: The Global Picture." *Bulletin of the World Health Organization* 68: 639–654.

de Sousa, Ronald. 1987. *The Rationality of Emotion.* Cambridge, Mass.: MIT Press.

Des Jarlais, Don C. 1992a. "The First and Second Decades of AIDS among Injecting Drug Users." *British Journal of Addiction* 87: 347, 349–350.

——— 1992b. "AIDS and the Transition to Illicit Drug Injection—Results of a Randomized Trial Prevention Program." *British Journal of Addiction* 87: 493–498.

Des Jarlais, Don C., and Patricia Case. 1992. "Increasing Access to Injection Equipment: Syringe Exchange and Other Examples of Harm Reduction Strategies." In Global AIDS Policy Coalition (1992): 685–699.

Des Jarlais, Don C., and Samuel R. Friedman. 1988. "The Psychology of Preventing AIDS among Intravenous Drug Users: A Social-Learning Conceptualization." *American Psychologist* 43: 865–870.

Des Jarlais, Don C., Samuel R. Friedman, and Cathy Casriel. 1990. "Target Groups for Preventing AIDS among Intravenous Drug Users: 2. The 'Hard' Data Studies." *Journal of Consulting and Clinical Psychology* 58: 50–56.

Detels, Roger, et al. 1989. "Seroconversion, Sexual Activity, and Condom Use among 2915 HIV Seronegative Men Followed for up to 2 Years." *Journal of Acquired Immune Deficiency Syndromes* 2: 77–83.

DeVita, Vincent T., Samuel Hellman, and Steven A. Rosenberg, eds. 1988. *AIDS: Etiology, Diagnosis, Treatment and Prevention.* Philadelphia: Lippincott.

DiClemente, Ralph J., et al. 1992. "Determinants of Condom Use among Junior High School Students in a Minority, Inner-City School District." *Pediatrics* 89: 197–202.

Diczfalusy, Egon. 1992. "Contraceptive Prevalence, Reproductive Health, and International Morality." *American Journal of Obstetrics and Gynecology* 166: 1037, 1039 (tab. 3).

Dietz, Klaus. 1988. "On the Transmission Dynamics of HIV." *Mathematical Biosciences* 90: 397–414.

Doll, Lynda S., et al. 1990. "High-Risk Sexual Behavior and Knowledge of HIV Antibody Status in the San Francisco City Clinic Cohort." *Health Psychology* 9: 253, 262.

——— 1991a. "Homosexual Men Who Engage in High-Risk Sexual Behavior: A Multicenter Comparison." *Sexually Transmitted Diseases* 18: 170–175.

——— 1991b. "Male Bisexuality and AIDS in the United States." In Tielman, Carballo, and Hendriks (1991): 27–39.

Donoghoe, Martin C. 1992. "Sex, HIV and the Injecting Drug User." *British Journal of Addiction* 87: 405–416.

Drug Store News staff. 1992. "Positioning for Change with OTC Contraceptives." *Drug Store News,* April 20: 50.

Druhot, Denise M. 1986. "Immigration Laws Excluding Aliens on the Basis of Health: A Reassessment after AIDS." *Journal of Legal Medicine* 7: 85–112.

Drummond, M. 1991. "Economic Studies." In Walter W. Holland, Roger Detels, and George Knox, eds., *Oxford Textbook of Public Health* (2nd ed.): vol. 2, *Methods of Public Health:* ch. 18. Oxford: Oxford University Press.

Dubin, Zan, and Kathleen Kelleher. 1991. "Dance Education and Specter of AIDS." *Los Angeles Times,* April 24: F1.

Dublin, Sascha, Philip S. Rosenberg, and James J. Goedert. 1992. "Patterns and Predictors of High-Risk Sexual Behavior in Female Partners of HIV-Infected Men with Hemophilia." *AIDS* 6: 475–482.

Duckett, Jodi. 1992. "Dating Services Confront AIDS." *Houston Chronicle,* May 25: 5.

Duleep, Harriet Orcutt. 1986. "Measuring the Effect of Income on Adult Mortality Using Longitudinal Administrative Record Data." *Journal of Human Resources* 21: 238–251.

Dwyer, Terence, Rosalie Viney, and Michael Jones. 1991. "Assessing School

Health Education Programs." *International Journal of Technology Assessment in Health Care* 7: 286–295.

Economist staff. 1991. "Street Cleaning: Legalised Prostitution." *Economist,* Sept. 7: 28, 29.

Edgar, Timothy, Sharon Lee Hammond, and Vicki S. Freimuth. 1989. "The Role of the Mass Media and Interpersonal Communication in Promoting AIDS-Related Behavioral Change." *AIDS and Public Policy Journal* 4 (no. 1): 3–9.

Ehrhardt, Anke A., and Judith N. Wasserheit. 1991. "Age, Gender, and Sexual Risk Behaviors for Sexually Transmitted Diseases in the United States." In Wasserheit et al. (1991): 97, 111–112.

Ehrlich, Isaac, and Hiroyuki Chuma. 1990. "A Model of the Demand for Longevity and the Value of Life Extension." *Journal of Political Economy* 98: 761–782.

Eisenberg, Bennett. 1989. "The Number of Partners and the Probability of HIV Infection." *Statistics in Medicine* 8: 83–92.

Eisenstaedt, Richard S., and Thomas E. Getzen. 1988. "Screening Blood Donors for Human Immunodeficiency Virus Antibody: Cost-Benefit Analysis." *American Journal of Public Health* 78: 450–454.

Eisenstat, Steven. 1991. "An Analysis of the Rationality of Mandatory Testing for the HIV Antibody: Balancing the Governmental Public Health Interests with the Individual's Privacy Interest." *University of Pittsburgh Law Review* 52: 327–387.

Ekstrand, Maria L. 1992. "Safer Sex Maintenance among Gay Men: Are We Making Any Progress?" *AIDS* 6: 875–877.

Ekstrand, Maria L., and Thomas J. Coates. 1990. "Maintenance of Safer Sexual Behaviors and Predictors of Risky Sex: The San Francisco Men's Health Study." *American Journal of Public Health* 80: 973–977.

Elford, Jonathan, Robert Bor, and Pauline Summers. 1991. "Research into HIV and AIDS between 1981 and 1990: The Epidemic Curve." *AIDS* 5: 1515–1519.

Ellickson, Phyllis L., et al. 1988. *Designing and Implementing Project ALERT: A Smoking and Drug Prevention Experiment* (R-3754-CHF, Dec.): 4–7. Santa Monica: RAND Corporation.

Epstein, Richard A. 1988. "AIDS, Testing and the Workplace." *University of Chicago Legal Forum* 1988: 33–56.

Ericksen, Karen Paige, and Karen F. Trocki. 1992. "Behavioral Risk Factors for Sexually Transmitted Diseases in American Households." *Social Science and Medicine* 34: 843–853.

Escobedo, Luis G., et al. 1990. "Sociodemographic Characteristics of Cigarette Smoking Initiation in the United States." *JAMA (Journal of the American Medical Association)* 264: 1550–1555.

Essock-Vitale, Susan M., and Michael T. McGuire. 1988. "What 70 Million Years Hath Wrought: Sexual Histories and Reproductive Success of a Random

Sample of American Women." In Laura Betzig, Monique Borgerhoff Mulder, and Paul Turke, eds., *Human Reproductive Behavior: A Darwinian Perspective*: 221, 228–230. Cambridge: Cambridge University Press.

European Study Group on Heterosexual Transmission of HIV. 1992. "Comparison of Female to Male and Male to Female Transmission of HIV in 563 Stable Couples." *British Medical Journal* 304: 809, 811.

Evans, William N., Wallace E. Oates, and Robert M. Schwab. 1992. "Measuring Peer Group Effects: A Study of Teenage Behavior." *Journal of Political Economy* 100: 966, 977.

Faden, Ruth R., and Nancy E. Kass. 1988. "Health Insurance and AIDS: The Status of State Regulatory Activity." *American Journal of Public Health* 78: 437–438.

Farizo, Karen M., et al. 1992. "Spectrum of Disease in Persons with Human Immunodeficiency Virus Infection in the United States." *JAMA (Journal of the American Medical Association)* 267: 1798–1805.

Feldstein, Paul J. 1990. "An Economic Perspective on Health Politics and Policy." *Quarterly Review of Economics and Business* 30: 117–135.

Felman, Yehudi M. 1989. "Syphilis: From 1495 Naples to 1989 AIDS." *Archives of Dermatology* 125: 1698–1700.

Field, Martha A. "Testing for AIDS: Uses and Abuses." *American Journal of Law and Medicine* 16: 33–106.

Fife, Daniel, and Charles Mode. 1992. "AIDS Incidence and Income." *Journal of Acquired Immune Deficiency Syndromes* 5: 1105–1110.

Fisher, Jeffrey D., and Stephen J. Misovich. 1990. "Evolution of College Students' AIDS-Related Behavioral Responses, Attitudes, Knowledge, and Fear." *AIDS Education and Prevention* 2: 322–337.

Ford, Nancy L., and Michael D. Quam. 1987. "AIDS Quarantine: The Legal and Practical Implications." *Journal of Legal Medicine* 8: 353–396.

Fordyce, E. James, et al. 1991. "A Method of Estimating HIV Transmission Rates among Female Sex Partners of Male Intravenous Drug Users." *American Journal of Epidemiology* 133: 590, 595.

Forrest, Jacqueline Darroch, and Susheela Singh. 1990. "The Sexual and Reproductive Behavior of American Women, 1982–1988." *Family Planning Perspectives* 22: 206, 213.

Fox, Daniel M., Patricia Day, and Rudolf Klein. 1990. "The Power of Professionalism: Policies for AIDS in Britain, Sweden, and the United States." In Graubard (1990): 309–328.

Fox, Daniel M., and Emily H. Thomas, eds. 1989. *Financing Care for Persons with AIDS: The First Studies, 1985–1988*. Frederick, Md.: University Publishing Group.

Fox, Robin, et al. 1987. "Effect of HIV Antibody Disclosure on Subsequent Sexual Activity in Homosexual Men." *AIDS* 4: 241–246.

Frazer, Ian H., et al. 1988. "Influence of Human Immunodeficiency Virus Antibody Testing on Sexual Behaviour in a 'High-Risk' Population from a 'Low-Risk' City." *Medical Journal of Australia* 149: 365–368.

Frech, H. E., ed. 1988. *Health Care in America: The Political Economy of Hospitals and Health Insurance.* San Francisco: Pacific Research Institute for Public Policy.

Friedland, Gerald H., and Robert S. Klein. 1987. "Transmission of the Human Immunodeficiency Virus." *New England Journal of Medicine* 317: 1125–1135.

Friedman, Milton. 1966. *Price Theory: A Provisional Text.* 2nd ed: 56–67. Chicago: Aldine Press.

Fuchs, Victor R., ed. 1982a. *Economic Aspects of Health.* Chicago: University of Chicago Press.

———— 1982b. "Time Preference and Health: An Exploratory Study." In Fuchs (1982a): 93–120.

Fuchs, Victor R., and Richard Zeckhauser. 1987. "Valuing Health—A 'Priceless' Commodity." *American Economic Review* 77 (May, Papers and Proceedings): 263, 267.

Fullilove, Mindy Thompson, et al. 1990. "Black Women and AIDS Prevention: A View towards Understanding the Gender Rules." *Journal of Sex Research* 27: 47–64.

Fumento, Michael. 1990. *The Myth of Heterosexual AIDS* 302–311. New York: Basic Books.

Gail, Mitchell H., and Ron Brookmeyer. 1988. "Methods for Projecting Course of Acquired Immune Deficiency Syndrome Epidemic." *Journal of the National Cancer Institute* 80: 900–911.

Gail, Mitchell H., Philip S. Rosenberg, and James J. Goedert. 1990. "Therapy May Explain Recent Deficits in AIDS Incidence." *Journal of Acquired Immune Deficiency Syndromes* 3: 296–306.

Gallup, George, Jr., and Frank Newport. 1991. "Large Majorities Continue to Back AIDS Testing." *Gallup Poll Monthly No. 308,* May: 25, 26.

Gallup Poll. 1988. *The Gallup Report No. 276,* Sept.: 17.

———— 1989. *The Gallup Report No. 290,* Nov.

Gardner, Lytt I., et al. 1989. "Evidence for Spread of the Human Immunodeficiency Virus Epidemic into Low Prevalence Areas of the United States." *Journal of Acquired Immune Deficiency Syndromes* 2: 521–532.

Garland, Frank C., et al. 1992. "Decline in Human Immunodeficiency Virus Seropositivity and Seroconversion in US Navy Enlisted Personnel: 1986 to 1989." *American Journal of Public Health* 82: 581–584.

Garrett, Laurie. 1992. "The Next Epidemic." In Global AIDS Policy Coalition (1992): 825.

Gayle, Helene D., et al. 1990. "Prevalence of the Human Immunodeficiency Virus among University Students." *New England Journal of Medicine* 323: 1538–1541.

Giesecke, Johan, et al. 1991. "Efficacy of Partner Notification for HIV Infection." *Lancet* 338: 1096–1100.

Ginzberg, Eli, and Anna B. Dutka. 1989. *The Financing of Biomedical Research.* Baltimore: The Johns Hopkins University Press.

Global AIDS Policy Coalition (Jonathan Mann, Daniel J. M. Tarantola, and Thomas W. Netter, eds.). 1992. *AIDS in the World, 1992.* Cambridge, Mass.: Harvard University Press.

Gohmann, Stephen F., and Robert L. Ohsfeldt. 1992. "The Demand for Abortions." Unpublished paper, University of Louisville and University of Alabama.

Goldsmith, Marsha F. 1989. " 'Silent Epidemic' of 'Social Disease' Makes STD Experts Raise Their Voices." *JAMA (Journal of the American Medical Association)* 261: 3509–3510.

——— 1991. "Can't Find One AIDS Vaccine? Try for a Few!" *JAMA (Journal of the American Medical Association)* 266: 763–764.

Goleman, Daniel. 1988. "Lies Men Tell Women in Danger of AIDS." *New York Times,* August 14: 29.

Golombok, Susan, John Sketchley, and John Rust. 1989. "Condom Failure among Homosexual Men." *Journal of Acquired Immune Deficiency Syndromes* 2: 404–409.

Gori, Gio B., and Brian J. Richter. 1978. "Macroeconomics of Disease Prevention in the United States: Prevention of Major Causes of Mortality Would Alter Life Table Assumptions and Economic Projections." *Science* 200: 1124–1130.

Gostin, Lawrence O. 1989. "Public Health Strategies for Confronting AIDS: Legislative and Regulatory Policy in the United States." *JAMA (Journal of the American Medical Association)* 261: 1621–1630.

——— 1990. "The AIDS Litigation Project: A National Review of Court and Human Rights Commission Decisions, Part I: The Social Impact of AIDS." *JAMA (Journal of the American Medical Association)* 263: 1961, 1966.

Gottfried, Robert S. 1983. *The Black Death: Natural and Human Disaster in Medieval Europe.* New York: The Free Press.

Graubard, Stephen R., ed. 1990. *Living with AIDS.* Cambridge, Mass.: MIT Press.

Gravelle, H. S. E. 1985. "Economic Analysis of Health Service Professions: A Survey." *Social Science and Medicine* 20: 1049–1061.

Greeley, Henry T. 1989. "AIDS and the American Health Care Financing System." *University of Pittsburgh Law Review* 51: 73–166.

Green, Jesse, and Peter S. Arno. 1990. "The 'Medicaidization' of AIDS." *JAMA (Journal of the American Medical Association)* 264: 1261–1266.

Green, Richard. 1992. *Sexual Science and the Law:* 63–84. Cambridge, Mass.: Harvard University Press.

Green, Timothy A., John M. Karon, and Okey C. Nwanyanwu. 1992. "Changes in AIDS Incidence Trends in the United States." *Journal of Acquired Immune Deficiency Syndromes* 5: 547–555.

Griffin, Jean Latz. 1992. "Prevention Distant Second in Race for AIDS Funds." *Chicago Tribune,* March 25: 1, 11.

Griffin, Mary. 1991. "AIDS Drugs and the Pharmaceutical Industry: A Need for Reform." *American Journal of Law and Medicine* 17: 363–410.

Grossman, Michael. 1972. *The Demand for Health: A Theoretical and Empirical Investigation.* New York: Columbia University Press.

Gupta, Sunetra, Roy M. Anderson, and Robert M. May. 1989. "Networks of Sexual Contacts: Implications for the Pattern of Spread of HIV." *AIDS* 3: 807–817.

Haaga, John G., Richard Scott, and Jennifer Hawes-Dawson. 1992. *Drug Use in the Detroit Metropolitan Area: Problems, Programs, and Policy Options* (R-4085-SKF/DPRC): 31. Santa Monica: RAND Corporation.

Handsfield, H. Hunter. 1985. "Decreasing Incidence of Gonorrhea in Homosexually Active Men—Minimal Effect on Risk of AIDS." *Western Journal of Medicine* 143: 469–470.

Harding, T. W. 1987. "AIDS in Prison." *Lancet* 1987-ii: 1260–1263.

Hardy, Ann M. 1990. "National Health Interview Survey Data on Adult Knowledge of AIDS in the United States." *Public Health Reports* 105: 629–634.

Hardy, Ann M., et al. 1991. "Characterization of Long-Term Survivors of Acquired Immunodeficiency Syndrome." *Journal of Acquired Immune Deficiency Syndromes* 4: 386, 387.

Harris, Jeffrey E. 1990. "Reporting Delays and the Incidence of AIDS." *Journal of the American Statistical Association* 85: 915–924.

Hart, Gavin. 1975. *Chancroid, Donovanosis (Granuloma Inguinale), Lymphogranuloma Venereum:* 2. Atlanta: Centers for Disease Control.

Hart, Graham, et al. 1992. " 'Relapse' to Unsafe Behaviour among Gay Men: A Critique of Recent Behavioural HIV/AIDS Research." *Sociology of Health and Illness* 14: 216–232.

Haseltine, William A. 1990. "Prospects for the Medical Control of the AIDS Epidemic." In Graubard (1990): 21–41.

Haskell, Richard J. 1984. "A Cost-Benefit Analysis of California's Mandatory Premarital Screening Program for Syphilis." *Western Journal of Medicine* 141: 538–541.

Hay, Joel W. 1989. "Econometric Issues in Modeling the Costs of AIDS." *Health Policy* 11: 125–145.

Hearst, Norman, and Stephen B. Hulley. 1988. "Preventing the Heterosexual Spread of AIDS: Are We Giving Our Patients the Best Advice?" *JAMA (Journal of the American Medical Association)* 259: 2428–2432.

Heckmann, Wolfgang. 1991. "HIV Prevention among IVDUs in the Federal Republic of Germany: Stability and Change." *International Journal of the Addictions* 26: 1321, 1329.

Hellinger, Fred. J. 1990. "Forecasting the Number of AIDS Cases: An Analysis of Two Techniques." *Inquiry* 27: 212, 215 (tab. 2).

———— 1991. "Forecasting the Medical Care Costs of the HIV Epidemic: 1991–1994." *Inquiry* 28: 213–225.

Henriksson, Benny, and Hasse Ytterberg. 1992. "Sweden: The Power of the Moral(istic) Left." In Kirp and Bayer (1992): 317–338.

Henry, Keith, and Scott Campbell. 1992. "The Potential Efficiency of Routine HIV Testing of Hospital Patients—Data from a CDC Sentinel Hospital." *Public Health Reports* 107: 138–141.

Henshaw, Stanley K. 1990. "Induced Abortion: A World Review, 1990." *Family Planning Perspectives* 22: 76, 78 (tab. 2).

Hessol, Nancy A., et al. 1989. "Prevalence, Incidence, and Progression of Human Immunodeficiency Virus Infection in Homosexual and Bisexual Men in Hepatitis B Vaccine Trials, 1978–1988." *American Journal of Epidemiology* 130: 1167, 1173.

Hethcote, Herbert W., and James A. Yorke. 1984. *Gonorrhea: Transmission Dynamics and Control* (vol. 56 of S. Levin, ed., *Lecture Notes in Biomathematics*). Berlin: Springer-Verlag.

Hethcote, Herbert W., James A. Yorke, and Annett Nole. 1982. "Gonorrhea Modeling: A Comparison of Control Methods." *Mathematical Biosciences* 58: 93–109.

Higgins, Donna L., et al. 1991. "Evidence for the Effects of HIV Antibody Counseling and Testing on Risk Behaviors." *JAMA (Journal of the American Medical Association)* 266: 2419–2429.

Hingson, Ralph, Lee Strunin, and Beth Berlin. 1990. "Acquired Immunodeficiency Syndrome Transmission: Changes in Knowledge and Behaviors among Teenagers, Massachusetts Statewide Surveys, 1986–1988." *Pediatrics* 85: 24–29.

Hinman, Alan R. 1991. "Strategies to Prevent HIV Infection in the United States." *American Journal of Public Health* 81: 1557–1559.

Hirshleifer, Jack. 1985. "The Expanding Domain of Economics." *American Economic Review* 75 (Dec.; Special Anniversary Issue): 53–68.

Hofferth, Sandra L., Joan R. Kahn, and Wendy Baldwin. 1987. "Premarital Sexual Activity among U.S. Teenage Women over the Past Three Decades." *Family Planning Perspectives* 19: 46–53.

Holle, Axel W. 1986. "Chancroid." In Yehudi M. Felman, ed. *Sexually Transmitted Diseases:* ch. 8. New York: Churchill Livingstone.

Holmberg, Scott D., et al. 1989. "Biologic Factors in the Sexual Transmission of Human Immunodeficiency Virus." *Journal of Infectious Diseases* 160: 116–125.

Hook, Edward W. III. 1991. "Approaches to Sexually Transmitted Disease Control in North America and Western Europe." In Wasserheit et al. (1991): 269–280.

Hooper, R. R., et al. 1978. "Cohort Study of Venereal Disease, I: The Risk of Gonorrhea Transmission from Infected Women to Men." *American Journal of Epidemiology* 108: 136–144.

Horn, Miriam. 1989. "The Artists' Diagnosis." *U.S. News and World Report*, March 27: 62–63.

Horsburgh, C. Robert, Jr., et al. 1989. "Duration of Human Immunodeficiency Virus Infection before Detection of Antibody." *Lancet* 1989-ii: 637, 638.

—— 1990. "Seroconversion to Human Immunodeficiency Virus in Prison Inmates." *American Journal of Public Health* 80: 209–210.

Hunter, Nan D., and William B. Rubenstein, eds. 1992. *AIDS Agenda: Emerging Issues in Civil Rights*. New York: The New Press.

Huszti, Heather C., James R. Clopton, and Patrick J. Mason. 1989. "Acquired Immunodeficiency Syndrome Educational Program: Effects on Adolescents' Knowledge and Attitudes." *Pediatrics* 84: 986–994.

Hyman, James, and E. Ann Stanley. 1988. "Using Mathematical Models to Understand the AIDS Epidemic." *Mathematical BioSciences* 90: 415–473.

Institute of Medicine, National Academy of Sciences. 1985. *Vaccine Supply and Innovation*. Washington, D.C.: National Academy Press.

—— 1988. *Confronting AIDS: Update 1988:* 67. Washington, D.C.: National Academy Press.

—— 1990. *Funding Health Sciences Research: A Strategy to Restore Balance*. Washington, D.C.: National Academy Press.

Isomura, Shin, and Masashi Mizogami. 1992. "The Low Rate of HIV Infection in Japanese Homosexual and Bisexual Men: An Analysis of HIV Seroprevalence and Behavioural Risk Factors." *AIDS* 6: 501–503.

Jacobs, Philip. 1987. *The Economics of Health and Medical Care:* chs. 7, 8, and 12. 2nd ed. Rockville, Md., and Royal Tunbridge Wells: Aspen.

James, Nicola J., Christopher J. Bignell, and Pamela A. Gillies. 1991. "The Reliability of Self-Reported Sexual Behaviour." *AIDS* 5: 333–336.

Jarvis, Robert M., et al. 1991. *AIDS Law in a Nutshell*. St. Paul: West.

Johnson, Arne M., et al. 1992. "Sexual Lifestyles and HIV Risk." *Nature* 360: 410–412.

Johnson, Ernest H., et al. "Do African-American Men and Women Differ in Their Knowledge about AIDS, Attitudes about Condoms, and Sexual Behaviors?" *JAMA (Journal of the American Medical Association)* 84: 49–64.

Jones, Robert B., and Judith N. Wasserheit. 1991. "Introduction to the Biology and Natural History of Sexually Transmitted Diseases." In Wasserheit et al. (1991): 11–37.

Judson, Franklyn N. 1990. "Gonorrhea." *Medical Clinics of North America* 74: 1353, 1355.

Jurich, Joan A., Rebecca A. Adams, and John E. Schulenberg. 1992. "Factors Relating to Behavior Change in Response to AIDS." *Family Relations* 41: 97–103.

Käll, Kerstin I., and Robert G. Olin. 1990. "HIV Status and Changes in Risk Behaviour among Intravenous Drug Users in Stockholm 1987–1988." *AIDS* 4: 153–157.

Kanouse, David E., et al. 1991. *AIDS-Related Knowledge, Attitudes, Beliefs, and Be-

haviors in Los Angeles County (R-4054-LACH). Santa Monica: RAND Corporation.

Kantner, John F., and Melvin Zelnik. 1973. "Contraception and Pregnancy: Experience of Young Unmarried Women in the United States." *Family Planning Perspectives* 5: 21, 22.

Karon, John M., and Ruth L. Berkelman. 1991. "The Geographic and Ethnic Diversity of AIDS Incidence Trends in Homosexual/Bisexual Men in the United States." *Journal of Acquired Immune Deficiency Syndromes* 4: 1179–1189.

Karon, John M., Timothy J. Dondero, Jr., and James W. Curran. 1988. "The Projected Incidence of AIDS and Estimated Prevalence of HIV Infection in the United States." *Journal of Acquired Immune Deficiency Syndromes* 1: 542–550.

Katz, Barry P. 1992. "Estimating Transmission Probabilities for Chlamydial Infection." *Statistics in Medicine* 11: 565–577.

Keeter, Scott, and Judith B. Bradford. 1988. "Knowledge of AIDS and Related Behavior Change among Unmarried Adults in a Low-Prevalence City." *American Journal of Preventive Medicine* 4: 146–152.

Kegeles, Susan M., Joseph A. Catania, and Thomas J. Coates. 1988. "Intentions to Communicate Positive HIV-Antibody Status to Sex Partners." *JAMA (Journal of the American Medical Association)* 259: 216–217.

Kelly, Jeffrey A. 1991. "Changing the Behavior of an HIV-Seropositive Man Who Practices Unsafe Sex." *H&CP (Hospital and Community Psychiatry)* 42: 239–240, 264.

Kelly, Jeffrey A., et al. 1990. "AIDS Risk Behavior Patterns among Gay Men in Small Southern Cities." *American Journal of Public Health* 80: 416–418.

Kelly, Jeffrey A., Janet S. St. Lawrence, and Ted L. Brasfield. 1991. "Predictors of Vulnerability to AIDS Risk Behavior Relapse." *Journal of Consulting and Clinical Psychology* 59: 163–166.

Kenkel, Donald S. 1991. "Health Behavior, Health Knowledge, and Schooling." *Journal of Political Economy* 99: 287–305.

Kessel, Reuben A. 1980. *Essays in Applied Price Theory:* chs. 1–3. R. H. Coase and Merton H. Miller, eds. Chicago: University of Chicago Press.

Kingma, Bruce Robert. 1989. "An Accurate Measurement of the Crowd-out Effect, Income Effect, and Price Effect for Charitable Contributions." *Journal of Political Economy* 97: 1197, 1203–1204.

Kingsley, Lawrence A., et al. 1990. "Sexual Transmission Efficiency of Hepatitis B Virus and Human Immunodeficiency Virus among Homosexual Men." *JAMA (Journal of the American Medical Association)* 264: 230–234.

Kirby, Philip K., et al. 1991. "The Challenge of Limiting the Spread of Human Immunodeficiency Virus by Controlling Other Sexually Transmitted Diseases." *Archives of Dermatology* 127: 237–242.

Kirp, David L., and Ronald Bayer, eds. 1992. *AIDS in the Industrialized Democracies: Passions, Politics, and Policies.* New Brunswick, N.J.: Rutgers University Press.

Klein, Daniel E., et al. 1987. "Changes in AIDS Risk Behaviors among Homosexual Male Physicians and University Students." *American Journal of Psychiatry* 144: 742–747.

Kleinman, Lawrence C. 1992. "To End an Epidemic: Lessons from the History of Diphtheria." *New England Journal of Medicine* 326: 773–777.

Kline, Anna, Emily Kline, and Emily Oken. 1992. "Minority Women and Sexual Choice in the Age of AIDS." *Social Science and Medicine* 34: 447–457.

Koehl, Carla. 1991. "Trump: The Art of the Heel." *Newsweek,* July 8: 47.

Kolata, Gina. 1991. "AIDS in U.S. May Be Near Peak." *Chicago Tribune,* August 8: 28.

——— 1992. "After 5 Years of Use, Doubt Still Clouds Leading AIDS Drug." *New York Times,* June 2: C3.

Kraft, Joe W., Jeff Q. Bostic, and Mary K. Tallent. 1990. "West Texas Teenagers and AIDS: A Survey of Their Knowledge, Attitudes, Behavioral Changes, and Information Sources." *Texas Medicine/The Journal* 86 (Sept.): 74–78.

Krajick, Kevin. 1988. "Private Passions and Public Health." *Psychology Today* 22 (May): 50–58.

Krueger, Leigh E., et al. 1990. "Poverty and HIV Seropositivity: The Poor Are More Likely to Be Infected." *AIDS* 4: 811–814.

Lampinen, Thomas M., et al. 1992. "HIV Seropositivity in Community-Recruited and Drug Treatment Samples of Injecting Drug Users." *AIDS* 6: 123–126.

Landes, William M., and Richard A. Posner. 1987. *The Economic Structure of Tort Law.* Cambridge, Mass.: Harvard University Press.

Landis, Suzanne E., et al. 1992. "Results of a Randomized Trial of Partner Notification in Cases of HIV Infection in North Carolina." *New England Journal of Medicine* 326: 101–106.

Leigh, J. Paul. 1990. "Schooling and Seat Belt Use." *Southern Economic Journal* 57: 195–207.

Lemp, George F., et al. 1990a. "Survival Trends for Patients with AIDS." *JAMA (Journal of the American Medical Association)* 263: 402, 406.

Lemp, George F., et al. 1990b. "Projections of AIDS Morbidity and Mortality in San Francisco." *JAMA (Journal of the American Medical Association)* 263: 1497–1501.

Leonard, Terri L., Matthew Freund, and Jerome J. Platt. 1989. "Behavior of Clients of Prostitutes." *American Journal of Public Health* 79: 903.

Levine, Carol, and Ronald Bayer. 1989. "The Ethics of Screening for Early Intervention in HIV Disease." *American Journal of Public Health* 79: 1661–1667.

Lewis, Diane K., and John K. Watters. 1991. "Sexual Risk Behavior among Heterosexual Intravenous Drug Users: Ethnic and Gender Variations." *AIDS* 5: 77, 82.

Lindan, Christina P., et al. 1990. "Underreporting of Minority AIDS Deaths in San Francisco Bay Area, 1985–86." *Public Health Reports* 105: 400–404.

Lippincott, Ronald C., and James W. Begun. 1982. "Competition in the Health Sector: A Historical Perspective." *Journal of Health Politics, Policy and Law* 7: 460–487.

Lloyd, P. J. 1991. "AIDS: An Economic Approach to the Choice of Policies." *Economic Record* 67: 126–138.

Lui, Kung-Jong, William W. Darrow, and George W. Rutherford, III. 1988. "A Model-Based Estimate of the Mean Incubation Period for AIDS in Homosexual Men." *Science* 240: 1333–1335.

Lyter, David W., et al. 1987. "The HIV Antibody Test: Why Gay and Bisexual Men Want or Do Not Want to Know Their Results." *Public Health Reports* 102: 468–474.

McCaig, Linda F., Ann M. Hardy, and Deborah M. Winn. 1991. "Knowledge about AIDS and HIV in the US Adult Population: Influence of the Local Incidence of AIDS." *American Journal of Public Health* 81: 1591–1595.

McCusker, Jane, et al. 1988. "Effects of HIV Antibody Test Knowledge on Subsequent Sexual Behaviors in a Cohort of Homosexually Active Men." *American Journal of Public Health* 78: 462–467.

McCusker, Jane, Anne M. Stoddard, and Ellen McCarthy. 1992. "The Validity of Self-Reported HIV Antibody Test Results." *American Journal of Public Health* 82: 567–569.

McKillip, Jack. 1991. "The Effect of Mandatory Premarital HIV Testing on Marriage: The Case of Illinois." *American Journal of Public Health* 81: 650–653.

McNally, James W., and William D. Mosher. 1991. "AIDS-Related Knowledge and Behavior among Women 15–44 Years of Age: United States, 1988." *Advance Data from Vital and Health Statistics of the National Center for Health Statistics*, May 14: 1, 6.

McNeil, John G., et al. 1991. "Trends of HIV Seroconversion among Young Adults in US Army, 1985 to 1989." *JAMA (Journal of the American Medical Association)* 265: 1709–1714.

Magura, Stephen, et al. 1989. "Determinants of Needle Sharing among Intravenous Drug Users." *American Journal of Public Health* 79: 459, 460.

Mann, Jonathan, Daniel J. M. Tarantola, and Thomas W. Netter. See Global AIDS Policy Coalition.

Mantell, Joanne E., Steven P. Schinke, and Sheila H. Akabas. 1988. "Women and AIDS Prevention." *Journal of Primary Prevention* 9: 18–40.

Marin, Gerardo. 1989. "AIDS Prevention among Hispanics: Needs, Risk Behaviors, and Cultural Values." *Public Health Reports* 104: 411–415.

Mariotto, Angela B., et al. 1992. "Estimation of the Acquired Immunodeficiency Syndrome Incubation Period in Intravenous Drug Users: A Comparison with Male Homosexuals." *American Journal of Epidemiology* 135: 428, 436.

Marks, Gary, et al. 1992. "HIV-Infected Men's Practices in Notifying Past Sexual Partners of Infection Risk." *Public Health Reports* 107: 100–105.

Martin, David J. 1990. "A Study of the Deficiencies in the Condom-Use Skills of Gay Men." *Public Health Reports* 105: 638–640.

May, Robert M., and Roy M. Anderson. 1987. "Transmission Dynamics of HIV Infection." *Nature* 326: 137–142.

May, Robert M., Roy M. Anderson, and Sally M. Blower. 1990. "The Epidemiology and Transmission Dynamics of HIV-AIDS." In Graubard (1990): 65–103.

Mays, Vickie M., and Susan D. Cochran. 1987. "Acquired Immunodeficiency Syndrome and Black Americans: Special Psychosocial Issues." *Public Health Reports* 102: 224–231.

——— 1990. "Methodological Issues in the Assessment and Prediction of AIDS Risk-Related Sexual Behaviors among Black Americans." In Voeller et al. (1990): 97–120.

Meirik, Olav, and Timothy M. M. Farley. 1990. "Oral Contraceptives and HIV Transmission." In Nancy J. Alexander, Henry L. Gabelnick, and Jeffrey M. Spieler, eds., *Heterosexual Transmission of AIDS:* 247–254. New York: Wiley-Liss.

Meltzer, David. 1992. "Mortality Decline, the Demographic Transition and Economic Growth." Unpublished Ph.D. dissertation, Department of Economics, University of Chicago.

Mertz, Gregory J. 1992. "Risk Factors for the Sexual Transmission of Genital Herpes." *Annals of Internal Medicine* 116: 197–202.

Metzger, David, et al. 1991. "Risk Factors for Needle Sharing among Methadone-Treated Patients." *American Journal of Psychiatry* 148: 636–640.

Miller, Heather G., et al. 1990. *AIDS: The Second Decade:* 82–83. Washington, D.C.: National Academy Press.

Miller, Jill Young. 1991. "Straight Talk on Safe Sex." *Calgary Herald,* Nov. 10: B2.

Mills, John, and Henry Masur. 1990. "AIDS-Related Infections." *Scientific American* 263 (Aug.): 50–57.

Mockler, Richard W., and Mark A. R. Kleiman. 1988. "With This Test I Thee Wed: Evaluating Premarital AIDS Testing." *Journal of Policy Analysis and Management* 7: 557–567.

Mohr, Richard D. 1988. *Gays/Justice: A Study of Ethics, Society, and Law.* New York: Columbia University Press.

Molgaard, Craig A., et al. 1988. "Assessing Alcoholism as a Risk Factor for Acquired Immunodeficiency Syndrome (AIDS)." *Social Science and Medicine* 27: 1147–1152.

Moran, John S., et al. 1990. "Increase in Condom Sales Following AIDS Education and Publicity, United States." *American Journal of Public Health* 80: 607–608.

Morgan, W. M., and J. W. Curran. 1986. "Acquired Immunodeficiency Syndrome: Current and Future Trends." *Public Health Reports* 101: 459–465.

Morse, Dale L., et al. 1990. "AIDS behind Bars: Epidemiology of New York State Prison Inmate Cases, 1980–1988." *New York State Journal of Medicine* 90: 133–138.

Morse, Edward V., et al. 1992. "Sexual Behavior Patterns of Customers of Male Street Prostitutes." *Archives of Sexual Behavior* 21: 347–357.

Mosher, William D. 1988. "Fertility and Family Planning in the United States: Insights from the National Survey of Family Growth." *Family Planning Perspectives* 20: 207, 210.

——— 1990. "Contraceptive Practice in the United States, 1982–1988." *Family Planning Perspectives* 22: 198–205.

Mosher, William D., and William F. Pratt. 1990. "Contraceptive Use in the United States, 1973–88." *Advance Data from Vital and Health Statistics of the National Center for Health Statistics,* March 20: 1–7.

Muirhead, Greg. 1992a. "AIDS Transforms Condom Marketing." *Supermarket News,* Jan. 20: 44.

——— 1992b. "Condoms Get an Assist." *Supermarket News,* Feb. 3: 17.

Muñoz, Alvaro, et al. 1989. "Acquired Immunodeficiency Syndrome (AIDS)-Free Time after Human Immunodeficiency Virus Type 1 (HIV-1) Seroconversion in Homosexual Men." *American Journal of Epidemiology* 130: 530–539.

Nakamura, Robert M. 1990. "Condoms—Manufacturing and Testing." In Voeller et al. (1990): 337–343.

National Commission on Acquired Immune Deficiency Syndrome. 1991. *Report: HIV Disease in Correctional Facilities* (March): 16. Washington, D.C.: National Commission on AIDS.

Newsday staff. 1991. "The Caregivers." *Newsday,* June 4: 63.

O'Brien, Maura. 1989. "Needle Exchange Programs: Ethical and Policy Issues." *AIDS and Public Policy Journal* 4: 75–82.

O'Connor, Anne-Marie. 1991. "Cuba Changes Its Tack on AIDS." *Atlanta Journal and Constitution,* Aug. 14: A2.

Ohi, Gen, et al. 1988. "Notification of HIV Carriers: Possible Effect on Uptake of AIDS Testing." *Lancet* 1988-ii: 947–949.

Ohsfeldt, Robert L., and Stephan F. Gohmann. 1992. "The Economics of AIDS-Related Health Insurance Regulations: Interest Group Influence and Ideology." *Public Choice* 74: 105–126.

Olson, Mancur, Jr. 1965. *The Logic of Collective Action: Public Goods and the Theory of Groups.* Cambridge, Mass.: Harvard University Press.

Oriel, J. D., and P. G. Walker. 1990. "Genital Papilloma Virus Infections." In Csonka and Oates (1990a): 153, 155.

Orr, Donald P., et al. 1992. "Factors Associated with Condom Use among Sexually Active Female Adolescents." *Journal of Pediatrics* 120: 311, 314.

Ostrow, David G. 1990. "AIDS Prevention through Effective Education." In Graubard (1990): 261–286.

Padian, Nancy S., Stephen C. Shiboski, and Nicholas P. Jewell. 1991. "Female-to-Male Transmission of Human Immunodeficiency Virus." *JAMA (Journal of the American Medical Association)* 266: 1664–1667.

Palca, Joseph. 1989. "Is the AIDS Epidemic Slowing?" *Science* 246: 1560.

Paltiel, A. David, and Edward H. Kaplan. 1991. "Modeling Zidovudine Therapy: A Cost-Effectiveness Analysis." *Journal of Acquired Immune Deficiency Syndromes* 4: 795, 799–800.

Panem, Sandra. 1988. *The AIDS Bureacracy.* Cambridge, Mass.: Harvard University Press.

Papaevangelou, G., et al. 1988. "Education in Preventing HIV Infection in Greek Registered Prostitutes." *Journal of Acquired Immune Deficiency Syndromes* 1: 386–389.

Pappas, Victoria P. 1988. "In Prison with AIDS: The Constitutionality of Mass Screening and Segregation Policies." *University of Illinois Law Review* 1988: 151–190.

Pascal, Chris B. 1988. "Intravenous Drug Abuse and AIDS Transmission: Federal and State Laws Regulating Needle Availability." In Robert J. Battjes and Roy W. Pickens, eds., *Needle Sharing among Intravenous Drug Abusers: National and International Perspectives* (NIDA Monograph 80): 119–136. Washington, D.C.: U.S. Government Printing Office.

Peltzman, Sam. 1976. "Toward a More General Theory of Regulation." *Journal of Law and Economics* 19: 211–240.

Pendergrast, Robert A., Robert H. DuRant, and Gregory L. Gaillard. 1992. "Attitudinal and Behavioral Correlates of Condom Use in Urban Adolescent Males." *Journal of Adolescent Health* 13: 133–139.

Penkower, Lili, et al. 1991. "Behavioral, Health and Psychosocial Factors and Risk for HIV Infection among Sexually Active Homosexual Men: The Multicenter AIDS Cohort Study." *American Journal of Public Health* 81: 194–196.

Pépin, Jacques, et al. 1992. "Association between HIV-2 Infection and Genital Ulcer Diseases among Male Sexually Transmitted Disease Patients in the Gambia." *AIDS* 6: 489–493.

Pérez-Stable, Eliseo J. 1991. "Cuba's Response to the HIV Epidemic." *American Journal of Public Health* 81: 563–567.

Perlman, Jeffrey A., et al. 1990. "HIV Risk Difference between Condom Users and Nonusers among U.S. Heterosexual Women." *Journal of Acquired Immune Deficiency Syndromes* 3: 155–165.

Perry, Samuel, et al. 1990. "Voluntarily Informing Others of Positive HIV Test Results: Patterns of Notification by Infected Gay Men." *Hospital and Community Psychiatry* 41: 549–551.

Petersen, Lyle R., et al. 1990. "Premarital Screening for Antibodies to Human Immunodeficiency Virus Type 1 in the United States." *American Journal of Public Health* 80: 1087–1090.

Phair, John, et al. 1992. "Acquired Immune Deficiency Syndrome Occurring within 5 Years of Infection with Human Immunodeficiency Virus Type-1: The Multicenter AIDS Cohort Study." *Journal of Acquired Immune Deficiency Syndromes* 5: 490–496.

Phelps, Charles E. 1992. *Health Economics*. New York: HarperCollins.

Philipson, Tomas. 1992a. "Choice-Based Epidemiology and the Prevalence of Sexually Transmitted Disease." Unpublished paper, Department of Economics, University of Chicago.

——— 1992b. "Choice-Based Infectious Disease and Public Health." Unpublished paper, Department of Economics, University of Chicago.

——— 1993. "The Empirical Content of the Heterogeneous Mixing Model of Infectious Disease." Unpublished paper, Department of Economics, University of Chicago.

Phillips, Kathryn A. n.d. "The Relationship of 1988 State Policies to Past and Future Voluntary Utilization of Human Immunodeficiency Virus (HIV) Testing." Unpublished paper, University of California at Berkeley.

Pleak, Richard R., and Heino F. L. Meyer-Bahlburg. 1990. "Sexual Behavior and AIDS Knowledge of Young Male Prostitutes in Manhattan." *Journal of Sex Research* 27: 557–587.

Plummer, Francis A., Stephen Moses, and Jackoniah O. Ndinya-Achola. 1991. "Factors Affecting Female-to-Male Transmission of HIV-1: Implications of Transmission Dynamics for Prevention." In Lincoln C. Chen, Jaime Sepulveda Amor, and Sheldon J. Segal, eds., *AIDS and Women's Reproductive Health*: 35–45. New York: Plenum Press.

Poku, Kwabena A. 1992. "Knowingly Exposing Others to HIV: Four Case Reports and Critique." *AIDS Patient Care* 6 (Feb.): 5–10.

Posner, Richard A. 1971. "Taxation by Regulation." *Bell Journal of Economics and Management Science* 2: 22–50.

——— 1981. *The Economics of Justice*. Cambridge, Mass.: Harvard University Press.

——— 1992. *Sex and Reason*. Cambridge, Mass.: Harvard University Press.

Potterat, John J., Richard L. Dukes, and Richard B. Rothenberg. 1987. "Disease Transmission by Heterosexual Men with Gonorrhea: An Empiric Estimate." *Sexually Transmitted Diseases* 14: 107–110.

Presidential Commission on the Human Immunodeficiency Virus Epidemic. 1988. *Report*. Washington, D.C.: The Commission.

Price, Vincent, and Mei-Ling Hsu. 1992. "Public Opinion about AIDS Policies: The Role of Misinformation and Attitudes toward Homosexuals." *Public Opinion Quarterly* 56: 29–52.

Quam, Michael, and Nancy Ford. 1990. "AIDS Policies and Practices in the

United States." In Barbara A. Misztal and David Moss, eds., *Action on AIDS: National Policies in Comparative Perspective:* 25, 38–44. New York: Greenwood Press.

Quinn, Thomas C., et al. 1990. "The Association of Syphilis with Risk of Human Immunodeficiency Virus Infection in Patients Attending Sexually Transmitted Disease Clinics." *Archives of Internal Medicine* 150: 1297–1302.

Ramstedt, Kristina, et al. 1991. "Choice of Sexual Partner according to Rate of Partner Change and Social Class of the Partners." *International Journal of STD and AIDS* 2: 428–431.

Reid, T. R. 1992. "Japan, Fearful of AIDS, to Continue Longtime Ban on Birth Control Pill." *Washington Post,* March 19: A20.

Reinisch, June Machover, Mary Ziemba-Davis, and Stephanie A. Sanders. 1990. "Sexual Behavior and AIDS: Lessons from Art and Research." In Voeller et al. (1990): 37–80.

Research Triangle Institute. 1990. *National Household Seroprevalence Survey Feasibility Study Final Report.* (RTI Rep. No. RTI/4190–01/01F (Apr. 30): vol. 1, pp. 4–80 (Exh. 4.45). Research Triangle Park: Research Triangle Institute.

Rhodes, Fen, et al. 1990. "Risk Behaviors and Perceptions of AIDS among Street Injection Drug Users." *Journal of Drug Education* 20: 271, 285.

Riesenberg, Donald E. 1986. "AIDS-Prompted Behavior Changes Reported." *JAMA (Journal of the American Medical Association)* 255: 171–176.

Rietmeijer, Cornelis A. M., et al. 1988. "Condoms as Physical and Chemical Barriers against Human Immunodeficiency Virus." *JAMA (Journal of the American Medical Association)* 259: 1851–1853.

Rhame, Frank S., and Dennis G. Maki. 1989. "The Case for Wider Use of Testing for HIV Infection." *New England Journal of Medicine* 320: 1248–1254.

Robert, Claude-Françoise, et al. 1990. "Behavioural Changes in Intravenous Drug Users in Geneva: Rise and Fall of HIV Infection, 1980–1989." *AIDS* 4: 657–660.

Robertson, D. H. H., A. McMillan, and H. Young. 1989. *Clinical Practice in Sexually Transmissible Diseases* (2nd ed.): 440–441. Edinburgh: Churchill Livingstone.

Robertson, J. R., C. A. Skidmore, and J. J. Roberts. 1988. "HIV Infection in Intravenous Drug Users: A Follow-Up Study Indicating Changes in Risk-Taking Behaviour." *British Journal of Addiction* 83: 387–391.

Rogers, Susan M., and Charles F. Turner. 1991. "Male-Male Sexual Contact in the U.S.A.: Findings from Five Sample Surveys, 1970–1990." *Journal of Sex Research* 28: 491–519.

Rolfs, Robert T., and Willard Cates, Jr. 1989. "The Perpetual Lessons of Syphilis." *Archives of Dermatology* 125: 107–109.

Rolfs, Robert T., and Allyn K. Nakashima. 1990. "Epidemiology of Primary and Secondary Syphilis in the United States, 1981 through 1989." *JAMA (Journal of the American Medical Association)* 264: 1432–1437.

Roper, William L. 1991. "Current Approaches to Prevention of HIV Infections." *Public Health Reports* 106: 111, 113–114.

Rosenberg, Michael J., and Jodie M. Weiner. 1988. "Prostitutes and AIDS: A Health Department Priority?" *American Journal of Public Health* 78: 418–423.

Rosenberg, Philip S., et al. 1991a. "Backcalculation of the Number with Human Immunodeficiency Virus Infection in the United States." *American Journal of Epidemiology* 133: 276–285.

—— 1991b. "National AIDS Incidence Trends and the Extent of Zidovudine Therapy in Selected Demographic and Transmission Groups." *Journal of Acquired Immune Deficiency Syndromes* 4: 392–401.

Ross, Michael W. 1983. *The Married Homosexual Man: A Psychological Study:* 110–111 and tab. 11.1. London: Routledge and Kegan Paul.

—— 1988. "Personality Factors That Differentiate Homosexual Men with Positive and Negative Attitudes toward Condom Use." *New York State Journal of Medicine* 88: 626–628.

Ross, Michael W., Brook Freedman, and Ralph Brew. 1989. "Changes in Sexual Behaviour between 1986 and 1988 in Matched Samples of Homosexually Active Men." *Community Health Studies* 13: 276–280.

Rowe, Mona J., and Caitlin C. Ryan. 1988. "Comparing State-Only Expenditures for AIDS." *American Journal of Public Health* 78: 424–429.

Rutherford, George W., and Jean M. Woo. 1988. "Contact Tracing and the Control of Human Immunodeficiency Virus Infection." *JAMA (Journal of the American Medical Association)* 259: 3609–3610.

St. Lawrence, Janet S., et al. 1989. "Differences in Gay Men's AIDS Risk Knowledge and Behavior Patterns in High and Low AIDS Prevalence Cities." *Public Health Reports* 104: 391–395.

Sacks, Michael, et al. 1992. "Undetected HIV Infection among Acutely Ill Psychiatric Inpatients." *American Journal of Psychiatry* 149: 544–545.

Samuel, Michael C., et al. 1991. "Changes in Sexual Practices over 5 Years of Follow-up among Heterosexual Men in San Francisco." *Journal of Acquired Immune Deficiency Syndromes* 4: 896–900.

Sandberg, Sonja, and Tamara E. Awerbuch. 1989. "Mathematical Formulation and Studies of the Risk Parameters Involved in HIV Transmission." *Bulletin of Mathematical Biology* 51: 467, 473.

Sattenspiel, Lisa, and Carl P. Simon. 1988. "The Spread and Persistence of Infectious Diseases in Structured Populations." *Mathematical Biosciences* 90: 341–366.

Schleifer, Steven J., et al. 1990. "HIV Seropositivity in Inner-City Alcoholics." *Hospital and Community Psychiatry* 41: 248–254.

Schmid, George P., et al. 1987. "Chancroid in the United States: Reestablishment of an Old Disease." *JAMA (Journal of the American Medical Association)* 258: 3265–3268.

Schneider, Lynne, Benjamin Klein, and Kevin M. Murphy. 1981. "Governmental Regulation of Cigarette Health Information." *Journal of Law and Economics* 24: 575, 598.

Schneiderman, Lawrence J., and Robert M. Kaplan. 1992. "Fear of Dying and HIV Infection vs. Hepatitis B Infection." *American Journal of Public Health* 82: 584–586.

Schoenstein, Richard Carl. 1989. "Note, Standards of Conduct, Multiple Defendants, and Full Recovery of Damages in Tort Liability for the Transmission of Human Immunodeficiency Virus." *Hofstra Law Review* 18: 37–87.

Schwefel, Detlef, et al., eds. 1990. *Economic Aspects of AIDS and HIV Infection.* Berlin: Springer-Verlag.

Scitovsky, Anne A., and Dorothy P. Rice. 1987. "Estimates of the Direct and Indirect Costs of Acquired Immunodeficiency Syndrome in the United States, 1985, 1986, and 1991." *Public Health Reports* 102: 5–17.

Sebastian, Pamela. 1992. "Funding a Cause: AIDS Groups Refine Strategies and Many Court Same Donors." *Wall Street Journal,* Dec. 30: A1, A8.

Seltzer, Vicki L., Jill Rabin, and Fred Benjamin. 1989. "Teenagers' Awareness of the Acquired Immunodeficiency Syndrome and the Impact on Their Sexual Behavior." *Obstetrics and Gynecology* 74: 55–59.

Selwyn, Peter A., et al. 1987. "Knowledge about AIDS and High-Risk Behavior among Intravenous Drug Users in New York City." *AIDS* 1: 247–254.

Shavell, Steven. 1987. *Economic Analysis of Accident Law.* Cambridge, Mass.: Harvard University Press.

Shilts, Randy. 1987. *And the Band Played On: Politics, People and the AIDS Epidemic:* 619 (index references under "Dugas, Gaetan"). New York: St. Martin's Press.

Sibthorpe, Beverly, et al. 1991. "Needle Use and Sexual Practices: Differences in Perception of Personal Risk of HIV among Intravenous Drug Users." *Journal of Drug Issues* 21: 699–712.

Sickles, Robin, and Paul Taubman. 1991. "Who Uses Illegal Drugs?" *American Economic Review* 81 (May; Papers and Proceedings): 248, 250 (tabs. 1–2).

Siegel, J. E., J. D. Graham, and M. A. Stoto. 1990. "Allocating Resources among AIDS Research Strategies." *Policy Sciences* 23: 1, 7 (tab. 2).

Siegel, Joanna E., Milton C. Weinstein, and Harvey V. Fineberg. 1991. "Bleach Programs for Preventing AIDS among IV Drug Users: Modeling the Impact of HIV Prevalence." *American Journal of Public Health* 81: 1273–1279.

Siegel, Karolynn, and Marc Glassman. 1989. "Individual and Aggregate Level Change in Sexual Behavior among Gay Men at Risk for AIDS." *Archives of Sexual Behavior* 18: 335–348.

Sisk, Jane E. 1987. "The Costs of AIDS: A Review of the Estimates." *Health Affairs* 6: 5–21.

Smith, Tom W. 1991. "Adult Sexual Behavior in 1989: Number of Partners, Frequency of Intercourse and Risk of AIDS." *Family Planning Perspectives* 23: 102, 104.

Snyder, Leslie B. 1991. "The Impact of the Surgeon General's 'Understanding AIDS' Pamphlet in Connecticut." *Health Communication* 3: 37–57.

Sparling, P. F., and Sevgi O. Aral. 1991. "The Importance of an Interdisciplinary Approach to Prevention of Sexually Transmitted Diseases." In Wasserheit et al. (1991): 1, 7.

"Special Section—The Sentinel HIV Seroprevalence Surveys." 1990. *Public Health Reports* 105: 113–171.

Spencer, Bruce D. 1989. "On the Accuracy of Current Estimates of the Numbers of Intravenous Drug Users." In Turner et al. (1989): 429, 445.

Stall, Ron, et al. 1992. "A Comparison of Younger and Older Gay Men's HIV Risk-Taking Behaviors: The Communication Technologies 1989 Cross-Sectional Survey." *Journal of Acquired Immune Deficiency Syndromes* 5: 682–687.

Stall, Ron D., Thomas J. Coates, and Colleen Hoff. 1988. "Behavioral Risk Reduction for HIV Infection among Gay and Bisexual Men: A Review of Results from the United States." *American Psychologist* 43: 878–885.

Stein, Michael D., et al. 1991a. "Differences in Access to Zidovudine (AZT) among Symptomatic HIV-Infected Persons." *Journal of General Internal Medicine* 6: 35, 39.

——— 1991b. "HIV-Positive Women: Reasons They Are Treated for HIV and Their Clinical Characteristics on Entry into the Health Care System." *Journal of General Internal Medicine* 6: 286, 287.

Stevens, Cladd E. 1990. "Sexual Activity and Human Immunodeficiency Virus Type 1 Infection in a Cohort of Homosexual Men in New York City." In Voeller, Reinisch, and Gottlied (1990): 20–34.

Stiffman, Arlene Rubin, et al. 1992. "Changes in Acquired Immunodeficiency Syndrome–Related Risk Behavior after Adolescence: Relationships to Knowledge and Experience concerning Human Immunodeficiency Virus Infection." *Pediatrics* 89: 950–956.

Stigler, George J. 1975. *The Citizen and the State: Essays on Regulation.* Chicago: University of Chicago Press.

Sunderland, Ann, et al. 1992. "The Impact of Human Immunodeficiency Virus Serostatus on Reproductive Decisions of Women." *Obstetrics and Gynecology* 79: 1027–1031.

Tan, W. Y., and H. Hsu. 1989. "Some Stochastic Models of AIDS Spread." *Statistics in Medicine* 8: 121–136.

Tanfer, Koray, Lisa A. Cubbins, and Karin L. Brewster. 1992. "Determinants of Contraceptive Choice among Single Women in the United States." *Family Planning Perspectives* 24: 155, 159.

Taylor, Jeremy M. G., Jo-Mei Kuo, and Roger Detels. 1991. "Is the Incubation

Period of AIDS Lengthening?" *Journal of Acquired Immune Deficiency Syndromes* 4: 69, 70.

Thomas, Stephen B., Aisha G. Gilliam, and Carolyn G. Iwrey. 1989. "Knowledge about AIDS and Reported Risk Behaviors among Black College Students." *Journal of American College Health* 38: 61–66.

Thompson, C., and D. H. H. Robertson. 1989. "Trends in Sexual Behaviour and HIV Incidence in Homosexual Men." *British Medical Journal* 298: 673.

Tielman, Rob, Manuel Carballo, and Aart Hendriks. 1991. *Bisexuality and HIV/AIDS: A Global Perspective.* Buffalo: Prometheus Books.

Timmerman, Tina, Stephen McDonough, and Philip Harmeson. 1991. "AIDS Awareness in North Dakota—A Knowledge and Attitude Study of the General Population." *Public Health Reports* 106: 120–123.

Tolley, George, Donald Kenkel, and Robert Fabian, eds. 1992. *Valuing Health for Policy: An Economic Approach.* Chicago: University of Chicago Press (forthcoming).

Tolley, George, et al. 1992. "Use of Health Values in Policy." In Tolley, Kenkel, and Fabian (1992): ch. 16.

Tollison, Robert D., and Richard E. Wagner. 1991. "Self-Interest, Public Interest, and Public Health." *Public Choice* 69: 323–343.

Trussell, James, et al. 1990. "A Guide to Interpreting Contraceptive Efficacy Studies." *Obstetrics and Gynecology* 76: 558, 565 (tab. 3).

Trussell, James, and Charles F. Westoff. 1980. "Contraceptive Practices and Trends in Coital Frequency." *Family Planning Perspectives* 12: 246–249.

Turner, Charles F., et al. 1989. *AIDS: Sexual Behavior and Intravenous Drug Use* (National Research Council, Committee on AIDS Research and the Behavioral, Social, and Statistical Sciences). Washington, D.C.: National Academy Press.

Turnock, Bernard J., and Chester J. Kelly. 1989. "Mandatory Premarital Testing for Human Immunodeficiency Virus: The Illinois Experience." *JAMA (Journal of the American Medical Association)* 261: 3415–3418.

Tversky, Amos, and Daniel Kahneman. 1981. "The Framing of Decisions and the Psychology of Choice." *Science* 211: 453–458.

Tyden, Tanja, Cecilia Björkelund, and Sven-Eric Olsson. 1991. "Sexual Behavior and Sexually Transmitted Diseases among Swedish University Students." *Acta Obstetricia et Gynecologica Scandinavica* 70: 219, 223.

Tyden, Tanja, Lillemor Norden, and Leena Ruusuvaara. 1991. "Swedish Adolescents' Knowledge of Sexually Transmitted Disease and Their Attitudes to the Condom." *Midwifery* 7: 25, 30.

University Publishing Group. *AIDS Literature and News Review* (monthly).

U.S. Bureau of the Census. 1991. *Statistical Abstract of the United States: 1991.* 111th ed. Washington, D.C.: U.S. Government Printing Office.

U.S. Congress. 1991. *Departments of Labor, Health and Human Services, Education, and Related Agencies Appropriations for 1992.* Hearings before a Subcommittee of the House Committee on Appropriations, 102nd Cong., 1st Sess., pt. 3, 1042–1052.

U.S. Congress, Office of Technology Assessment. 1979. *A Review of Selected Federal Vaccine and Immunization Policies, Based on Case Studies of Pneumococcal Vaccine:* 5. Washington, D.C.: U.S. Government Printing Office.

———— 1985. *Review of the Public Health Service's Response to AIDS: A Technical Memorandum:* 32 (tab. 1). Washington, D.C.: U.S. Government Printing Office.

U.S. Department of Health and Human Services, Public Health Service, Centers for Disease Control. *See* Centers for Disease Control.

U.S. Department of Labor, Occupational Safety and Health Administration. 1991. "Occupational Exposure to Bloodborne Pathogens." *Federal Register* 56: 64,004–64,182.

U.S. Public Health Service. 1988. *Vital Statistics of the United States, 1988:* 338 (tab. 1-35). Washington, D.C.: U.S. Government Printing Office.

van de Laar, M. J. W., et al. 1990. "Declining Gonorrhoea Rates in The Netherlands, 1976–88: Consequences for the AIDS Epidemic." *Genitourinary Medicine* 66: 148–155.

van den Hoek, J. A. R., H. J. A. van Haastrecht, and R. A. Coutinho. 1990. "Increase in Unsafe Homosexual Behaviour." *Lancet* 336: 179–180.

———— 1992. "Little Change in Sexual Behavior in Injecting Drug Users in Amsterdam." *Journal of Acquired Immune Deficiency Syndromes* 5: 518–522.

van Griensven, Godfried J. P., et al. 1988a. "Impact of HIV Antibody Testing on Changes in Sexual Behavior among Homosexual Men in the Netherlands." *American Journal of Public Health* 78: 1575–1577.

———— 1988b. "Failure Rate of Condoms during Anogenital Intercourse in Homosexual Men." *Genitourinary Medicine* 64: 344–346.

———— 1990. "Risk Factors for Progression of Human Immunodeficiency Virus (HIV) Infection among Seroconverted and Seropositive Homosexual Men." *American Journal of Epidemiology* 132: 203, 209.

Viscusi, W. Kip. 1985. "A Bayesian Perspective on Biases in Risk Perception." *Economic Letters* 17: 59–62.

———— 1990. "Do Smokers Underestimate Risks?" *Journal of Political Economy* 98: 1253–1269.

———— 1991. "Age Variations in Risk Perceptions and Smoking Decisions." *Review of Economics and Statistics* 73: 577–588.

Viscusi, W. Kip, and Michael J. Moore. 1989. "Rates of Time Preference and Valuations of the Duration of Life." *Journal of Public Economics* 38: 297–317.

Vlahov, David, et al. 1991. "Prevalence of Antibody to HIV-1 among Entrants to US Correctional Facilities." *JAMA (Journal of the American Medical Association)* 265: 1129–1132.

Voeller, Bruce. 1991. "AIDS and Heterosexual Anal Intercourse." *Archives of Sexual Behavior* 20: 233–276.

Voeller, Bruce, June Machover Reinisch, and Michael Gottlied, eds. 1990. *AIDS and Sex: An Integrated Biomedical and Biobehavioral Approach.* New York: Oxford University Press.

Vogel, Kenneth. 1989. "Discrimination on the Basis of HIV Infection: An Economic Analysis." *Ohio State Law Journal* 49: 965–998.

Volberding, Paul A., et al. 1990. "Zidovudine in Asymptomatic Human Immunodeficiency Virus Infection." *New England Journal of Medicine* 322: 941–949.

Wachter, Robert M. 1992. "AIDS, Activism, and the Politics of Health." *New England Journal of Medicine* 326: 128, 130.

Waldholz, Michael. 1992. "Stymied Science: New Discoveries Dim Drug Makers' Hope for Quick AIDS Cure." *Wall Street Journal,* May 26: A1, A6.

Wall Street Journal Staff. 1992. "Despite AIDS and Safe-Sex Exhortations, Sales of Condoms in U.S. Are Lackluster." *Wall Street Journal,* Nov. 24: B1, B12.

Warner, Kenneth E. 1977. "The Effects of the Anti-Smoking Campaign on Cigarette Consumption." *American Journal of Public Health* 67: 645–650.

——— 1989. "Effects of the Antismoking Campaign: An Update." *American Journal of Public Health* 79: 144–151.

Wasserheit, Judith N., et al., eds. 1991. *Research Issues in Human Behavior and Sexually Transmitted Diseases in the AIDS Era.* Washington, D.C.: American Society for Microbiology.

Watters, John K., et al. 1990. "AIDS Prevention for Intravenous Drug Users in the Community: Street-Based Education and Risk Behavior." *American Journal of Community Psychology* 18: 587–596.

Weingast, Barry R. 1980. "Physicians, DNA Research Scientists, and the Market for Lemons." In Roger D. Blair and Stephen Rubin, eds., *Regulating the Professions: A Public-Policy Symposium:* 81–96. Lexington, Mass.: D. H. Heath.

Weinstein, Milton C., et al. 1989. "Cost-Effectiveness Analysis of AIDS Prevention Programs: Concepts, Complications, and Illustrations." In Turner et al. (1989): 471–499.

Weisbrod, Burton A. 1983. *Economics and Medical Research.* Washington, D.C.: American Enterprise Institute for Public Policy Research.

Wells, James A. 1987. "GrantWatch: Foundation Funding for AIDS Programs." *Health Affairs* 6(3): 113, 116 (exhibit 2).

Wenger, Neil S., et al. 1991. "Reduction of High-Risk Sexual Behavior among Heterosexuals Undergoing HIV Antibody Testing: A Randomized Clinical Trial." *American Journal of Public Health* 81: 1580–1585.

Westoff, Charles F. 1974. "Coital Frequency and Contraception." *Family Planning Perspectives* 6: 136–141.

Westoff, Charles F., Larry Bumpass, and Norman B. Ryder. 1969. "Oral Contraception, Coital Frequency, and the Time Required to Conceive." *Social Biology* 16: 1–10.

Wickwire, Kenneth. 1977. "Mathematical Models for the Control of Pests and Infectious Diseases: A Survey." *Theoretical Population Biology* 11: 182–238.

Wiktor, Stefan Z. 1990. "Effect of Knowledge of Human Immunodeficiency Virus Infection Status on Sexual Activity among Homosexual Men." *Journal of Acquired Immune Deficiency Syndromes* 3: 62, 67.

Wiley, James A., and Stephen J. Herschkorn. 1988. "The Perils of Promiscuity." *Journal of Infectious Diseases* 158: 500–501.

Wiley Law Publications Editorial Staff, eds. 1992. *AIDS and the Law.* 2nd ed. New York: John Wiley and Sons.

Winkenwerder, William, Austin R. Kessler, and Rhonda M. Stolec. 1989. "Federal Spending for Illness Caused by the Human Immunodeficiency Virus." *New England Journal of Medicine* 320: 1598–1603.

Wolchok, Carol Leslie. 1989. "AIDS at the Frontier: United States Immigration Policy." *Journal of Legal Medicine* 10: 127–142.

Woodard, Catherine. 1991. "Buyer Beware: Condom Quality Varies." *Newsday,* Nov. 26: 27.

Woollely, Robert J. 1989. "The Biologic Possibility of HIV Transmission during Passionate Kissing." *JAMA (Journal of the American Medical Association)* 262: 2230.

World Health Organization. 1991. "Update: AIDS Cases Reported to Surveillance, Forecasting and Impact Assessment Unit." Unpublished. Oct. 1.

Wykoff, Randolph F., et al. 1988. "Contact Tracing to Identify Human Immunodeficiency Virus Infection in a Rural Community." *JAMA (Journal of the American Medical Association)* 259: 3563, 3565.

———— 1991. "Notification of Sex and Needle-Sharing Partners of Individuals with Human Immunodeficiency Virus in Rural South Carolina: 30-Month Experience." *Sexually Transmitted Diseases* 18: 217–222.

Zeckhauser, Richard, and Donald Shepard. 1976. "Where Now for Saving Lives?" *Law and Contemporary Problems* 40 (Autumn): 5, 41.

Ziegler, Philip. 1969. *The Black Death.* New York: Harper and Row.

Index